KATE SCHARFF, M.S.W.

MW00827367

Mastering Crucial Moments in Separation and Divorce

A Multidisciplinary Guide to Excellence in Practice and Outcome

AMERICAN BAR ASSOCIATION
**Defending Liberty
Pursuing Justice**

SECTION OF
FAMILY LAW

Cover by Mary Anne Kulchawik/ABA Publishing.

Printed in the United States of America.

20 19 18 17 16 5 4 3 2 1

Library of Congress Cataloging-in-Publication Data

Names: Scharff, Kate, author. | Herrick, Lisa, author.
Title: Mastering crucial moments in separation and divorce / by Kate Scharff
    and Lisa Herrick.
Description: First edition. | Chicago : American Bar Association, [2016] |
    Includes bibliographical references and index.
Identifiers: LCCN 2016029740 | ISBN 9781634254083 (print : alk. paper)
Subjects: LCSH: Divorce—Law and legislation—United States. | Separation
    (Law)—United States.
Classification: LCC KF535 .S255 2016 | DDC 346.7301/66—dc23
LC record available at https://lccn.loc.gov/2016029740

Discounts are available for books ordered in bulk. Special consideration is given to state bars, CLE programs, and other bar-related organizations. Inquire at ABA Publishing, American Bar Association, 321 North Clark Street, Chicago, Illinois 60654-7598.

www.ShopABA.org

Contents

About the Authors

Kate Scharff, MSW, is an individual, couple, and family psychotherapist with over 25 years of clinical experience. She is also a senior divorce consultant, mediator, parenting coordinator, and Collaborative Divorce practitioner. Ms. Scharff is a founder and principal of the Collaborative Practice Center of Greater Washington. She teaches internationally on divorce, psychodynamic psychotherapy, parenting, and alternate dispute resolution. She regularly conducts workshops and seminars for family law attorneys, mental health professionals, and multidisciplinary audiences. Ms. Scharff is the author of many journal articles and book chapters, and of the books *Therapy Demystified: An Insider's Guide to Getting the Right Help* (Marlowe & Co., 2004) and (with Lisa Herrick) *Navigating Emotional Currents in Collaborative Divorce: A Guide to Enlightened Team Practice* (American Bar Association, 2010). Her pieces appear frequently in online and print media; she is a regular contributor to the Divorce section of *The Huffington Post*.

Ms. Scharff maintains a private practice in Washington, D.C., and Bethesda, Maryland.

Her website is www.katescharff.com.

Lisa Herrick, PhD, is a licensed clinical psychologist who has worked with children, families, and couples for more than 25 years. Dr. Herrick's practice includes psychotherapy, family mediation, Collaborative Divorce, and providing expert testimony in cases related to custody and parenting coordination. She is a founder and principal of the Collaborative Practice Center of Greater Washington and has been at the leading edge of the Collaborative Practice movement. Dr. Herrick is an internationally known trainer in parenting coordination, the impact of divorce on children, and working with divorcing couples in mediation, and Collaborative Practice. She is the co-author (with Kate Scharff) of *Navigating Emotional Currents in Collaborative Divorce, A Guide to Enlightened Team Practice* (American Bar Association, 2010).

Dr. Herrick maintains a private practice in Washington, D.C., and Northern Virginia.

Her website is www.lisaherrick.com.

Praise for...

Mastering Crucial Moments in Separation and Divorce: A Multidisciplinary Guide to Excellence in Practice and Outcome

Families in transition are desperate for capable professionals to provide insight and guidance on how best to navigate toward the successful outcome of a separation and divorce. Kate Scharff and Lisa Herrick, two highly experienced and enormously well-respected practitioners, have set forth in clear and concise terms concrete strategies that will enable professionals in many disciplines to better accomplish those admirable goals.

Scharff and Herrick's thoughtful work is unique in the breadth of its scope and in the creative strategies it offers to ease the pain of clients experiencing the trauma of separation and divorce and giving them the tools they need to move forward in a positive and constructive way with the remainder of their lives. There is something for everyone in this exceptional and insightful work.

Mastering Crucial Moments in Separation and Divorce *has been a pleasure for me to read in its clarity, its cutting edge ideas, and its inspiring pragmatic applications for our everyday work. Even though this is my area of expertise, I learned an enormous amount and found the book informative and insightful. You will be pleased that you read it and anxious to share what you have learned with your professional colleagues.*

—Sanford K. Ain, Esq., Co-founder and Principal, Ain & Bank, P.C.; Fellow, American Academy of Matrimonial Lawyers; President, District of Columbia Chapter of American Academy of Matrimonial Lawyers

What an extraordinarily abundant and nuanced gift Kate Scharff and Lisa Herrick have given to the divorce community! This book resonates with intelligence, compassion, and wisdom while offering psychologically sound and practical tools to help all professionals— from beginners to old-timers—get better at navigating the deep waters of divorce with our clients. The authors bring an authoritative yet kind and humble perspective from their years of multidisciplinary divorce experience, giving readers a rich mix of theoretical anchors, case studies, and concrete guidance. Although they are careful to acknowledge points at which the responsibilities of lawyers differ from those of mental health or financial professionals, the understandings they share with us transcend professional boundaries. They write with grace and clarity and have a knack for asserting complex and important truths like this one straightforwardly and powerfully:

*"When a case flounders or falls out, the culprit is almost always problems in and among the personalities of professional team members, **not** the difficult behaviors of the clients. Collaboration is a state of mind that exists first, primarily, and sometimes **only** in the minds of the professionals. In other words, we are not dependent on our clients for good outcomes; they are dependent on us."*

—Pauline Tesler, Esq., Fellow, American Academy of
Matrimonial Lawyers; Co-founder and First President,
International Academy of Collaborative Professionals;
Founding Director, Integrative Law Institute at Commonweal

Kate Scharff and Lisa Herrick have once again brought forth their wisdom and compassion to enhance the evolution of the interdisciplinary practice of separation and divorce. Considering divorce as a "developmental crisis" creates a wide-open field of possibilities. Many of the authors' previously articulated ideas come together in new ways, along with new, original conceptualizations that take the reader further into the experience of clients and of the professionals who are trying to help them. With their characteristic thoroughness and true-to-life illustrations, Scharff and Herrick create a rich yet accessible tapestry of possibilities for the practitioner to consider at their next client meeting. Presenting such delicious terms as "metabolizing an idea," such robust models as "the Three Conditions for Positive

Change," and extending their scope to include mindfulness practices, their work is continually evolving, practical, creative, and inspiring.

—Dr. Susan Gamache, Psychologist, Clinical Fellow in Marriage & Family Therapy; Senior Collaborative Practitioner & Trainer; Founding Co-Chair, Vancouver Collaborative Divorce Group

Once in a great while something surprising happens at the frontier of psychotherapeutic thinking. A creative mind emerges that has deeply and personally integrated established theories, infused them with original ideas, and shaped them into new conceptualizations with the power to expand our collective thinking and raise the bar of professional practice. In their inspiring second book on the universally relevant topic of divorce, Kate Scharff and Lisa Herrick have done just that.

Drawing from the most important lessons of psychotherapy, the authors offer a developmental paradigm for learning how best to help couples and families through this challenging life phase. Whether you're an individual or couple psychotherapist, mediator, or divorce attorney of any stripe everything you need is here—plain English theory, lively vignettes, common-sense techniques, and an exploration of the importance of self-awareness.

Mastering Crucial Moments in Separation and Divorce *is another deceptively simple work by two experts in both the art and the science of their craft. Like its predecessor,* Navigating Emotional Currents in Collaborative Divorce *(American Bar Association 2010), it's beautifully written—sophisticated, yet accessible and often funny—and all helping professionals who deal in fractured human relationships should read it.*

—Jane Prelinger, MSW, LICSW, Founding Co-Director, Center for Existential Studies; Faculty, The International Psychotherapy Institute and the Washington School of Psychiatry; Former Director, Treatment Centers of the Washington School of Psychiatry; International Speaker and Trainer

Kate Scharff and Lisa Herrick have made another major contribution to our professional library. This is a must-have book for divorce professionals who aspire to improve their level of practice by expanding their

understanding of the complex dynamics between themselves and their clients. Along the way, the authors remind us of the powerful impact of our own life experiences and biases, and of the importance of our willingness to uncover and explore our vulnerabilities.

The organization and layout of the book is exceptional and designed to make the material highly accessible. Important ideas are pulled from the text and highlighted, and each chapter ends with a help-ful summary. These, along with chapter-by-chapter "learning modules" and a comprehensive glossary, make it easy for the reader to dip back into the book when reviewing a concept or looking for a quick answer.

I found the section on "Modes of Advocacy" extremely useful, especially the observation that "empathy doesn't equate with endorse-ment." It is often challenging to persuade an angry, upset client that acknowledging their spouse's point of view does not mean abandon-ing their own. And attorneys can find it equally difficult to avoid ally-ing with their own client's story and dismissing that of their client's spouse. The authors offer a powerful reminder that advocacy can either suck us into the vortex of our client's experience or lift us above and beyond so we can offer perspective and reality testing.

—Rita S. Pollak, MA, JD, Former President of International Academy of Collaborative Professionals and the Massachusetts Collaborative Law Council

Scharff and Herrick inject a psychodynamic perspective into divorce work in order to help professionals from the fields of law and mental health understand their clients and react to them in ways that are growth-promoting. The authors turn sophisticated concepts into tools, using language designed to support working at a deeper level. They write in a conversational style that makes you feel as if they are right there, talking to you.

—Marsha Kline Pruett, PhD, MSL, ABPP, Smith College School for Social Work

Kate Scharff and Lisa Herrick, both seasoned psychotherapists who have worked in the field of divorce for many years, have written an invaluable multidisciplinary primer to help professionals working

with divorcing couples move beyond the win-lose paradigm and forward with their lives. Mastering Crucial Moments in Separation and Divorce *will raise the skill level and self-awareness of attorneys, divorce coaches and financial experts so they can become attuned facilitators of change. As a professional who works regularly with couples struggling to resolve money problems amid the stress of separation and divorce, I found Scharff and Herrick's book to be a gift— packed with sound advice, surprising insights, and new techniques for navigating even the toughest moments of a couple's divorce.*

—Olivia Mellan, National Speaker, Money Coach,
Business Consultant, Author of *Money Harmony:*
A Guide for Individuals and Couples

Many highly trained divorce professionals put great emphasis on learning to work with a wide range of clients but neglect to explore (or choose not to explore) their own impact on the matter. In Mastering Crucial Moments in Separation and Divorce: A Multidisciplinary Guide to Excellence in Practice and Outcome, *Kate Scharff and Lisa Herrick bring attention to the professionals involved in all manner of divorce processes, and to the impact we have on case outcomes. Early on they make the powerful point that, "The success of any case is predicated on the self-awareness and self-management of every professional involved."*

This book is filled with practical techniques and the clinical reasoning behind them. I particularly found the "Seven Factors to Consider When Deciding What to Do or Say" and the "Supplemental Study Modules" to be very effective. I believe that all divorce professionals could work together more productively if they were to read this book and use it as a guide.

Kate and Lisa, thank you for explaining so many concepts in such a usable, reader-friendly manner. All of us in the world of multidisciplinary divorce work will benefit from your wisdom.

—Linda Solomon, LPC, LMFT, Collaborative Facilitator,
Therapist, Trainer, Recipient of the Collaborative Law Institute
of Texas 2015 Gay C. Cox Collaborative Law Award

For the families who invite us to accompany them on their journeys. Your trust, courage and wisdom inspire us, enrich our lives, and infuse the pages of this book.

Acknowledgments

We are grateful to Dan Morris and to Doug Lederman, for their keen eyes, discerning ears, and generous editorial guidance. Dan gave our project liftoff; Doug gave it a final elevating boost.

We want to thank our friends and colleagues at our professional home, The Collaborative Practice Center of Greater Washington. Your vibrant presence turns what would otherwise be a suite of offices and conference rooms into a perfect container for ongoing personal and professional development. We feel lucky every day for our shared support, thought-provoking conversations, laughter and sense of family.

We did not get here on our own. Our primary partner in crime from the beginning has been Barbara Burr, JD. She has been so integral to our professional "growing up" that separating out her contributions to our work is a tough challenge. Barb offers a bridge of understanding between our world of psychotherapy and her world of family law. She helps us to identify and extract the most helpful aspects of our theoretical concepts and to ground them in a language and form that make them easily accessible to a multi-disciplinary audience. The three of us have spent many exciting hours engaged in lively discussion, with Barb's insights and curious questions often sparking "aha moments" that led us down new paths of inquiry and resulted in fresh conceptualizations. Barb is our co-trainer, teammate on Collaborative and cooperative cases, and a colleague to whom we frequently turn for guidance and perspective. Over the years, the feedback loop created by our ongoing three-way conversation has created a rich matrix for friendship and learning. That shared experience has deepened our understanding of our clients and ourselves, and made us better practitioners. Without it, this would be a lesser work.

If we climb high enough we will reach a height from which tragedy ceases to look tragic.

—Irvin D. Yalom, *When Nietzsche Wept*

To Our Readers: A Note on Our Use of Language

Before you dive in, there are a few important things we'd like you to know about us and about this book. As you read, you'll notice that we make heavy reference to husbands, wives, spouses, ex-partners ("exes"), mothers, and fathers. But here is how we see things:

Our Definition of a Parent

A parent is any person who identifies as a parent and who is identified by a child as being a parent. A parent has or shares primary ethical responsibility for meeting the physical and emotional needs of a child. A parent may or may not be called "Mom" or "Dad." They may or may not share DNA with the child, or be in (or have ever been in) a relationship with the other parent or parents. There may never have been another parent. A parent may or may not be recognized as such in the eyes of the law. A parent can fall anywhere on the spectrums of gender and sexual orientation.

Our Definition of a Couple

A couple is any two people who have made a mutual commitment to share life, love and intimacy.

A Few Words on Our Use of Pronouns

We make inconsistent use of pronouns in this book. It's pretty hodgepodge. But that's not because we didn't think things through or forgot to proofread.

In some cases, we employ gender-specific, singular pronouns, such as *him*, *her*, *his*, and *hers*. Because we don't want to favor either fathers or mothers, we switch back and forth across various vignettes—choosing in each instance whether to feature a "he" or a "she." At other times, we deal with the issue differently, opting not to choose one gender-specific pronoun. This practice is more egalitarian but is unwieldy. It results in sentences like "Each professional must choose for him- or herself how much personal information he or she is comfortable to disclose." It also doesn't address the fact that some people are neither male nor female, or that some parents are neither mothers nor fathers.

Finally, we often use plural pronouns to refer back to singular subjects. For example, we might say, "The client was happy with their outcome," or "If you don't respond to your client's email, you might upset them." This sentence structure has historically been considered a grammatical sin. But it's gaining acceptance in the media and in print and (although it's a matter of debate) is moving toward common usage.

We use plural pronouns with increasing frequency. We're working toward a point where either the larger community reaches consensus or we are ready to give up the complicated and awkward attempt to speak to individual preferences in our audience—in favor of employing a simpler, more inclusive language that is consistent with our values.

Language is about respect. Our goal is to write in a way that conveys nondiscriminatory recognition and acceptance. The social, political, and linguistic landscape is changing for the better. We admit to being at a new phase in our own development. As individuals, we have a lot to learn. As writers, we clearly have not cracked the code. It's an ongoing process.

Introduction

We are a clinical social worker and a psychologist. Each of us has been a psychotherapist for over 25 years and has completed extensive training in individual, couple, and family psychotherapy. We also share a love of play therapy and work with children as young as two years old (or even younger, when we're seeing them together with their parents). About 15 years ago, each of us wandered into the field of separation and divorce. It happened gradually—a case here, a case there. We both have personalities that propel us toward novel experiences; we prefer to err on the side of trying something new. We found ourselves working for the first time with professionals of other disciplines and wearing new hats. We performed roles for which we did not always have names or roadmaps but which are now familiar to all of us, such as *parenting coordination* and *divorce coaching.* We also had our earliest experiences of testifying in custody cases. We learned mostly on the job (and by making mistakes!), but we found good mentors and gobbled up all the relevant training we could find—the best of which came from that wonder of an organization, the Association of Family and Conciliation Courts (AFCC).

We were driven by personal interest, too. Both of us were in the late recovery phase of our own divorces. We were engaged in quests to understand why our interpersonal lives had played out as they had, and to minimize the negative impact on our (then young) children. Kate was a child of divorce and thought a lot about ways things might have gone better if her well-intentioned, psychologically minded parents had had more supportive process options available to them.

We found our work with divorcing families and their attorneys stimulating and interesting, and we knew it was important. But our experiences were uneven. Sometimes we were effective in helping separating partners relate in less acrimonious ways, make child-centered decisions, and reach mutually acceptable compromises without squandering their mutual goodwill and their kids' college funds. Other times we felt like cogs in a massive, destructive machine—unwillingly complicit players in an adversarial system in which complex, interpersonal difficulties were reduced to judicial disputes and human vulnerabilities were exploited as legal liabilities.

In the beginning we were pretty naive. We didn't understand why some attorneys seemed wedded to a narrow definition of zealous advocacy. We were thrown off-kilter whenever an attorney we liked and considered reasonable (maybe because we were friendly with him or her in social settings) took on the mantle of a clearly vindictive or mentally unstable client. We felt like we were in the *Twilight Zone* whenever we listened to two lawyers (who had perhaps played a friendly game of tennis the day before) hurl invectives at each other as though they were avatars of the clients themselves. We found ourselves wanting to blurt out "Wait! Don't you see that if you switched clients you'd each start speaking the other's lines with equal conviction?"

Eventually, we came to know so many family lawyers (as well as mental health professionals and financial experts who worked alongside them) that we experienced a wide range of professional perspectives and approaches. We became acutely aware of how complex and difficult divorce work really is—the content is upsetting and provocative, the clients are reeling, there are *children* involved, and every fact pattern is different. Once you layer in the infinite combinations of variables relating to the professionals' characters and levels of experience and skill—whew! It's quite a web. We weren't alone in struggling to learn how to do our best with every client. Nearly all our colleagues were struggling too, some with stunning success, others with more difficulty. We also became more attuned to the profound nature of the paradigm shift required of *us* in learning to apply psychotherapeutic concepts in a multidisciplinary, task-focused process. We became humbler and more curious.

As therapists, we're trained to eschew the notion of objective truth. Our responsibility to our patient is to understand and accept their narrative without judgment, but from a questioning stance. We listen for clues that our patient is distorting reality. But we do this so we can help them to develop a deeper understanding of their own thinking and behavior and, with our support, to make healthy adjustments. We don't want to show our patient that they're wrong; we want to help them find ways to be happier. We don't want to use what we know against them; we want to work collaboratively to develop shared insight. We want to help them get out of their own way. But our job is made easier by the fact that (with a few rare exceptions) we have no legal or ethical responsibility for the outcome of our work.

As we became more familiar with the work of attorneys and gained a more nuanced understanding of their ethical responsibilities to clients, we became more interested in their stylistic differences. We noticed that some colleagues who were highly successful and effective litigators were gifted at creating deep, powerfully supportive relationships with clients. Other colleagues who swore allegiance to mediation and other alternate dispute resolution processes didn't seem to understand their clients at all, and fomented more conflict than did their litigating peers. We wondered: Since it's clear that effectiveness isn't tied simply to process (e.g., litigation or mediation), what is it tied to? Which skills are innate? Which can be learned? What's the best way to teach them? What determines which divorce professionals will seek or be open to more humanistic perspectives? And while we're at it, we thought, let's ask the same question with respect to mental health professionals and financial experts.

Although we both live and work in the Washington, D.C., area, we did not meet until our first Collaborative Practice training in 2006 (a multidisciplinary team training offered by our now friend and colleague Sue Brunsting, JD, of Rochester, NY). We were immediately hooked on the model. Collaborative Practice offered an opportunity to pull together and apply our entire toolbox of accumulated knowledge and skills, and a way to reach families at the beginning of their divorce process—before damage had been done by an adversarial system. Collaborative Practice was a door. Through it we entered into a community of people who, like us, search for ways to practice within the realities of the law but in a manner consistent with our identities as helping professionals. Our Collaborative colleagues don't think in lockstep on every issue. But they share a commitment to an integrated approach in which the needs of a family can be seen in three dimensions (legal, financial, emotional), and clients can be supported in making decisions based on a mutual understanding of underlying interests and concerns—rather than out of fear.

We joined the larger Collaborative world when we became members of the International Association of Collaborative Professionals. We attended IACP annual forums and conferences. Soon we began presenting at those forums and, with increasing frequency, to be invited to conduct trainings for local and statewide Collaborative groups and bar associations. Every community we visited gave us fresh perspectives. Our learning expanded exponentially, and our minds crackled with new ideas.

The lawyers, mental health professionals, and financial professionals who attended that training in 2006 began to work together on a regular basis—sharing cases and talking together about what did and didn't work. In 2007 we formed the first Board of Directors of the D.C. Academy of Collaborative Professionals (DCACP), an extraordinary organization we both hold dear to our hearts. The authors still fondly think of that group as our "graduating class." Its members are many of our closest friends and colleagues.

In those first few years the two of us had nearly daily conversations (sometimes many in the same day) about how to apply our psychological understanding to the Collaborative model. We learned best when we thought backwards. We deconstructed meetings retrospectively, putting countless fraught moments under our metaphorical microscope, examining them for clues about why things had unfolded the way they had. From those conversations emerged our first book, *Navigating Emotional Currents in Collaborative Divorce: A Guide to Enlightened Team Practice*. *Navigating* is a study of how unconscious personality conflicts (both inside each client and between them) play out in a Collaborative Divorce process, often working their way into the professional team in ways that can be either problematic or transformative (or both).

Over time, we've integrated the concepts from *Navigating* so deeply into our own work and teaching that they've become reflexive; we have "muscle memory" for working with our clients' emotional dynamics in the multidisciplinary divorce context. Armed with that solid foundation, we are less preoccupied with the nuts and bolts of our work. This has freed up mental bandwidth, and given us freedom to be curious in new ways and to take creative risks.

Since 2010, our ongoing conversation about the application of psychotherapeutic concepts to divorce work has continued—but our focus has shifted. We remain interested in the interplay of individual, couple, and team dynamics, but we've pulled our perspective back, expanding our visual field.

The shift began when we were ready to look at our beloved Collaborative model through a more critical lens. We did a lot of postmortems, and here is what we learned: A Collaborative team can be a rocket to the moon or a plane spiraling earthward. The success of any Collaborative case is predicated on the self-awareness and self-management of every professional involved. When a case flounders or falls out, the culprit is almost always (with a few notable categories of exception, such as active substance abuse or severe mental illness) problems in and among the personalities of professional team members, *not* the difficult behaviors of the clients—even when the clients are very high conflict.

We came to understand that collaboration is a state of mind that exists first, primarily, and sometimes *only* in the minds of the professionals. In other words, we are not dependent on our clients for good outcomes; they are dependent on us. We began to approach each new case— whether it was Collaborative,

> *When a case flounders or falls out, the culprit is almost always problems in and among the personalities of professional team members, **not** the difficult behaviors of the clients. Collaboration is a state of mind that exists first, primarily, and sometimes **only** in the minds of the professionals. In other words, we are not dependent on our clients for good outcomes; they are dependent on us.*

cooperative, litigation, mediation, settlement negotiation, parenting coordination, or one of many hybrid varieties—from the same collaborative state of mind.[1]

But could that state of mind be taught? How? To whom? We'd come full circle to our original questions.

A couple of years ago, while once again pondering the conundrum of what makes a great divorce professional great, we had a lightbulb moment in which we hit upon the notion that *the people who are doing this work really well (whether they're lawyers, mental health professionals, or financial experts) are providing an emotional environment that allows their clients to do really hard things under really hard circumstances.* Like all basic truths, it should have been obvious all along, but it was a revelation. The recipe to the "secret sauce"—that ineffable quality of mastery we'd been struggling to capture in the wild so we could study it—was simply a reflection of what good parents have been doing since time began: creating psychological conditions for growth under conditions of stress.

Pauline Tesler, JD, author of *Collaborative Law: Achieving Effective Resolution Without Litigation* (now heading into its third edition) and a pioneer in the multidisciplinary practice of family law, has been one of our most important teachers. Here's what she had to say on the complicated question of what can be taught versus what is hardwired (and the potential implications of that question):

> *For some time now, as a trainer, I have been trying to figure out what is teachable/learnable in what the innate peacemakers are doing naturally, and to figure out how it can be taught to those who have the capacity and intention to be*

---

1. We want to distinguish between the specific modality of "Collaborative Practice" (a legal divorce process the primary distinguishing feature of which is the Participation Agreement, signed by both parties and their counsel, stipulating that their respective attorneys cannot represent the parties in any subsequent litigation) and "collaborative" (an adjective describing a nonadversarial approach to our work). Because "Collaborative Practice" (also known as "Collaborative Divorce" and "Collaborative Law") is a proper noun, we capitalize it. We do not capitalize the adjective "collaborative."

*pretty good collaborative lawyers. I'm also interested in how those who **do** seem to have the peacemaker gene can build small groups to support highest, best practices. What they do by nature includes much that can't be taught but also some elements that can. We will still have a bell curve—some who are excellent, some who are just okay at the work, and some who don't bother to do well at anything. Training doesn't change that, but I do believe that capturing what's effective about what master practitioners do by nature can help float all the boats higher.[2]*

As the Director of the Integrative Law Institute at Commonweal, Pauline works at the leading edge, gathering up emerging ideas from the worlds of positive and social psychology, neuroeconomics, cognitive psychology, and other natural and social sciences. She synthesizes these ideas into practical concepts that speak directly and powerfully to divorce lawyers, who in turn put them to immediate use with their clients. We find Pauline's work important for many reasons, not the least of which is that it offers empirical evidence for the efficacy of practicing law as a healing profession. She reminds us that as human beings we are born with the capacity and desire to understand each other, to connect in ways that promote emotional growth.

In this book we present a developmental model for highly effective practice in the multidisciplinary field of separation and divorce. We offer it as a new point of entry, another vector for understanding how to help when human relationships falter. We hope the stream of our ideas will flow to meet the river already swirling with the contributions of Pauline and other leaders in our field. We like to imagine it there—mixing with the currents, playing in the eddies, joining the rising tide.

---

2. Personal communication with Pauline Tesler, 2015.

PART I

A New Perspective
on Our Work:
The Elements of
Successful Outcomes in
Separation and Divorce

Chapter 1

Divorce Reimagined as a Developmental Experience

"How does one become a butterfly?" she asked.
"You must want to learn to fly so much that you
are willing to give up being a caterpillar."

—Trina Paulus, *Hope for the Flowers*

None of us are untouched by divorce. Approximately half of marriages end before the death of a spouse,[1] and if you haven't experienced divorce firsthand (as a child or as an adult), then your once-married sibling, your son's best friend, or your next-door neighbor has. Yet, the fact that divorce is statistically normal doesn't seem to have done much to change our cultural view. Our reflexive use of phrases like "broken home" and words like "visitation" support the notion that the original nuclear family has more intrinsic value than any other kind, and that any postseparation family configuration is, at best, a watered-down substitute.

In political discourse the perceived collapse of the "traditional family" is blamed for societal ills. Those who seek to characterize

---

1. Centers for Disease Control National Center for Health Statistics, *Change in the Reporting of Marriage and Divorce Statistics.* 2010, http://www.cdc.gov/nchs/pressroom/96facts/mardiv.htm.

the decision to divorce as a moral failure often cite studies describing children's poor adaptive responses to divorce. All this, despite research indicating that it is the conflict between parents, more than the fact of the divorce, that places children at risk.[2]

We propose the introduction of a new idea for professionals working in the area of separation and divorce: That divorce can be best understood as an experience embedded in ordinary human development. We view divorce not as a failure, but as a point of temporary breakdown in the ongoing evolution of a family. By extension, we view divorce professionals as healers, with the job of helping the family to reconstitute itself in a way that allows each of its members to get back on a healthy developmental track.

> *The fact that divorce is statistically normal doesn't seem to have done much to change our negative cultural view. We propose that divorce can be best understood as an experience embedded in ordinary human development. We view divorce professionals as healers, with the job of helping the family to restructure in a way that allows it to get back on a healthy developmental track.*

What Do We Mean by "Development"?

The inborn propensity to move from a state of total dependence, through the achievement of a personal identity, and into a state of relative independence is universal within our species. Even if you're not familiar with any particular theory of human development you know that as individuals we grow up, to some extent, along a predestined path.[3] It starts from the moment we are

2. Heatherington E. Mavis and John Kelly, *For Better or Worse: Divorce Reconsidered*. W. W. Norton (2003).
3. Our description of human development as being composed of an unfolding series of "phases" (with each phase serving as the foundation for subsequent phases) is an idea so widely held among mental health researchers, theoreticians, and practitioners that it has reached the stature of a concept that "goes without saying." However, the model of development that the authors present here represents an integration of the seminal work of several iconic theorists, notably that of Sigmund Freud (drive theory, psychosexual stages of development), Erik Erickson (psychosocial stages of development), Jean Piaget (biological/cognitive/intellectual phases of development), Margaret Mahler (separation-individual theory of child development), and W.R.D. Fairbairn (model of endopsychic organization).

born (many would argue it starts in the womb) and continues throughout our lives. We face a series of increasingly complex challenges—learning to sleep through the night, to tolerate the absences of our parents, to delay gratification, to leave the home of our youth, to becoming increasingly financially and emotionally independent, to form intimate partnerships, to become a parent, to tolerate our child's increasing independence from us, to care for and eventually lose a parent, to adjust to our own aging—and confronting these challenges is inevitable. Each developmental phase calls on us to master new concrete and emotional tasks and to achieve new capacities in the service of emotional growth.

All developmentally important moments carry transformative potential. Whether they occur in infancy or old age, these important moments challenge us to overcome fear, relinquish the familiar, and take on new experience. These are moments of dynamic tension in which we stand on the precipice of change. If we are to let go of the known in favor of the unknown—if we are to take that leap—we'll need to draw on a reservoir of established emotional, cognitive, and perhaps even physical capacities. And we'll need to develop new ones.

Some common life challenges are not predictable in the way that, for example, the onset of adolescence is. But sometimes an unforeseen challenge is so profound, and the successful navigation of it requires the mastery of so many complex concrete and emotional tasks, that it *becomes* a development phase—a new stage in an individual's personal evolution. Though not anticipated, such a challenge is not unique to the individual and contains universal themes such as fear, grief, and loss. As with predictable developmental phases, such challenges offer the opportunity for significant psychological growth. Examples of these challenges

> All developmentally important moments carry transformative potential. These are moments of dynamic tension in which we stand on the precipice of change. If we are to let go of the known in favor of the unknown—if we are to take that leap—we'll need to draw on a reservoir of established emotional, cognitive, and perhaps even physical capacities. And we'll need to develop new ones.

include having a developmentally challenged child, being laid off from a job, facing a serious medical diagnosis, or getting divorced.

Now let's dig into one illustration of a developmental experience, so we'll have a context for moving these concepts into a discussion of our divorce work.

Think back to your own transition from home to college. Remember how you screwed up your courage to wave goodbye to your parents, then turned back toward your dorm room and the new roommate who was a stranger to you. Remember how you mustered enough courage to enter the dining hall for the first time, how you coped with the anxiety of being suddenly on your own. Perhaps after a week or two on campus, you had pangs of feeling at sea and ached for the familiar safety of your old life. But these moments soon gave way to the thrill of freedom and the excitement of meeting new challenges, new people, and new experiences.

Your personal experience may have been quite different from the one we described. But our point is that if your desire to master the task of adjusting to college outstripped your fear and doubt, the pleasure of your new success built on itself and propelled you onward to master new challenges of increasing difficulty. Eventually, college became your new normal.

All emotional development is like that. Each time we face a compelling new idea that offers the possibility of growth but challenges us to relinquish aspects of the known and the safe and we are able to successfully navigate that moment, we add a brick to the foundation of further growth.

On the other hand, development isn't really linear. Let's consider a hypothetical college student who struggles with his ambivalence about leaving the comfort of home. He might choose college and even separate from his family fairly easily at first. His first weeks at school might go smoothly, and he may feel thrilled to be coping so well. But if a new stressor is introduced into his life (perhaps his mother becomes ill or he starts failing chemistry), he will likely need a bit more reassurance and support—at least for a while.

Let's say that the effect of the new stressor increases (the student's mother gets sicker or he flunks chemistry) and this boy begins to regress. He loses the ability to self regulate; he starts skipping meals, develops insomnia, and is too tongue-tied and insecure to contribute during class discussions. In the evenings, he plays video games alone in his room, just as he had during the summer before he entered middle school (another tough transition for him). As days stretch into weeks and he stops participating in his college life, we now describe him as in a "developmental crisis." He is faced with the task of mastering important challenges associated with a new life phase, but he has slipped back to an earlier phase of his development and is stuck there. At that moment, under those psychological conditions, the pull backward is greater than his desire for the next big thing.

Divorce as a Developmental Crisis

A primary function of a couple and the family it creates is to provide a unique environment in which its members can face and successfully master new developmental phases and their attendant challenges. If there comes a time when the original configuration of the nuclear family can no longer do its work, we hope the couple or family will seek help in the form of counseling or therapy. But if they don't, or if efforts to rectify the situation fail, it makes sense that there be an organizational restructuring. Even though couples come to us "because my husband slept with his secretary," or "because my wife and I have grown apart," they are really in our offices because they can no longer work together to facilitate their own (and their children's, if they have them) continued evolution into more accomplished, nuanced, authentic versions of themselves. Rather than viewing divorce as a sign of moral weakness or a selfish choice, the authors view it as a developmental crisis with transformative potential.

> Couples come to us because they can no longer work together to facilitate their own (and their children's) continued evolution into more accomplished, nuanced, authentic versions of themselves. Rather than viewing divorce as a moral failure or selfish parental choice, the authors view it as a developmental crisis with transformative potential.

Divorce involves family members at different ages and with differing levels of inherent psychological and cognitive capacity, all facing a rapid succession of significant changes while experiencing a roller coaster of powerful emotions. For many of our clients, the simple acts of getting out of bed and putting one foot in front of the other require Herculean effort. And yet, somehow, they have to make a series of complex and frightening decisions that carry lifelong consequences.

In our developmental model, divorce is not simply a series of legal disputes, conflicts to be resolved, or problems to be solved—though it is a legal process usually requiring the resolution of conflict-laden, problematic questions (Who will keep the house? How will we share time with our children?). Viewed as a developmental crisis in the life of a couple and family, divorce becomes a stage of life in which there is a dynamic and shifting tension between the old, dysfunctional way of doing things and an array of new options.

> In our developmental model, divorce is not simply a series of conflicts to be resolved or problems to be solved. It is a stage of life in which there is a dynamic and shifting tension between the old, dysfunctional way of doing things and an array of new options.

The process of getting divorced tasks us with letting go of established traditions and familiar routines of daily life. It requires adapting to new rhythms, to the loss of a partner, to new financial and social realities, and to the intermittent absence of children. Divorce often requires learning new skills, such as balancing a checkbook, resetting a circuit breaker, or establishing bedtime rituals for kids. In the absence of a spouse we must learn to soothe ourselves, and to find new sources of comfort and support. Like all significant life passages (leaving the home of our youth, coupling, becoming a parent, losing a parent), dismantling a marriage means redefining our identities.

Although divorce will likely remain a painful chapter in the lives of all involved, it need not be a bad developmental turning point. A well-handled divorce can help a family regain its capacity to attend to the evolving needs of its members. A *very* well-handled divorced can raise the bar by improving the developmental trajectory of each family member. If, as helping professionals, we want to be agents of transformation, we need to know a lot about the conditions in which people can change in tough but important ways. And we need to learn how to create those conditions in our work.

> *A well-handled divorce can help a family regain its capacity to attend to the evolving needs of its members. A very well-handled divorce can raise the bar by improving the developmental trajectory of all involved. If, as helping professionals, we want to be agents of transformation, we need to know a lot about the conditions under which humans can change in tough but important ways.*

Summary of Concepts from Chapter 1

- Human beings "grow up" by facing a series of developmental phases and mastering the new challenges (emotional, cognitive, physical) associated with them. Some developmental phases are predictable and universal. Others are not predictable, but contain themes that are universal to human experience.
- Developmental phases have transformative potential; they offer opportunities for emotional growth.
- The function of a family is to support its members in moving through developmental phases in healthy ways, even under difficult conditions.
- A healthy family provides the conditions in which healthy development can proceed.
- Divorcing couples and their families have lost the ability to support each other in mastering new developmental phases and are in a "developmental crisis" with transformative potential.
- If, as helping divorce professionals, we want to help our clients to navigate their developmental crisis at their own highest level of transformative capacity, we need to understand the conditions under which humans can change in difficult and important ways and how to create those conditions in our work.

Chapter 2

Conditions for Positive Change

"People don't resist change, per se. They resist loss."

—Ronald A. Heifetz and Marty Linsky,
Leadership on the Line

The Human Relationship to Change

The desire to move toward or away from new experiences varies by individual. We all know people who instinctively light up when offered the opportunity for a novel undertaking, and others who meet the unfamiliar with apprehension. Some lead with "yes"; others with "no." But most of us eschew the extremes. We reasonably mistrust those who too easily abandon stable situations (the impulsive folks who never look before they leap) and resent the stultifying naysayers who cast a pall over spontaneity, creativity, and fun. Those of us who function best are comfortable in a range of registers. The flexibility that allows us to live responsibly in the real world while being open to moving beyond our comfort zones Is the same quality of grounded resiliency that helps us bounce back from life's challenges even if we have to adjust some expectations in the process.

But whether we are impulsive, apprehensive, or a healthy blend, the truth is that change—when it is significant, profound, and potentially life-altering—is hard for all of us. Why? Because it is predicated on loss.

> Change, when it is significant, profound and potentially life altering, is hard for all of us—because it is predicated on loss.

As we explored in Chapter 1, throughout our lives each of us faces a series of developmental phases that present us with new and complex challenges. To master each challenge (and move successfully through a given developmental phase), we have to overcome fear and relinquish the familiar in favor of the unfamiliar. In doing so, we grow emotionally; we are transformed.

When we struggle to master a new developmental challenge, we engage in a psychological dance between two polarities of desire that exist in a dynamic tension. One polarity is the primitive instinct to cling to the safe and known (think of the college freshman wishing to remain at home, or a divorcing client insisting on keeping a big house she can't afford). The other polarity is the fundamental human imperative to grow and adapt (think of the anxious freshman deciding to tough it out at school, or the divorcing client opting for a smaller—but cozy and affordable—new home). When the desire to grow and adapt triumphs over the instinct to cling to the safe and known, the result is what we refer to in this book as "positive change."

So how does one navigate the tension between competing polarities such that change, not stasis, wins the day? And when stasis is the victor, what's gone wrong?

Take a moment to consider the important and ultimately successful struggles of your life thus far—the hurdles you've tackled, the goals you've met. Zero in on one victory you're proud of. Don't focus on whether your accomplishment carries obvious status, or whether others would consider it a big deal. It *could* be something splashy (like landing a prestigious job or writing your first novel), but it could be something of quiet personal worth (such as standing up to a bully, or learning to live within a budget). Focus on an achievement that carries special significance to you because:

- You really wanted it to accomplish it.
- It was difficult to accomplish.

- It took what felt like a long time (perhaps with lots of false starts).
- It involved overcoming emotional obstacles such as fear, anxiety, self-doubt, intimidation, shame, or hopelessness.
- Your self-esteem went up as a result of your success.

Hold your example of positive change in mind as we move on in our discussion. You'll see that the forces that drove you in your quest and the conditions that made it possible for you to forge on through the rough spots can be distilled to the same three elements that make it possible for any one of us to successfully tackle the challenges associated with any new developmental phase.

The Three Conditions for Positive Change

The concepts that inform the authors' conceptualization of the "Three Conditions for Positive Change" are drawn from psychological theory, but they form the bedrock of good technique in any helping profession.[1] We'll list them first, and then look at each individually:

1. A new idea
2. A helping relationship (offering a holding environment, containment, empathy, and attunement)
3. Optimal anxiety

---

1. Many of the psychological ideas discussed in this book are so commonly accepted that citing a particular theorist is difficult. But we can trace many ideas close to their source. The notions of the "conscious" and "unconscious" mind as well as "transference" and "countertransference" originated with Sigmund Freud. Later, he and Anna Freud began the discussion of ego defenses or "defense mechanisms," which are now part of common parlance. In general, we lean most heavily on Object Relations Theory (ORT) and its therapeutic technique. ORT is an outgrowth of traditional psychoanalytic theory that holds with the notion that humans are born seeking relationships and that our early experiences in relationships form templates for modes of later relating—the more trauma involved, the more rigidly predictive these templates become. Our Three Conditions for Positive Change are derived from ORT (including Donald Winnicott's "holding environment," "transitional space," "basic trust," "attunement" and "primary maternal preoccupation," and Wilfred Bion's "containment").

A New Idea

Why would any of us ever let go of a comfortable status quo? Only because a new, compelling, exciting idea comes along that offers us something important that we want and don't yet have. Sometimes the new idea is a fun challenge (jumping out of an airplane, learning a new language); other times it's overcoming a fear (remaining in a committed relationship despite having been dumped in the past, traveling to a foreign country when we've never felt brave enough to leave your hometown). Sometimes the new idea isn't shiny or sexy. Sometimes it's simply the desire to stop emotional pain, or the wish to avoid an unpleasant outcome. Whatever it is, this new idea has to have enough appeal—and the anticipation of mastering the necessary obstacles has to promise a large enough increment of enhanced self-esteem—that we want it more than we fear the journey toward it.

As divorce professionals we know that when clients participate fully in their divorce process and make proactive decisions (even when legal, financial, and interpersonal realities limit their range of options), they go on to live happier and more fulfilling lives than do clients who remain passive, intractably angry, or victimized. But most of our clients choose divorce after having exhausted every other available avenue; especially in the beginning, none of the choices are appealing. As a freshly separated, grieving father pointed out to Kate during a recent discussion of ways he and his wife could share time with their kids, "There's nothing good here, only the best of the worst."

In divorce, transformation exists on a continuum. Clients who achieve the most positive change are motivated by what the authors call "higher order new ideas," such as the desire to move on to a more intimate partnership, for self-understanding, for the peace of mind that comes with forgiveness, or to become a better parent. Clients who achieve less positive change (but still *some* change) are motivated by what we call "lower order new ideas." An example of a lower order new idea is a bitter wife's acceptance of the fact that since it's unlikely a judge would pillory her cheating ex in court, she might as well stick it out in mediation. Perhaps you're thinking "that's not positive change, that's just giving up on a hopeless strategy!" We would counter by pointing out that some clients go to court regardless of how hopeless their cases—perhaps because they're after some abstract sense of justice or they're hell-bent on destroying their future ex—even if they have to take themselves (and their kids) down in the process. So if your client starts out looking like a terrorist and ends up angry but resigned, that's positive change. Both higher and lower order new ideas can serve as motivators for positive growth *at a given client's level of transformative capacity.*

> *In divorce, transformation exists on a continuum. Clients who achieve the most positive change are motivated by what the authors call "higher order new ideas." Clients who achieve less positive change are motivated by what we call "lower order new ideas." Both higher and lower order new ideas can serve as motivators for positive growth at a given client's level of transformative capacity.*

But whether your client emerges from their divorce like a butterfly from a chrysalis or merely avoids a nasty court battle by the skin of their teeth, they're not going to get there on their own. They're going to need a helping relationship, and they're going to need you to create and sustain it.

A Helping Relationship

We are born into relationships, and we are born seeking relationships. No other animal on earth is as dependent on an early caregiver (or for as long) as is the human infant. We depend on our mothers, fathers, and other primary attachment figures to meet our physical needs, protect us from unwanted impingements, and keep us safe from potential dangers. And our caregivers are wired to provide us with the kind of protection we need. Good parents quickly learn to distinguish between a merely fussy cry and a cry that says, "You better stop what you're doing and come here right away!"

When development goes well, we gradually leave the sanctuary of our caregivers' embrace—exploring our world by traveling away, back, and away again in loops of increasing distance. When our caregivers remain consistently present to receive us, cheer us on as we become more adventurous, and meet our other needs in reasonable and predictable ways, we develop a sense of "basic trust." Basic trust is the idea that the world is essentially a safe place in which people can be counted on to be caring, available, and helpful. Armed with basic trust we acquire new skills and coping mechanisms—we navigate unfolding developmental phases until we can take independent care of ourselves and form new primary attachments.

Four Core Components of a Helping Relationship

The four core components of the helping relationship provided by a good early caregiver (or professional) are:

1. A holding environment
2. Containment
3. Empathy
4. Attunement

As you read the following descriptions of these components and how they form the foundation for a helping relationship that can facilitate healthy development, let your mind play. Think about the relevance of these ideas to your own experiences in important personal relationships, now and in the past. Think too about your relationships with colleagues and clients. How many of these conditions have been provided to you? How many of these conditions have you provided for others?

A Holding Environment

A holding environment is a safe, responsive, nurturing milieu that facilitates development. Our first experience of a holding environment begins in our relationship with our earliest caregivers. To illustrate, let's take a look at a father and his newborn baby.

Our father cradles his infant in his arms and holds her in his gaze. Through a process that has traditionally been termed "primary maternal preoccupation," but which we prefer to call "primary parental preoccupation," the father uses his mind and body to fully take in this infant who, after all, is still in many ways a stranger. His entire self is literally and metaphorically curved around his baby. His focus on her sometimes requires him to suspend familiar life rhythms and the gratification of his own desires.

In these early days many of the needs of parents and older children must take a backseat to those of the baby.

It's not that the father never becomes anxious or irritable. It's rather that the positive experiences between him and his baby far outweigh the negative. Dad is loving and steady; he meets the infant's needs consistently and well. In the inevitable instances in which he does struggle to understand his baby's needs ("Are you hungry or are you tired?") or fails to meet them right away (perhaps by being sleepily slow to respond when the baby wakes at night for the fourth time), the resultant anxiety can be borne, the minor failure corrected, and a sense of security reestablished and enhanced. These interactions help the infant to develop the basic trust that allows them to expand their attachments outward from the protective one-on-one relationship with their primary caregiver(s) into relationships with siblings, extended family, friends, community, and the wider world.

> *Basic trust is a sense that the world is essentially a safe place in which people can be counted on. It is what allows the baby to expand their attachments outward from the protective one-on-one relationship with their primary caregiver(s) into relationships with siblings, extended family, friends, community, and the wider world.*

The holding environment provided by the father and the baby we just described is composed of both physical comfort (food, warm air, a soft crib, comfortable clothing, protection from loud sounds) and the loving relationship itself. It is a setting in which healthy development can unfold. A good physical and emotional professional environment replicates the essential qualities of that holding environment.

> *The holding environment provided by the parent is composed of both physical comfort (food, warm air, a soft crib, comfortable clothing, protection from loud sounds) and the loving relationship itself. It is a setting in which healthy development can unfold. A good physical and emotional professional environment replicates the essential qualities of that holding environment.*

We will discuss the holding environment as it applies to divorce work in detail in Chapters 4, 5, and 6.

Containment

While the holding environment is composed of the more visible, interpersonal aspects of the parent-baby relationship, containment occurs internally, between the minds of the caretaker and his or her charge. Containment is the act of allowing someone else's painful experience to enter into you in such a way that you can understand it on a gut level and can empathize with it *without being taken over by it.* In the beginning the baby does not know where he ends and the mother or father begins. The baby has bodily experiences, some of which are unpleasant. In response Mom or dad coos comfortingly, watches and listens, and attempts to find a solution to the problem. Perhaps he or she changes the baby's diaper and, if that doesn't soothe, offers the breast or bottle. Eventually he or she hits on the right solution, and the baby settles into a state of sated calm. Parent and baby enjoy a mutual sense of success, satisfaction, and connectedness.

> Containment is the act of allowing someone else's painful experiences to enter into you in such a way that you can understand it on a gut level without being taken over by it.

In this simple, ordinary set of interactions, many important things have happened. The baby has had an overwhelming experience. The parent has registered it and (because he or she loves the baby and wants to relieve its distress) has become somewhat anxious. But mom or dad has not become overwhelmed; they have maintained a steady, calm, caring stance. They have allowed the baby's distress to flow into their own mind and body where they could experience it closely and, without moving too quickly to action, formed hypotheses about what the baby was feeling and how to help. Based on those hypotheses they have offered one potential solution, then another—without becoming discouraged or frustrated when they didn't succeed right away. Without being aware of it, the parent has communicated to the baby that pain (physical and emotional) can be borne without causing damage, that together they can understand the source of the distress, and that a solution will emerge from that understanding.

A crucial aspect of this interaction is that while the parent's emotional energy remains powerfully focused on the baby, he or she doesn't merge with the baby. He or she is *with* him, but not *in it* with him. This increment of separation is what, in psychotherapeutic parlance, is known as "transitional space." It represents a crucial distance between parent and child that allows room for reflection. It is not an empty space, but rather a bridge between the parent's maturity and the baby's immaturity. Within the safety of the holding environment (and perhaps while (physically *holding*) the baby), mom or dad reaches across the space between them with their mind, gathers up the not-yet-understood bits of the baby's experience, contains them in his or her psyche and body, and begins to form hypotheses about their meaning ("Is he hungry?" "Does he need a diaper change?"). Rather than becoming frantic, the adult holds open the space between him- or herself and the baby. He or she exercises caring restraint, "taking in" the baby's experience until they can feed it back to him along with a new understanding of it. In this way they metabolize the baby's experience.

Through containment, our parent has communicated a faith in their and their baby's shared capacity to work things out in a mutually satisfactory way, even if it takes a while for the solution to come into focus. In time and over thousands of such interactions, the baby will internalize a sense of his own capacity to bear and make meaning of his own experience.

When we are working optimally with a client, we register their overwhelming feelings without becoming overwhelmed. We are with them, but not overidentified with them. We don't take their distress personally (even when it comes at us in the form of aggression), but maintain a calm,

> *While the parent's emotional energy remains powerfully focused on the baby, he or she doesn't merge with the baby. He or she is with him, but not in it with him. This increment of separation is known as "the transitional space." Similarly, when we are working optimally with a client we register their overwhelming feelings without becoming overwhelmed. We are with them, but not overidentified with them.*

client-centered stance in which we invite, take in, and try to make meaning of their experience. We hold open a space for reflection, and, once we have a working understanding of the problem, we convey our client's experience back to them in a metabolized form (more on that concept in a moment). In this way we communicate our care and concern as well as our competence to take in and tolerate even powerfully negative emotion. We convey our calm conviction that together we can successfully navigate tough moments.

Containment

If you have ever sat quietly with someone who recently learned that his beloved wife of 20 years has fallen in love with another man, you know well how difficult it can be to allow yourself to *simply be* with him in that moment—to resist the urge either to dissociate from his feelings or to move too quickly to comfort him. Containment is the act of being completely present with someone in their moment of deep distress, and of taking their experience inside you so you can understand and empathize with it *without taking it on as your own.* Offering containment can be not only emotionally but *physically* difficult. But it is one of the most powerful tools in your professional toolbox.

Understanding Containment More Fully: The Concept of Metabolizing Experience Let's take a look at a typical exchange between the parent and baby we described earlier so we can unpack it a bit. The conversation (spoken and unspoken) goes something like this:

(*Baby is crying. The parent, cradling the baby, offers a bottle.*)
Parent: (*in a voice of caring concern*) Are you hungry, sweetheart?
    (*Baby screws up his face and turns away, his muscles tightening.*)
    Parent: (*voice softening*) No, that's not it (*rocking the baby gently and withdrawing the bottle*) Are you wet? Do you need a fresh diaper?

(*Baby continues to cry.*)

Parent: (*his body unconsciously swaying gently back and forth*) No, not wet. (*changing the baby's position so his head lies against the parent's shoulder. The baby's cries subside to a whimper*)

Parent: Oh, that's better. It's a bit early for bedtime, but I think you're sleepy. You did have a short nap today. Would you like to go in your crib, Little One?

(*The parent places the baby in his crib, turns down the lights, and rubs the infant's back as the baby quiets, relaxes, and falls peacefully to sleep*).

Now, let's consider what the baby has learned from this set of interactions:

- He is in competent, caring hands in which his needs are the focus of attention.
- His neediness is not destructive.
- His distress can be tolerated and meaning can be made of it.

Now, let's consider what else has happened:

- The baby has had an experience of empathy that over the years he will internalize as the ability to be empathic towards others.
- The baby has begun to develop a sense of basic trust (the foundation for self-esteem leading to the ability to become increasingly independent over time).
- The bond between the parent and baby has been strengthened.
- The parent has learned new information about the baby that will help in future interactions.
- The baby has learned information about himself ("Oh, that feeling is sleepiness!")
- Now you've seen it in action: The parent takes in a baby's distress, contains it without rushing to make sense of it or take it away, develops an empathic understanding of it, then feeds it back to the baby- but in an elevated form. The parent's response is fortified by new understanding, *metabolized* into a better idea with the power to facilitate transformation- within and between each of them. When

the baby receives the response ("You're sleepy") and it hits the mark, his capacity to master the primary task associated with his developmental phase (to develop a sense of basic trust) has been raised another notch.

We like the word "metabolize" and use it in our writing about divorce because we think it captures an essential aspect of our work. The verb itself comes from the world of biology, and refers to a process in which an organism ingests nutrients and transforms them into usable energy. When we invoke this concept we are referring to a process in which an individual or group of individuals takes in raw experience and enriches it through self-reflection, thus raising it to a higher order idea that includes insight and empathy. Metabolized ideas move an individual and a process forward because they contain the perspective of the "other."

> We metabolize our client's experience when we enrich it through self-reflection. Metabolized ideas move an individual and a process forward because they contain the perspective of the other.

More distressed or rigid clients rely on us to metabolize their ideas for them, less distressed or healthier clients bring this capacity to their divorce process (though they'll still need our support to gain and maintain new perspectives, especially when emotions run high). The process of metabolizing a position ("I want to bury my spouse financially") into a new idea that exists further along the developmental continuum ("I am hurt and angry, but I realize that behaving destructively isn't good for any of us") is part and parcel of the transformational process.

Understanding Containment More Fully: Transitional space in divorce work. To facilitate transformation in our client is to participate in a mutually improvised dance. Our client leads *us* by communicating how far, in any given moment, she can allow us to stretch her toward the next step on her developmental journey. We lead *her* by metaphorically taking her hand, lending her our belief in her ability to take that step, and (while holding her in mind) turning our attention toward her horizon and trusting her to follow.

Here's another metaphor: If we think of our client's journey as a garden path and of each new divorce challenge as a paving stone, the transitional space is the unoccupied paving stone between the one on which our client stands and the one—two paving stones further ahead—on which we choose to stand. It is the increment of psychological distance between our client and us into which we invite our client and from which we guide her. Without it, in order to meet our client we would have to move backward to stand with her in the exact same space she occupies. Rather than reaching emotionally across the developmental divide and supporting her in taking a step forward (offering empathy in the service of growth), we would be taking *on* her feelings. If we "Over-identifying with our clients robs them of their volition and leads to stasis or regression."

The transitional space is also the incubator of transformation. As we take in our client's experience, mull it over (like the parent containing and trying to make sense of their baby's distress), and feed it back in a metabolized form that regulates their anxiety up or down to an optimal level (more on that in a moment), we invite our client (sometimes nudge her) onto the next paving stone. It is in that safe but open space where our client's mind meets ours that their new idea—not yet imagined or fully realized—can emerge and come into focus. And, as it does ("Oh, maybe I *could* tolerate a shared custody arrangement!"), we stay on our paving stone long enough for the new idea to take solid hold. Once our client has taken a step forward along the path we do too—thus maintaining the expectation of further growth and maintaining the transitional space in which it can occur.

> *The transitional space is the increment of psychological distance between our client and us into which we invite our client and from which we guide her. The transitional space is the incubator of transformation, a creative space in which new ideas are generated.*

Empathy

The most therapeutic of all human experiences is to be deeply understood and accepted. Where sympathy is the capacity to feel

The most therapeutic of all human experiences is to be deeply known and accepted. Unless your client feels that you understand him or her profoundly and without judgment, nothing else you do will ever matter.

for another, empathy is the capacity to feel *with* them—to understand in our bones what it means to walk in their shoes. You may be a skilled lawyer, coach, or financial expert, but unless your client feels you understand him or her profoundly and without judgment, nothing else you do will ever matter.

Attunement

An emotionally present mother absorbs her infant's experiences through all of her senses. And it's a mutual process. She and her baby are exquisitely connected to each other, unconsciously noting nearly invisible shifts in muscular movement. The mother tracks her infant – intuitively matching her actions, tone of voice and posture to the child's changing states of being. If the baby is happy, the mother mirrors the pleasure back. If the baby is in pain, the mother communicates calm concern. Through their mutual and intense gaze the two establish a feedback loop that allows the mother to gauge and match her baby's needs. This process is called attunement.

When to be silent? When to offer comfort? When to open up emotion? When to focus on the task? The concept of attunement is relevant in our offices every day. Our ability to intuitively track our client's emotional and cognitive states is crucial in leveraging our helping relationship in the service of positive change.

The concept of attunement is relevant in our offices every day. When to be silent? When to offer comfort? When to open up emotion? When to focus on the task? These moment-to-moment questions are the very stuff of our work. Once we've built a safe relationship of trust characterized by holding, containment and empathy, our ability to intuitively track our clients' emotional and cognitive states will become crucial in leveraging our helping relationship in the service of positive change.

Optimal Anxiety

Imagine the following scenario:

A couple whose divorce you are mediating sits in charged silence. The issue on the table is whether or not the wife, who has been out of the workforce for several years, will go back to work to help cover the gap between the husband's income and their projected expenses. She is terrified and angry. The couple has spent several hours on this topic and explored a number of scenarios. It becomes increasingly clear that the only viable alternative to the wife's going back to work is to sell the only home their children have ever known. The couple falls silent what seems an eternity. Should you . . .

- Remain silent for as long as it takes one of them to speak?
- Remind the wife that she doesn't have to make a decision today?
- Remind the wife that she has already said she thinks going back to work is better than selling the house?
- Remind the wife that the vocational counselor with whom she consulted gave her good reason to be optimistic about her earning potential?
- Ask the husband to reassure the wife that he is ok with her going back to work part-time to start?
- Something else?

The answer is, *it depends.*

Good parents fail their children incrementally over time. Think back to the college freshman in Chapter 1 who wanted to succeed but had some difficulty adapting to his new independence. Now, rewind the clock to when that young man was one year old. Back then, his parents picked him up whenever he seemed frightened or wanted their loving care. But, by the time he was 18 months old, they sometimes let him whine for a few minutes—making reassuring eye contact but perhaps finishing a phone call before giving him a cuddle. When the little boy was three and asked for help completing a simple wooden puzzle, his parents guided his hands. When he was four, they encouraged him to work harder to find the right fit for each piece—even when he grumbled a bit. But if his grumbling turned into tears or his frustration grew too great, they'd quickly relent and offer help. Each time their son faced a new challenge he faced a familiar quandary – he wanted his parents' help because it was comforting and a good short-cut, but he also wanted the pleasure of "doing it *myself.*"

What these well-attuned parents knew intuitively is that development requires optimal anxiety – the right amount of tension between *worry about the difficulty of the task and the desire to accomplish the task.* They assessed each moment, and offered carefully considered responses that regulated his anxiety and matched his needs in a given moment. They didn't move in too quickly to help—if they had, he wouldn't have had the time, space, and opportunity to struggle for mastery. But they didn't hold back so long that he became overwhelmed to the point of giving up.

After thousands of such interactions throughout childhood and adolescence, this boy became a young adult ready to leave home for the exciting but scary world of college. Knowing that his parents empathized both with his nervousness and his excitement but ultimately had faith in his ability to handle more independence gave the boy the confidence he needed.

Development requires optimal anxiety – the right amount of tension between worry about the difficulty of the task and the desire to accomplish the task. In any given moment we must honor the part of our client that wants to stay safe, while "siding" with the part that wants to move forward. Like the best-attuned parents, the best-attuned divorce professional knows when to comfort, when to push, and when to hold back—all in the service of our ultimate goal.

Just as the job of a parent is to facilitate their child's successful "growing up," our job is to help our client move through their divorce process toward their own best outcome. In any given moment we must honor the part of them that wants to stay safe, while "siding" with the part that wants to move forward. Like the best-attuned parents, the best-attuned divorce professional knows when to comfort, when to push, and when to hold back—all in the service of our ultimate goal.

Some Final Thoughts for this Chapter

We can't see your face as you read, but we've presented this material to lots of audiences whose faces we could see. We're guessing that by now some readers may be struggling to understand certain concepts, or feeling skeptical about some concepts' practical applicability. Others of you might like our ideas, but feel worried you'll never be confident enough to put them to use with clients. If you're feeling any of those ways, we invite you to simply allow yourself to be confused, skeptical, or worried. Don't fight the feelings, but read on. If at any point you become flooded (with either information or emotion), tell yourself, "Yup, this stuff is new to me. But I'm reading this book because I want to up my professional game. That's a developmental task I've set for myself. If this task were easy, it wouldn't be a challenge. There'd be no opportunity for positive change." Guess what? If you're carrying on in the face of uncertainty, allowing yourself to linger in a state of not yet knowing, holding on to the faith that sense and meaning will eventually emerge because you are motivated by curiosity and an authentic desire to learn how to be helpful to another person, you're already doing everything a good parent does. You're creating a holding environment—this time for yourself.

And by the way, in this moment your authors are doing it too. Even though we can't see you, we're imagining ourselves in your shoes. We don't want to presume anything about you, but we're taking a moment to make space for any uncomfortable feelings you might be having. And we're not leaving you alone with them; we're supporting you in tolerating them for now. There are eight chapters to go and, if we've done our job right, each of them will help bring things into clearer focus.

We also invite you to remember what we said in the introduction—*we are all wired to be able to do this work.* We recently ran across an article by the psychologist and science writer Daniel Goleman in which he explains this point succinctly and well:

> *The circuitry for compassion is based in the mammalian parenting circuitry—and because of the brain's neuroplasticity you can be very systematic in strengthening it. Not only do*

*you become stronger but you actually become kinder, and
more likely to help other people.*[2]

So, essentially, you came out of the box preloaded with the soft-
ware you need to apply the concepts in this book. As you read
further and are kind to yourself when you don't "get it" right away,
the meaning and practical significance of new ideas will assemble
themselves in your mind; you'll begin to integrate them.

Summary of Concepts from Chapter 2

- Human development involves relinquishing safe, familiar
  positions, mastering of new challenges, and taking leaps of
  faith.
- Every developmental crossroad represents a struggle
  between two emotional polarities—one pulling us toward
  stasis, the other pulling us forward along our own developmental trajectory.
- Change is particularly difficult under conditions of stress
  (such as divorce), in which our cognitive abilities are often
  impaired and our natural inclination is to cling to familiar
  positions.
- There are three elements necessary to make positive
  change: a new idea, a special kind of helping relationship
  modeled on a good parent/child attachment paradigm, and
  optimal anxiety.
- An effective helping relationship has four components: a
  holding environment, containment, empathy and attunement.
- Helping our clients to successfully navigate their divorce
  involves helping them to stretch emotionally in ways that
  are often painful and frightening.
- If, as divorce professionals, we want to help our clients
  reach their own highest transformative potential, we need
  to create the conditions for change within the context of
  our work.

---

2. Goleman, Daniel. *Interview, Vineyard Gazette,* August, 2015.

Chapter 3

Understanding Our Clients

"Tell me what you fear and I'll tell you what happened to you."

—Donald Winnicott, *The Child, the Family and the Outside World (Classics in Child Development)*

This book is about helping our clients reach their own highest outcomes. In Chapter 2, we explained that great outcomes emerge from creating the Three Conditions for Positive Change. We explained that our ability to create and maintain those conditions depends on our capacity to create and maintain a very special kind of helping relationship that includes a holding environment, containment, empathy, and attunement. We are the instruments of change; the conditions for change exist first in our minds and are maintained by our own emotional and cognitive capacities. But we are human, and therefore our states of mind are affected by the states of mind of those around us—by every person with whom we are in a relationship. And the more intimate the relationship, the more affected we are by its vicissitudes. Because our clients depend on us in a time of crisis, their relationship with us is, in its own way, highly intimate. So it's often difficult to maintain the frame of our professional roles, especially when our clients reject our best advice, act against their own interests, or attack our motivations or competence.

If you've worked on even a few family law cases, you know that convincing clients to relinquish entrenched positions, consider new options, and craft compromises they can live with is tough work. Even our most seemingly reasonable clients sometimes behave in frustratingly irrational ways, shooting themselves (and us) in the foot just when things are going their way. In this chapter we are going to explore the "why" beneath our clients' seemingly inscrutable behavior.

Common Examples of Irrational and Self-Defeating Behaviors in Clients

- Asking for advice, then failing to take it
- Holding to unreasonable or illogical positions
- Behaving in provocative or needling ways toward their spouse, particularly when their spouse is on the verge of making a concession or agreeing to a proposal
- Rejecting generous settlement offers
- Overvaluing advice from their "Greek Chorus" (friends, family members) and devaluing yours
- Withholding important information that, when it inevitably surfaces, might torpedo the process
- Failing to comply with agreements (e.g., to pay pendente lite support, or to inform a co-parent in advance of taking children out of town)
- Delaying progress by failing to complete important tasks (e.g., to gather documents, to get an appraisal of the marital home), then complaining about the glacial pace of the process
- Being unavailable to schedule meetings, missing/being late to/repeatedly asking to reschedule meetings, failing to respond to your calls/e-mails
- Introducing provocative/spurious/already discussed-to-death issues at the end of a tough meeting or just before final settlement
- Driving up the cost of the process and then complaining about the cost of the process
- Relentlessly seeking recompense or revenge for real or perceived acts of deceit by their spouse

(Continued)

Common Examples of Irrational and Self-Defeating Behaviors in Clients (*Continued*)

- Appearing to listen closely and to understand information or instructions, then denying the conversation took place
- Behaving with/toward their spouse in ways that have a powerfully undermining effect on the divorce process (e.g., having sex with their spouse on the eve of litigation)

Our first co-written book included an in-depth exploration of the way a person's accumulated experiences with important other people in their life (especially from early childhood) form "templates," ways of relating to others that are typical for that individual but that often don't match their current day reality. When someone (us, our clients, our colleagues) brings these ingrained patterns and assumptions from the past into the moments of our work, that person is likely to view the present situation in negatively distorted ways that can cause trouble in the case.

> *When someone brings ingrained patterns and assumptions from the past into the moments of our work, that person is likely to view the present situation in negatively distorted ways that can cause trouble in the case.*

You may be thinking, "Come on, none of us has a perfect childhood. My dad ran the house like a military barracks and I don't have trouble with authority!" It's true: Some people are more resilient than others. But, by and large, the difference between someone who recreates traumatic experiences and someone who doesn't is the extent to which that person has faced and worked through the feelings associated with the trauma.

> *The difference between someone who recreates traumatic experiences and someone who doesn't is the extent to which that person has faced and worked through the feelings associated with the trauma.*

For example, let's say you *did* grow up with a dad who ran the house like a military barracks, with the result that you grew up feeling criticized, on edge, and like you could never be "good enough" in the eyes of any authority figure. But let's say that over time (either on your own or through discussions with other helpful people—perhaps a therapist) you've been able to recognize, understand, and accept the ways your dad made you feel when you were a child. The feelings are still there, but they don't sting as much anymore. And they're out in the open; you can separate them from current reality. You have insight, both about yourself and about your dad. There are still times when you overreact to criticism, but it doesn't happen as often and when it does you recover quickly.

But the scenario ends differently if you decide *not* to deal with the emotional impact of your negative experiences with your dad in favor of adopting a "whatever doesn't kill you makes you stronger" attitude toward life. You think you're "fine," but you're not. Those old feelings of anxiety and shame aren't really gone; they're just banished (repressed) to the dark recesses of your mind. They lurk there, in your unconscious, and break through when they're activated by a present-day person or situation that reminds you of your upsetting past. Because you haven't dealt with your old conflicts, you're vulnerable to seeing other people as strictly authoritarian—even when they're not. You do this frequently, and, because you lack insight and don't *know* you're distorting reality, you have a lot of trouble recovering. Plus, every time you accuse a well-meaning person of being unfairly critical of you, they are likely to react angrily. So, in effect, you've created a feedback loop that reinforces your negative expectations.

> If you adopt a "whatever doesn't kill you makes you stronger" attitude toward life, old feelings of anxiety and shame aren't really gone— they're just banished (repressed) to the dark recesses of your mind. They lurk there, in your unconscious, and break through when they're activated by a present-day person or situation, even when that person or situation doesn't fit the feelings.

The unconscious conflicts that our clients haven't fully processed and that come alive in confusing or problematic ways are their "emotional dynamics." These dynamics have a pesky way of cropping up repeatedly in our work. We ask you to consider the following basic assumptions:

- The ways our clients think, feel, and behave are often driven by unconscious factors.
- Those unconscious factors play strong, sometimes problematic roles in the course of a divorce case.
- It is only by developing an understanding of the dynamics underlying our clients' patterns of thinking, feeling, and behaving that we can help them to reach successful outcomes.

Let's put these basic assumptions into a practical context with some examples of . . .

Why Developing an Understanding of Our Clients' Emotional Dynamics is Important for Our Work

Maintaining Empathy

It is impossible to fully dislike someone you know well. The process of learning another's personal narrative puts us in touch with their vulnerability, even if they are trying to appear invulnerable—it fosters connection. A colleague told us of her recent experience sitting with a particularly hard-to-like client. He was, she explained, "your classic corporate 'master of the universe'"—handsome, wealthy, entitled, demeaning. She described her client as a large, imposing middle-aged man; our colleague is in her early thirties, diminutive and reserved. As her client (red-faced, with finger pointed) loudly berated her for her failure to get his wife's "poor excuse for a lawyer to keep his client in line!" and threatened to call a senior partner in our colleague's law firm to complain about her incompetence, our colleague felt her heart begin to race, her thoughts to scramble, and a sense of floating above her own body.

"I was flooded," she told us. "All I could think was 'make this horrible man shut up and go away.'" But then she did something wonderful; she made an internal shift that would be hard for the most seasoned among us to accomplish. And it started with self-reflection.

Our colleague continued: "This guy made me feel so humiliated. Then I thought, 'Wow, this is the same way I felt as a kid at my family's dinner table when my father humiliated me in front of my older brothers because I didn't know the answers to one of his famous pop quizzes.' Suddenly I found myself imagining my client as a young boy in short pants, terrified, and feeling horrible while a contemptuous adult yelled at him. That made sense to me, because I know there's a scared child inside every bully. Once I came to see my client that way, my mind came back into the room and I was able to think again. And, I didn't hate or fear him anymore. Actually, I could relate to him."

Understanding your client helps you manage your negative reactions to aggressive or otherwise unpleasant behaviors. Remember: While these behaviors feel personal to you, they're not. Work to remain empathic, even when you're under attack.

> *It is impossible to fully dislike someone you know well. The process of learning another's personal narrative puts us in touch with their vulnerability and fosters connection. Understanding your client helps you manage your negative reactions to aggressive or otherwise unpleasant behaviors.*

Gaining a Realistic Sense of Your Client's Strengths and Limitations

If your gracious, smart, and grateful client stimulates in you a rescue fantasy that has you taking her calls at eleven o'clock at night, your professional boundaries have collapsed. Seeing her plaintive cries for help as reflecting echoes of her past relationships (perhaps with her husband, perhaps with her unavailable mother) can empower you to set better limits—crucial if she is to take responsibility for herself in her divorce process. As we discussed in Chapter 2, containing our client's feelings while setting reasonable limits that are based on knowing our client

> *Your clients should get as much of you as they need, but never quite as much as they want. That's what makes growth possible.*

well and being attuned to their needs and capacities is an important aspect of the holding environment. Maintaining a sturdy professional structure allows us to support our clients emotionally while remaining allied with the part of them that seeks to stride forward on their developmental path. Your clients should get as much of you as they need, but never quite as much as they want. That's what makes growth possible.

Assessing Transformative Capacity

Over the years we've become humbled by our inability to predict with any reliability which clients will settle in and surprise us with their willingness to make reasonable compromises and which clients will become increasingly locked into unreasonable positions. It's important to enter each new case without preconceptions about your client's transformative capacity (we'll discuss this issue in depth in Chapters 5 and 7). Especially since clients nearly always come to us in pain and under stress, it takes time (and many opportunities to experience how our clients respond to the support we offer as our work with them unfolds) to develop a real understanding of our client's strengths and vulnerabilities. We like to say, "We don't know until we know."

On the other hand, lots of well-intentioned professionals fail to recognize and accept their own client's emotional or intellectual limitations, even when those limitations are clearly in evidence. It's as if these professionals believe that in taking a more realistic view they're giving up on their client. The opposite is true. If we want our client to experience us as empathic—if we want to remain helpfully attuned—we need to learn what works for them *as they are*. Insisting that a given client is emotionally healthier than they are despite mounting evidence to the contrary can unintentionally damage our relationships with both our client and our colleagues.

> It's important to enter each new case without preconceptions about your client's character or transformative capacity. Overestimating your client's transformative capacity can unintentionally damage your relationships with both your client and your colleagues.

Consider a client who appears cheerfully accommodating during the initial meeting, impressing you with his capacity to see his situation and his spouse in what seems to be reasonable perspective. You perceive this client as able to see life in shades of gray. Because the couple is recently separated, tensions are high, and they don't yet have a plan for moving forward, you make some suggestions for ways this client and his wife might handle finances and custody on an interim basis. But let's say that beneath the surface of this client's character lies a deeply insecure younger version of himself who (because he longs for approval) leads with what appears to be an accommodating posture but (because he also fears exploitation and rejection) is unable to sustain a reasonable stance. This client may actually be exquisitely sensitive to any subtle indication that you are not going to be 100 percent supportive of his positions at every moment of your work. This individual (especially before he has come to know and trust you) is likely to pick up the slightest trace of evidence that you think he should agree to a compromise on any issue, and experience it as a betrayal. It will trigger mistrust in your capacity to advocate for him in the way *he* defines advocacy.

> *A client may initially impress you with his capacity to see his situation in reasonable perspective. But beneath the surface of this client's character may lie a deeply insecure younger version of himself who is unable to sustain a reasonable stance. This individual is likely to pick up the faintest trace of evidence that you think he should agree to a compromise, and experience it as a betrayal.*

Here's a vignette that shows how our professional effectiveness is diminished when we fail to see our clients clearly:

Our case includes two opposing teams of professionals who are working cooperatively, ostensibly to find solutions that work for both parties. At a point about midway through the process, it becomes clear that the clients are running out of money and have to decide which of their assets to draw on in order to create cash flow while they work toward settlement.

The husband in this case is unemployed (having stayed home to raise the couple's children) and is dependent on his wife for financial support. He tells one of his professionals that he feels financially disadvantaged and vulnerable. He runs up the professional's fees by spending hours on the phone with her, ruminating about how he can't afford the divorce and saying things like "My wife is going pull out of this process, go to court, and bankrupt me." The professional is worried on her client's behalf, and makes a side agreement allowing him to hold off paying her mounting fees until the client has access to funds from the sale of the marital home. The couple is planning to sell the home, but there is no official agreement to do so.

The husband's professional believes that the manner in which she has chosen to handle payment of her fees is a reasonable "personal decision." She informs her colleagues, but is resistant to discussing the issue. None of her colleagues perceive her client as she does. They talk with her about their shared perception that the husband is not so much a victim as someone who is having a hard time accepting his wife's decision to divorce. The team thinks the husband feels less frightened than angry, and that what he really wants is to punish his wife by refusing to engage in productive discussions. Still, the husband's professional sticks to her decision to delay billing for her fees. Tension rises between that professional and her colleagues.

Soon relationships between all professionals and both clients begin to deteriorate. The colleagues of the professional who has made special fee arrangements with her client begin to experience an unwelcome pressure to match her financial flexibility. The wife, the breadwinner, begins to resent her husband's "special treatment," and feels anxious that his professional has tied payment of fees to the sale of their home. After all, they haven't made a final decision about whether or when to sell, or about what will happen to the proceeds. The wife's satisfaction with the process wanes, along with her trust in all the professionals.

In the end, the husband terminates the cooperative process and takes the case to court. He doesn't pay his portion of any of his outstanding fees. His wife, disgusted with the way the process plays out, doesn't either.

This example illustrates a common phenomenon. As professionals, we all sometimes make well-intentioned decisions without being aware that we're acting in response to our own distorted

We all sometimes make well-intentioned decisions without being aware that we're acting in response to our own distorted or idiosyncratic views. The conscious effort to develop an accurate perception of our client and his or her motivations contributes to better outcomes.

or idiosyncratic views. Sometimes we overestimate our client's capacities or inaccurately believe they're acting in good faith. Other times we underestimate our client's capacities, or wrongly believe them to have malicious intent toward their spouse. The conscious effort to develop an accurate perception of our client and his or her motivations contributes to better outcomes.

Developing Shared Understanding

One of the toughest parts of working with colleagues in any divorce process is developing a shared and balanced perspective of both of the clients involved—the marital dance in which both partners play a role. Light bulb moments in which a colleague helps us to understand an aspect of our own (or their) client's emotional dynamics are always turning points. These flashes of shared expanded insight instantly raise the transformative possibilities for all involved.

At this juncture you may reasonably ask, "Yeah, but what about when the other side doesn't want to play ball?" Unfortunately, we've all been there: A colleague is convinced that zealous advocacy means simply championing their own client's explicit desires and perspectives, and refuses to engage in an honest discussion with us (the "opposing" side) in which they might be asked to share any of their client's vulnerabilities.

This leads us to . . .

Avoiding Falling into Counterproductive Modes of Advocacy

Consider this scenario:

You're meeting a new client, Mrs. A. She is furious. Her husband of 20 years has precipitously asked for a divorce. She describes him as work-obsessed and emotionally unavailable to her and to their three children. She wants sole custody; after all, he barely knows the kids. He's shown up for the occasional dinner and soccer game. Makes sense to you. In an early settlement proposal you float an access schedule in which Mr. A would have limited time with his children—alternate partial weekends (from Friday at 6 p.m. until Saturday at 3 p.m.) and one night during the week. You're not trying to be provocative; you accept your client's depiction of her husband as a largely absent father whose primary interest is his work. You're expecting to settle custody quickly.

*Then comes the angry response from Mr. A's attorney: "My client is offended by your client's implication that he is anything but a loving father who should have equal time with his children." Mr. A and his attorney propose a 50/50 time-sharing schedule. Mrs. A is panicked and furious, and you're off to the races: thrust, parry, proposal, counter-proposal, mounting acrimony, and mounting fees. Six miserable months and a custody evaluation later, they arrive at a compromise agreement—one that might have been achieved relatively quickly and much less painfully if the attorneys had started off not by sending the messages their clients **wanted** them to send, but by having a thoughtful conversation about the couple's history and co-parenting relationship.*

Our clients come to us with vivid, compelling stories, full of feeling and detail. Whether you're working in a traditional settlement model or some form of alternate dispute resolution in which you're allied with one party (as opposed to being a sole neutral), you're an advocate. It is your job to represent your client's interests. But are your client's interests best served by you becoming the standard bearer of their cause as they define it?

Empathy does not equate with endorsement. In fact, accepting our client's narrative as the exclusive truth shuts down the transitional space we described in Chapter 2. It puts us *in* our client's position, rather than in a position to understand and reflect on our client's positions. It also shuts down the possibility of coming to understand the perspective of the

> *Empathy does not equate with endorsement. Accepting our client's narrative as the exclusive truth puts us in our client's position, rather than in a position to understand and reflect on our client's position.*

other spouse—a crucial element in our ability to help our clients achieve their best outcome.

By way of further illustration, let's return to Mrs. A. Let's assume for purposes of this vignette that you are an attorney (as opposed to a mental health professional or financial neutral). What if, as you listened to her story, you asked yourself: "How would Mr. A tell the same story?" What if, instead of leading with an aggressive custody proposal, you had called Mr. A's attorney and asked some questions? You'd have learned that while Mr. A had worked a gazillion hours per week, he had done so in order to provide the large home and lavish lifestyle that his wife claimed she needed to compensate for the pain of growing up in an impoverished family. You'd also have learned that Mr. A had felt excluded from the unit created by Mrs. A and their children. He'd wanted to be more involved, but she had shut him out (perhaps because her identity was entirely wrapped up in her ideas about herself as a mother). You'd have learned, too, that Mr. A had reluctantly asked for the divorce after several years of failed marriage counseling. What if Mr. A's attorney conveyed Mr. A's acknowledgment that while he wanted to spend substantial time with his children, he knew that the children would have initial difficulty with long separations from their mother. What if he admitted to having a lot to learn before he'd be an effective day-to-day parent?

It's crucial to remember that our client's "side" of the story is one of multiple potential (and potentially realistic) perspectives. Not only does it shift and change shape with our client's mood and stage in the divorce process, but it represents only part of the family narrative. But this presents technical challenges for all of us. It's often difficult to help a client to understand that you're not serving their interests by simply supporting them in every idea, wish, and feeling. A healthier client may come to understand that in challenging them to consider new options you are helping to manage their expectations and get the outcome that is closest to their goals (in other words, they'll "stretch"). A less healthy client may become furious when you don't simply toe the line, and may accuse you of not understanding, not caring, or not being proactive on their behalf.

Resisting the pull to overidentify with a client can be a particular challenge for even the best family lawyers, since it dovetails with one of their toughest jobs—that of balancing the role of advocate with knowledge of the limits of the law and a realistic sense of what might be in a client's (or a child's) best interest. In other words, helping a client to get what he or she wants while accepting what he or she can't have. And, hopefully, doing all of this while keeping them out of the blood bath of a nasty negotiation or, worse, a court battle.

Seeing a Couple in Three Dimensions: Learning the Other Side of the Story

Here are some benefits of understanding the perspective of your client's future ex and of their professional(s):

- It allows you to help your client anticipate the needs/interests of their spouse—and thereby increases the chance of successful settlement.
- It helps you to empathize with the other client and their professional team—so you can avoid getting caught in counterproductive adversarial positions and maintain better relationships with colleagues.
- It helps you to realistically assess the validity of your client's claims so you can strategize appropriately.
- It helps you to see that your client isn't purely a victim and their spouse isn't purely a villain—a realization which may bolster you when its time to stretch your client toward accepting a reasonable compromise.

Now, a few tips for learning to listen to the other side of the story

- Listen nonjudgmentally, but always with a bit of skepticism.
- Ask yourself: "What might the other spouse say if he or she were here?"

(Continued)

Seeing a Couple in Three Dimensions: Learning the Other Side of the Story (*Continued*)

- If you're an attorney, begin the process with an exploratory conversation with opposing counsel, rather than with a provocative letter or an aggressive proposal.
- Ask yourself how you would advocate most effectively for the other client (if that person had walked into your office rather than their spouse).
- Learn more about the couple's dynamics—the emotional dance they've been doing for years. The more you learn about each of their contributions to the marriage and its dissolution, the more you'll be able to see things realistically. A broadened perspective increases your capacity to think creatively and—we would argue—increases your overall effectiveness as a divorce professional.[1]

Having Realistic Expectations of Ourselves, Our Clients, and Our Process

Lots of us confuse transformation in a divorce process with fundamental character change. For example, a stay-at-home dad with college-aged children who begins the divorce process with you feeling hopeless about his professional prospects and emerges with a new sense of hope and personal agency has had what we in the mental health field call a "corrective emotional experience." Because the divorce process was different from and better than he expected (and different from and better than his experiences with conflict in the past), his experience of himself and the world has been, to some extent, modified. That's a big, wonderful deal; we don't want to minimize the positive impact of your work.

---

1. For an in-depth exploration of the factors (conscious and unconscious) that bring two people together in an intimate partnership, what happens when they come apart, and how marital dynamics affect their helping professionals (including the authors' explanation of their concept of the "The Lock and Key") see Chapter 2: Couple Dynamics in *Navigating Emotional Currents in Collaborative Divorce: A Guide to Enlightened Team Practice* (Scharff and Herrick, ABA 2010).

But it's unhelpful (and anti-therapeutic) for us to overestimate the significance of the shift. In fact, when we behave in celebratory and congratulatory ways ("Wow, I'm so proud of you! You're going to do great now that you're divorced!"), we risk making our client feel emotionally dropped. After all, they're still in pain. We also risk raising their anxiety by sending the unintended message that feeling good and optimistic is somehow morally or intrinsically better than feeling depressed and hopeless. Setting up a dynamic in which a client feels that we're gratified by their happiness and disappointed by their distress represents a collapse of the holding environment, because it shifts the focus away from our client's needs and onto ours.

Clients need our emotional attunement right through to the end of our work with them. Even for clients who feel they have grieved their marriage and are impatient for the process to end, the final phase of the legal divorce can be surprisingly emotionally fraught. And many clients (especially those who did not initiate the split) are still in the early phase of their emotional divorce when they finalize their Agreement. Often for months or years beyond settlement, most of our clients continue to wrestle with a potent mixture of relief, regret, grief, fear, anticipation, guilt, depression and excitement. It takes a long time for the water to recede after a tsunami.

The best any of us can do for a given client is to open their eyes to new possibilities—set them on track for significant personal change over time. We can facilitate a shift in their trajectory, but we can't push them faster than their situation and emotional make-up will allow, nor can we change their fundamental character. The secret to professional satisfaction is finding pleasure in the idea that our job is to shepherd

Setting up a dynamic in which a client feels that we're gratified by their happiness and disappointed by their distress shifts the focus away from our client's needs and onto ours. The secret to professional satisfaction is finding pleasure in the idea that our job is to shepherd our client through a leg of their journey, and to leave them at a safe way station. But determining the ultimate outcome of their journey? That's out of our control and, thankfully, outside of our job descriptions.

our client through a leg of their journey, and to leave them at a safe way station—while remaining available to them should they need our help in the future. But determining the ultimate outcome of their journey? That's out of our control and, thankfully, outside of our job descriptions.

It's a tough balance. The work we do with and for our clients is meaningful and significant. But some humility on our part keeps our promises in check and protects our clients from idealizing us; it minimizes the development of inflated expectations and it helps us keep our personal, ego-driven agendas out of the work.

Now that we've examined the benefits of developing an understanding of our clients' dynamics, let's dig a little deeper—toward an understanding of how those dynamics are formed in the first place.

How Personality Develops: The Impact of Bad Childhood Experiences

We all know someone who is a genius at making a pig's ear out of a silk purse. They seem to have it all—money, intelligence, health—even a large support network of loving friends and family. Yet they're incapable of experiencing pleasure in their lives, and often sabotage themselves by, say, fleeing from intimacy, becoming inappropriately angry at inopportune moments, or failing to follow through on commitments. Likely, they disown their own contributions to the problem while projecting fault outward. They blame their insensitive spouse, their ungrateful children, their cruel boss, the stupidity of the grocery clerk, or the simple rotten luck of having been born cursed. On the other hand, we all also know someone who seems to defy the odds in the other direction. Their life has been a series of Jobean events—abusive parents, poverty, illness, loss after loss—yet they find pleasure in their work and make wonderful, loving relationships. Are some people hardwired for misery and others for joy?

The truth is that those who defy the odds are rare. As we acknowledged earlier in the chapter, some folks are unusually resilient. But most people display attitudes and behaviors that follow logically from their early lives. Important character traits—the capacity to find and maintain satisfying work, the ability to form loving relationships—can be linked directly to our formative experiences. To some extent there is a simple mathematical way of thinking about this: The better our early experience is, the happier we will be, and vice versa.

But this simplistic formula breaks down when we consider that we all have both bad and good experiences, right from the beginning. Because development is neither linear nor consistent across different aspects of a person's life, neither is personality. We are not simply happy or not, successful or not. As we described in Chapter 2, most of us are influenced by more than one caregiver right from the start. So, for example, someone with a domineering, critical mother may clash with authority figures. But if this same person had a loving, supportive father, she may become a confident, successful parent. And our personalities can evolve over time; they can be changed for the better through interactions with new people and new perspectives. If you sit down for a chat with someone who has risen above emotional and financial deprivation to become "good at life," what you'll likely find is that somewhere along the line they developed a relationship with at least one important older person (a teacher, a mentor, a caring divorce professional) who believed in them and was emotionally sturdy enough to provide the holding environment needed to get them back on developmental track.

Unfortunately, a bad experience, whether ongoing (like having a harsh, critical parent), or sudden (like the death of a loved one) exerts more influence over our lives than does a positive experience. And the earlier in our lives the bad experience occurs, the more influence it wields. Why? Because the more formative and traumatic the experience, the more emotional energy is required to cope with it over time. Here's what we mean.

> *A bad experience exerts more influence over our lives than a positive experience. And the earlier in our life it occurs, the more influence it wields. The more formative and traumatic the experience, the more emotional energy is required to cope with it over time.*

Emotional Defenses

All of us protect ourselves against (in other words, manage to go on in spite of) negative or traumatic experiences through various unconscious psychological strategies known in the mental health field as "defenses." We might push feelings or memories out of our awareness (repression), insist to ourselves and to others that our feelings are mild when they are actually intense (minimization), deny that an event affected us or even occurred (denial), or distract ourselves from an emotional situation by focusing on other issues or tasks (avoidance). There are other emotional defenses (and we'll get to some of them later), but we hope we've given you enough of the flavor of the phenomena that we can turn our attention to the larger impact of defenses on us and on our clients.

THE IMPACT OF DEFENSES ON OUR CAPACITY TO FUNCTION

Defenses are not always problematic; in fact, we couldn't make it through a day without them. We couldn't be productive workers (or parents or spouses) if we were steadily preoccupied with global crises or the dangers of everyday life. It is the extent of our reliance on defenses—how often we move into protective mode, how long we linger there, and how entrenched our defensive postures become—that shape the way we cope, both in our ordinary lives and during times of stress (such as divorce).

Here's why: Think of your emotional energy as money in your psychic bank. You have a finite amount. Choosing not to think about or to remember something (to defend against it) doesn't come free; in fact it's very costly. As we described early in the chapter (remember our hypothetical militant dad?), once you force a painful memory out of your conscious awareness it's not really buried. It's just exiled to your unconscious. You will have to continue to spend emotional capital in order to keep it there. Defenses are mentally expensive; trying to feel less or not feel at all costs a lot of emotional currency. That's currency that is then not avail-

Think of your emotional energy as money in your psychic bank. You have a finite amount. Choosing not to think about or remember something (to defend against it) doesn't come free; in fact it's very costly.

able to spend on other, more productive pursuits, like the two pillars of a fulfilling life—work and love.

So when a client behaves in perplexing or provocative ways, ask yourself, "Is this someone whose defenses are getting in the way of effective functioning?" For example, consider a client who appears upset at the end of a meeting but insists that he is "fine," only to send an enraged e-mail to his spouse that evening. This client is likely using the defense of denial to protect himself from uncomfortable feelings at the meeting, and then later experiencing a breakdown of his defense. Take another client who repeatedly forgets to complete homework assignments in preparation for financial meetings. This client may be employing avoidance as protection from her anxiety about finances.

We'll say it again: We don't expect divorce professionals to have the psychological understanding of therapists, and we're not interested in turning anyone into a therapist (in fact, every therapist reading this book has to learn how *not* to be a therapist in the context of this work!). But we do want to stress the importance of remembering that the ways our clients behave often reflect attempts to stave off painful states of mind. If you can stay tuned in to the existence of these latent feelings and try to make sense of them, you will have taken the first step in learning to help your clients more efficiently, compassionately and productively.

> *We don't expect divorce professionals to have the psychological understanding of therapists, and we're not interested in turning anyone into a therapist. But we do want to stress the importance of remembering that the ways our clients behave often reflect attempts to stave off painful states of mind.*

Understanding Mental Health and Ill Health

Mental health can be measured, in large part, by the extent to which an individual relies on emotional defenses in their everyday life and interactions. Emotionally healthy people live in the here-and-now, and so can relate to a broad range of people and situations in a broad range of ways. A healthy individual is capable of seeing the world in shades of gray, capable of seeing him- or herself in realistically nuanced ways, capable of recognizing others' points of view, and (perhaps most importantly for our work) capable of ownership of his or her own feelings and behaviors.

Less emotionally healthy people live in their psychological past. Think of a colleague who seems to meet every new situation in the same old way. Say, for example, he seems always to feel that people are ready to exploit or take advantage of him, even when there is no evidence to support that idea. Or think of a friend who seems always to experience you as disinterested or not listening, when, in fact, you are exhausted from her constant need for a sympathetic ear. What's going on?

Highly traumatized individuals behave in stereotypical ways. Why? Because the fact that that they have to work so hard to keep painful thoughts and feelings outside of their conscious awareness means that there is not much of their selves or of their psychic energy left over for spontaneous, realistic relating in the present. They must resort to living according to a few preset modes of relating—the templates we discussed earlier in this chapter. These templates are narrow in scope and number. They become caricatures.

Because none of us escapes trauma, we all use defenses to some extent to minimize the impact of painful memories and the feelings associated with them. So we all have emotional vulnerabilities, trigger points in our personalities that sometimes cause us to behave in predictably difficult ways and compromise our abilities to see the world as it is. We'll talk more about those emotional vulnerabilities in Chapter 7.

> *We all have emotional vulnerabilities, trigger points in our personalities that sometimes cause us to behave in predictably difficult ways and compromise our abilities to see the world as it is.*

As divorce practitioners, we should not ask ourselves whether or not our clients will sometimes adopt irrational positions, develop distorted ideas, or overreact. They are human, and they will. The important questions to ask are "how often?," "under what conditions?," and "how quickly can they recover?"

That brings us to . . .

A Model of Emotional Health and Ill Health: The Rigidity/Flexibility Continuum[2]

Most of our cases fall somewhere on the spectrum between the two poles of "transformative" and "nontransformative." Sometimes one member of the couple grows psychologically through the process of getting divorced, while the other remains stuck. Sometimes both members of the couple are able to grow in certain areas but remain stuck in others. Usually, even when both members of the couple are generally pleased with the final settlement, they feel battered and bruised by certain aspects of the experience and resentful about some of the compromises they have made.

Also, since recovery from the divorce process often takes years, feelings about the process itself and the capacity to learn from it do not freeze the moment the clients sign an Agreement. A healthier client will make evolving use, over time, of what he or she has internalized while working with his or her professional helpers. What determines where a client, or a couple, falls on this spectrum? We suggest that it is the levels of psychological health or ill health—in other words, flexibility or rigidity—within the characters of each.

Earlier we discussed the fact that when we experience early trauma we employ defenses to keep the feelings about those experiences at bay. We made the point that the more psychic energy we must expend in employing these defenses, the less energy is left over for more productive uses. Finally, we explained that an individual who must make heavy use of defenses has a more limited, caricatured, or rigid way of relating to the world. The latter individuals are the ones we often refer to as "character disordered." They are typically unable to see things from another person's point

---

2. Scharff and Herrick, *Navigating Emotional Currents in Collaborative Divorce: A Guide to Enlightened Team Practice*, 2010, pp. 64–71.

of view and are resistant to change. They are our most difficult clients.

As we've said, all of us utilize defenses to some degree. In other words, rigidity and flexibility exist on a continuum; we all move back and forth along it. In times of stress (such as early on in a divorce, or at difficult moments along the way) our feelings and behaviors may place us at the rigid end of the continuum. In better times, we may land closer to the flexible end.

Our clients will act in irrationally rigid ways. The important questions are "how often?," "under what conditions?," and "how quickly can they recover?" Rigidity and flexibility exist on a continuum; we all move back and forth along it. In times of stress (such as early on in a divorce or at difficult moments along the way) our clients feelings and behaviors may place them at the rigid end. In calmer times they may land closer to the flexible end.

It takes time to get to know our clients. Where their behaviors will "cluster" along the continuum is often not apparent at the start of a case. What you'll notice is that the more rigid your client, the less successfully you'll be able to stretch them to accept new ideas (and you'll have fewer effective techniques for doing so). We have learned the hard way that the sooner we can assess a given client (locate their character along the Rigidity/Flexibility Continuum) the better, because certain techniques, while they might work beautifully with a more flexible client, will have disastrous results with a rigid client.

Also, early assessment is important to your own morale and sense of professional competence. The quicker you can separate your client's more rigid behaviors *under stress* from where his behaviors *generally cluster* over time, the quicker you can develop realistic goals for your client in his divorce process. We are not advocating setting the bar too low, but we are suggesting that setting it too high can set up the professionals for disappointment

Early assessment is important to your own morale and sense of professional competence. The quicker you can separate your client's more rigid behaviors under stress from where his behaviors generally cluster over time, the quicker you can develop realistic goals for your client in his divorce process.

and frustration and can get in the way of meeting clients *where they really are.*

The Rigidity/Flexibility Continuum: A Way of Understanding Our Clients, Our Colleagues, and Ourselves

The authors introduced the Rigidity/Flexibility Continuum in 2010. This model for understanding and talking about mental health and ill health allowed us to bypass the unhelpful and pathologizing jargon associated with the diagnoses we'd been bandying about for years (such as narcissistic personality disorder and borderline personality disorder). We had been searching for a concept that would simplify the complicated process of describing and understanding the confusing behavior of real people—our clients, our colleagues, and ourselves.

Following are two diagrams. The first is a visual representation of the continuum itself; the second is a visual representation of the ways rigidity and flexibility often show up in our work. The two poles, rigidity and flexibility, as well as the polar pairs under "Common Emotional and Behavioral Manifestations," are intentionally connected by dotted lines moving in two directions, rather than by solid fixed lines. This design choice is intended to underscore two points. First, health and ill health exist not in two discrete categories, but rather on a continuum. The behaviors of an individual will move back and forth along this continuum in accordance with the individual's emotional state in a given moment—though over time their behaviors will usually group closer to one end or the other. Second, it is common for a person to be rigid in response to certain feelings and situations, and more flexible in response to others; we all display some unevenness. But highly rigid clients usually fall closer to the rigid end of the continuum with respect to most or all of the "Common Manifestations of Rigidity and Flexibility."

(Continued)

The Rigidity/Flexibility Continuum: A Way of Understanding Our Clients, Our Colleagues, and Ourselves (*Continued*)

The Rigidity/Flexibility Continuum

Rigidity <⋯⋯⋯⋯⋯> Flexibility

Significant Pathology <⋯⋯⋯⋯⋯> Relative Health

Less Transformative <⋯⋯⋯⋯⋯> More Transformative
Capacity   Capacity

Common Emotional and Behavioral Manifestations of Rigidity and Flexibility

Positionality <⋯⋯⋯⋯⋯> Willingness to Consider
                        Options

Lack of Insight <⋯⋯⋯⋯⋯> Self-Reflection/Insight

Blame/Projection <⋯⋯⋯⋯⋯> Ownership/Perspective

Anger/Vengefulness <⋯⋯⋯⋯⋯> Forgiveness

Entitlement/Self-Absorption <⋯⋯⋯⋯⋯> Generosity

Victimization/<⋯⋯⋯⋯⋯> Volition/
Passivity   Empowerment

Catastrophizing <⋯⋯⋯⋯⋯> Hope

Okay; now we have a framework for understanding whether a client has the inherent capacity for deep transformation, or whether he or she is likely to scrape through by the skin of their teeth. We've learned that where the practice of dispute resolution is concerned, one size definitely does not fit all. It is essential to understand where your client falls on the Rigidity/Flexibility Continuum and which techniques will work well for a client in that position, so you can intervene in effective ways.

Ready to throw up your hands and say "This is *waaaay* too complicated. I can't understand any of this, let alone use it with my clients!"? Breathe. First, much of this you already know intuitively. How many times have you said to your professional counterpart some version of: "My client is really touchy about the idea of spousal support. Let's find a way of talking about it that

We advocate treating each case, from the beginning, as if it were transformative. If necessary, adjust your expectations downward over time.

doesn't leave him feeling he's being taken advantage of"? Without knowing it, you've made some diagnostic assessments of your client and are putting those assessments to work. Second, we don't expect you to understand your client from the outset. We advocate treating each case, from the beginning, as if it were transformative. If necessary, adjust your expectations downward over time. Third, if you're not a mental health professional, you can and should consult with an experienced mental health colleague to help you understand the psychological makeup of your client and help you strategize about what techniques will work best for your case.

So far in this chapter we have explored a number of concepts that can help us understand our clients better and work more effectively with them—even when they behave in self-destructive, seemingly inscrutably ways. We've discussed the importance of being aware that our clients are often motivated by unconscious conflicts, and we've briefly reviewed the concept of psychological defenses against the memories and feelings associated with past painful experiences. We've noted the pitfalls of accepting our client's narrative as objective truth, and the usefulness of listening to the other side of the story. We introduced the Rigidity/Flexibility Continuum, our model for classifying and making sense of the ways clients behave in the context of our work.

None of these ideas is more important than or inconsistent with any other. Think of the multiple lenses that an optometrist flips down over our eyes—trying first one, then another, then back to the first—in an effort to clarify and sharpen our vision. The ideas we've offered here are like different lenses through which to view your clients; they're most useful when considered cumulatively.

"There's another important conceptual framework for us to consider before we move on-attachment."

A Few Words on Attachment in Divorce Work

The psychological literature on attachment is rich and complex, and a few divorce professionals have written and taught about its applicability to our work. We've chosen to include it here because it brings many aspects of our experience with clients into focus—it helps things make sense. Here we offer a brief overview of the two "umbrella" categories of human attachment—secure and insecure. We've divided insecure attachment into its the three broad subcategories: ambivalent, avoidant, and disorganized.[3] We encourage any reader who wants to learn more about attachment theory to consult our bibliography—it's a fascinating area of inquiry!

Secure Attachment

When children are raised by attentive, reliable, attuned, and empathic parents, they develop a sense of basic trust—the idea that the world is a safe place populated by people who are inclined to be reliable, helpful, and kind. In other words, positive early experiences form a blueprint for ongoing positive expectations that persist into adulthood and carry over into our clients' work with us.

Clients who have formed secure early attachments are the ones with whom we feel a strong mutual connection. They make good use of the holding environment we provide, and are not afraid to become temporarily emotionally dependent on us in the service of longer-term independence. Their general tendency is to attend meetings promptly with their homework done, to respect our boundaries, and to communicate with appropriate regularity. Securely attached clients tend to achieve higher levels of transformation in their divorce process—they often grieve and forgive, take responsibility, keep their children's needs front and center, compromise, and recover quickly when they regress to earlier positions during times of particular stress.

---

3. Ainsworth, Mary et al., *Patterns of Attachment: A Psychological Study of the Strange Situation* (Psychology Press and Routledge Classic Editions, July 2015 Ainsworth, 2015.

Insecure Attachment: Ambivalent, Avoidant, Disorganized

On the other hand, clients who were less well parented through infancy and childhood fail to develop basic trust. They develop insecure attachments, and tend to give us a run for our money through a variety of frustrating and baffling behaviors (some of which we listed at the top of this chapter).

AMBIVALENT ATTACHMENT

Clients with *ambivalent attachment styles* display bewilderingly inconsistent attitudes (e.g., soliciting then rejecting our advice, and doubling back on hard-won agreements). These folks continually worry about whether the process and the professionals will be able to help them reach a successful outcome, but never take a decisive stance on whether or not to switch to a new professional or to a different model of dispute resolution. They sometimes appear unquenchable in their thirst for guidance, input, and feedback, but after we take the time to e-mail our detailed feedback or spend an hour discussing potential next steps, they fall off the radar for a week—perhaps canceling meetings, ignoring voice mails, or failing to follow up on agreed-upon actions.

If, as you read the above description, you found yourself thinking of a difficult client with whom you often feel frustrated, try thinking of that client as having grown up with a caretaker who was inconsistently available and unpredictably responsive. Picture a child crying for a parent for 45 minutes, only to have the parent finally show up for a quick hug before disappearing again—leaving

> *Clients with ambivalent attachment styles display bewilderingly inconsistent attitudes. They continually worry about whether the process and the professionals will be able to help them reach a successful outcome, but never take a decisive stance on whether or not to switch to a new professional or to a different model of dispute resolution. They sometimes appear unquenchable in their thirst for guidance, input, and feedback, but after we take the time to e-mail our detailed feedback or spend an hour discussing potential next steps, they fall off the radar for a week.*

the child with a painful longing, a tantalizing hope, and a growing expectation of disappointment.

Adults with ambivalent attachment styles are often nervous marital partners. They often have endless complaints about their spouse's unavailability. But they don't seek divorce, and typically resist it vehemently.

AVOIDANT ATTACHMENT

Perhaps the *avoidant attachment style* is the easiest to recognize—because avoidant clients avoid *us*! These are the individuals who retain us but delay the beginning of the process. They complain that the process is moving too slowly, but they cancel meetings, forget to do their homework, and don't keep in touch. They appear to have no confidence in our ability to help, but don't articulate their disgruntlement until it has had time to ferment. These are the clients we never really get to know. When they are present, they're not really *there*. Their reactions seem muted, anesthetized. If you experience an emotionally intense moment with such a client, you might briefly feel that they *do* trust and like you. But before you know it, the client is looking at his phone, checking his watch, cutting the conversation short, and out the door. Any experience of closeness is short-lived.

The spouses of clients with avoidant attachment styles typically describe them as emotionally absent—perhaps even literally absent. Avoidant people often create lifestyles in which they travel a lot, are rarely home with the kids, and tend to forget birthdays and anniversaries. They may show love in concrete ways—birthday gifts, anniversary cruises—but they can't establish intimate partnerships. And when they leave a marriage, it's often in an abrupt, "out of the blue" fashion. Because they avoid connection, they avoid conflict. They are terrible listeners, and keep their cards close to the vest.

Avoidant clients appear to have no confidence in our ability to help, but they don't articulate their disgruntlement until it has had time to ferment. These are the clients we never really get to know. Sometimes they are not particularly difficult when it comes to reaching settlements, but they rarely express gratitude and are gone before the ink is dry on their Agreement.

Sometimes avoidant clients are not particularly difficult when it comes to reaching settlements, but they rarely express gratitude. They are gone before the ink is dry on their Agreement.

When you feel annoyed with your avoidant client, conjure the image of a child whose connection to his parents was dissatisfying, incomplete, sadistic, or perhaps *missing*. Or try imagining a child whose parents were so intrusive, so suffocating, that he or she grew up feeling invaded and desperately in need of space to breathe or to be an independent person with an independent mind. Avoidant attachment styles emerge from very sad histories— helpful to remember when you want to strangle your client for being a no-show at a meeting that took six weeks to schedule.

DISORGANIZED ATTACHMENT

Finally, there are people who have grown up with such chaotic or intermittently abusive parental figures that they have barely been able to develop a blueprint of attachment at all. These clients are both literally and psychologically inscrutable—they are "all over the place." Clients with a *disorganized attachment style* are often too emotionally disabled to work well within a mediation or collaborative process. They often have distorted perceptions of others and of reality, and odd reactions to events that don't jibe with the reactions of anyone else involved. These clients are extremely difficult to work with successfully, not necessarily because they are consistently angry or high conflict but because they are so hard to understand and to predict. Their narratives are jumbled and often don't make logical sense. Their marriages are severely dysfunctional, and they often have poor relationships with their children and bizarre (often disturbing) ideas about parenting.

When children grow up in frightening, confusing households in which there is virtually no emotional guidance and in which even their basic physical needs

> *Clients with disorganized attachment styles are extremely difficult to work with successfully; not necessarily because they are consistently angry and high conflict but because they are so hard to understand and to predict. Their narratives are jumbled and often don't make logical sense.*

are unmet, they become adults who have great difficulty navigating the world. Sometimes these children are lucky enough to have found one or more healthy adult—a teacher, coach, aunt, or uncle—who has had a therapeutic impact. If that has been part of your disorganized client's history, it's possible that while they may struggle mightily in most areas of their life, they may be able to navigate a divorce process moderately well if they have a sensitive, supportive team of helping professionals.

But disorganized clients are always vulnerable to falling back into irrational thinking, paranoid behavior, bizarrely ill-timed passive stances, and startlingly confusing approaches to decision-making. These are the clients who are highly unlikely to successfully move through a process like divorce without a mental health professional by their side.

Summary of Concepts from Chapter 3

- The ways our clients think, feel, and behave are often driven by unconscious factors.
- Those unconscious factors play a strong, often problematic, role in the course of our work.
- It is only by developing an understanding of the dynamics underlying our clients' patterns of thinking, feeling, and behaving that we can help them to navigate the process successfully.
- The quality of our relationships with early caregivers creates templates that determine how we will behave toward important others in our adult lives.
- We all utilize emotional defenses, but clients who are highly traumatized make heavier use of defenses, which can result in problematic behaviors during the divorce process.
- Our clients' personality organizations (healthy and unhealthy) can be viewed on a Rigidity/Flexibility Continuum that has predictive value and can help us to choose the techniques that will help them to reach their own best divorce outcomes.

- Our clients relate to us four broad categories of attachment styles: secure, ambivalent, avoidant, and disorganized. These styles give us windows into our clients' histories and clues as to how to be most helpful in their divorce process.

Chapter 4

Introduction to the Professional Container

And I say the sacred hoop of my people was one of the many hoops that made one circle, wide as daylight and as starlight, and in the center grew one mighty flowering tree to shelter all the children of one mother and one father.

—The Sixth Grandfather: Black Elk's
Teachings Given to John G. Neihardt

Just as parents take pleasure in and learn from their children, we care about and are deeply affected by our clients. But, like good parents, good divorce professionals have internalized the fundamental premise that our relationship with our client, while real, often intense, and crucially important, is not a relationship of equals. Although our client drives the *content* of discussions, we are responsible for establishing and maintaining the *structure* of the relationship within which those discussions take place.

Think of the families you have worked with or know in your personal life who, even if you're fond of them as individuals, you find off-putting as a group. Perhaps they induce in you a feeling of unease—or even panic. These are families whose structural integrity was either never established or has collapsed. The members of these families lack predictable routines, daily rhythms, limits, boundaries, clearly defined expectations, and effective modes of communication. Their roles are diffuse; the kids are out of control and disrespectful, the spouses are overwhelmed and at each other's throats.

When parents fail to form a couple that acts as a loving but firm "executive branch," everyone feels anxious. So, while it's true that we work for our clients, within the context of our professional role we must be the keepers of their process.

When parents fail to form a couple that acts as a loving but firm "executive branch," everyone feels anxious. Similarly, when we fail to provide and hold a steady frame for our divorcing clients they become emotionally destabilized and disorganized—not a state of mind from which we can reasonably expect them to make high-level, tough decisions. So, while it's true that we work for our clients, within the context of our professional role we must be the keepers of their process— even when they chafe against it.

In Chapter 2 we talked about the Three Conditions for Positive Change—the psychological components necessary for healthy development. One component, the "new idea," emerges primarily from the person who is the focus of the helping relationship—our client. It is often our job to help shine a light on, clarify, and nurture the new idea, but it is not *our* idea. In fact, as we've described, when we take ownership of our client's goals—when we become personally invested in any particular outcome—the transitional space between us collapses and we lose our professional helping capacity. The other components of the Three Conditions for Positive Change, "optimal anxiety" (which keeps the new idea alive) and "the helping relationship," are established by us and thrive only under our continued stewardship. They are co-constructions; we make thoughtful adjustments in response to our client's shifting states of mind. Like good parents we strive to provide what our client needs in each moment.

So how do we go about creating an environment in which a new idea can emerge and thrive? How do we establish a helping relationship? How do we facilitate the regulation of optimal anxiety in our clients? The answer: By constructing a sturdy professional "container."

If you have experience in mediation or other alternate dispute resolution models, you're likely to have heard reference to the concept of a container. But the authors find that while many professionals accurately think of the container as a safe zone in which clients can function best, there is general confusion in the field about the definition and components of the container in the context of divorce work. In our cowritten book, we unpacked the form and function of the container and presented our conceptualization as a clear schema. Let's review it now.

The Two-Part Container[1]

In ordinary life a container is a tangible object with form, function, fixed properties, and finite capacity—a milk carton, a mailbox. By contrast, the professional container is a construct that resides in our minds and hearts. When it is well designed and constructed, our container can withstand powerful attacks from both within and without. But it is flexible too, capable, when necessary, of expanding, contracting or changing shape to accommodate the evolving needs of the people within its boundaries.

The professional container is composed of two interrelated parts—the "Macrocontainer" and the "Microcontainer." The Macrocontainer is probably a lot like the container you've talked and thought about in your work so far. It offers a warm and strong "arms around" experience. Think back to the safe physical and psychological parent-baby relationship we described in Chapter 2. That relationship was crucially fortified by the support each parent or caregiver offers to the other, as well as the support they each receive from extended family and trusted others. Those interrelated relationships are the model for the Macrocontainer.

The Macrocontainer is composed of the protocols of our work (as well as thoughtful departures from them), the skill and

---

1. Kate Scharff and Lisa Herrick, *Navigating Emotional Currents in Collaborative Divorce: A Guide to Enlightened Team Practice* (American Bar Association, 2010), 31–37.

The Macrocontainer is like the safe physical and psychological environment offered by parents, as well as the support they each receive from extended family and trusted others. In our work, the Macrocontainer is composed of the protocols of our work, the skill and knowledge we offer, and any benefits to the client stemming from good relationships between our colleagues and us.

knowledge we offer, and any benefits to the client stemming from good relationships between and among our colleagues and us. The Macrocontainer is also the entire group of professionals (or team, if the process is cooperative or Collaborative) working with a given family. Macrocontainers come in a wide range of configurations. One example is two attorneys plus the mediator helping a couple through a settlement process. Another example is a Collaborative team of two attorneys, a financial neutral, and two coaches. And just as a baby's safe environment often includes grandparents and other ancillary helpers, a Macrocontainer often includes supportive people who are not at the work table—such as other partners in a lawyer's firm or the administrative assistant who keeps the complex lines of communication from becoming snarled.

The Microcontainer is like the focused relationship between the parent and the baby. In divorce practice, the Microcontainer is most obviously represented by the one-on-one support offered to a client by a member of his or her professional team. But there are equally important Microcontainers throughout the system. These relationships make it possible for us and for our clients to tolerate, navigate, and learn from the powerful feelings that are stirred up during the course of our work.

The Microcontainer, on the other hand, is analogous to the psychological functioning of the parent-baby relationship itself. In that one-on-one relationship, the parent (or other primary caregiver) is entirely focused on taking in, tolerating, and helping the baby to make sense of experience. In divorce practice, the Microcontainer is most obviously represented by the individual support offered to a client by one member of his or her professional team. But there are equally important Microcontainers throughout the system. Think of a time when you found yourself at a loss in dealing with a difficult client and turned to a trusted colleague for advice and support—that was you making use of the Microcontainer of you and your colleague. These relationships and their special qualities (we'll get to those) make it possible for us and our clients to tolerate, navigate, and learn from the powerful feelings that are stirred up during the course of our work.

The Macrocontainer and the Microcontainer are equally important. Without a well-functioning Macrocontainer, the Microcontainer could not exist. Just as a mother or father cannot parent well without a well-functioning emotional and physical support system, you cannot be fully focused on your client without the support of your colleagues and the structure of your professional protocols. Together these two levels of containment, the macro and the micro, provide a safe psychological space in which we and our clients can manage the challenges we face.

The Two-Part Professional Container

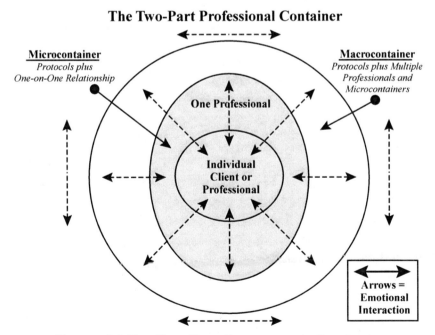

FIGURE 4.1 THE TWO-PART PROFESSIONAL CONTAINER

In practice, the Macrocontainer and Microcontainer are interrelated and interdependent. Also, the distinction between the container and the contained is often blurred, since there is a mutually beneficial feedback loop connecting them. For example, while it is our job (within the Microcontainer) to understand and be supportive of our client, we also learn from and are transformed by them.

The Macro- and Microcontainers are necessarily simplified models. In practice they are more complex—interrelated and interdependent. For example, departures from standard protocol (changes in the Macrocontainer) must be processed in the relationship between the client and his or her Collaborative professional (the Microcontainer). Similarly, difficulties in the relationship between a client and, say, his mental health professional (the Microcontainer) must be resolved by the whole team (the Macrocontainer). Also, the distinction between the container and the contained is often blurred, since there is a mutually beneficial feedback loop connecting them. While it is our job (within the Microcontainer) to understand and be supportive of our client, we also learn from and are transformed by them.

So why do these distinctions matter at all? What are their practical applications? We think the concept of a two-part container is useful because it offers a theoretical framework for thinking about the needs of our individual clients, larger process issues, and the interaction of the two. Consider the following vignette:

Years ago, Lisa had a Collaborative client with a volatile temper. This man had grown up with an abusive, bullying father. As a result, the client often became enraged and verbally abusive when he felt backed into a corner or disrespected by the professionals (e.g., when he had to wait in the reception area for 15 minutes because the team needed extra time to prepare for a meeting). Lisa understood and empathized with her client's fragility, and did not dislike him. But she felt unnerved when he expressed his displeasure by yelling—at her or at anyone else in the room. She came to understand that her coaching relationship with him (their Microcontainer) was compromised when she realized that she had become uncharacteristically slow to return his phone calls. She realized, too, that she had failed to set appropriate limits when her client yelled or used disrespectful language. Lisa needed her Macrocontainer (the team) in order to better manage the Microcontainer (her client and herself).

In a pre-meeting phone call, Lisa talked with her co-coach and both attorneys. She described negative reactions she now realized she was having to her client, as well as her own resulting problematic behaviors. Immediately she felt the emotional support and empathy of her team. While one attorney shared that she actually felt scared of the client, the other attorney admitted that he, too, found himself avoiding contact with the client. The whole team reassured Lisa that they recognized the challenges she faced in working with this client, and validated the hard work she had been doing in managing a difficult dynamic. They all brainstormed ways to help the man move through the process successfully.

Feeling well contained herself, and armed with new ideas about how to work more effectively, Lisa was able to forge a more productive relationship with her client. She had more confidence in setting appropriate limits when he expressed his frustration in aggressive ways, which made both of them less anxious. The team—the Macrocontainer—was also strengthened through this process. The attorneys' new insight into the psychological make-up of the client allowed them to feel empathy for him. As a result, they gained greater control over their negative reactions to him. The group became more cohesive, which ultimately led to a better outcome for both clients.

Now that we have defined the Macro- and Microcontainers and explored their interrelatedness and interdependence, let's take a closer look at how we establish each of them.

Summary of Concepts from Chapter 4

- In the same way that children do best when their parents maintain predictable (but not punitive or inflexible) structure and routine, our clients do best when we provide a sturdy "container."
- The container provides a safe psychological space in which we and our clients are able to do our work.

- The container is composed of two interrelated parts: the Microcontainer and the Macrocontainer.
- The Macrocontainer offers a warm "arms around" experience for the one-on-one relationship between us and our client or colleague. It is composed of the protocols of any given divorce process, as well as all the one-on-one relationships (Microcontainers) that support us in doing our work.
- The Microcontainer is any intense one-on-one relationship that provides focused attention, empathy, and containment—such as that between you and your client or you and a colleague.
- The Microcontainer and Macrocontainer are interrelated and interdependent.

PART II

Applying Our Understanding to Our Work with Clients

Chapter 5

The First Step in Establishing the Container:
Our One-on-One Relationship with Our Client

*Oh, the comfort, the inexpressible comfort of feeling safe
with a person; having neither to weigh thoughts nor measure words, but to pour them all out, just as they are,
chaff and grain together, knowing that a faithful hand
will take and sift them, keep what is worth keeping, and
then, with a breath of kindness, blow the rest away.*

—Dinah Maria Craik, *A Life for a Life*

Now that we're *conceptually* familiar with the special qualities of the Microcontainer—the one-on-one relationship between you and your client (or colleague) that provides a holding environment in which transformation is possible—let's get down to brass tacks. How do we build that relationship from the ground up? What does it look like in our ordinary everyday interactions with the wide range of clients we see in our offices?

Ask Yourself: "When Does the Helping Relationship Begin?"

As you read the following scenario, try to note your emotional responses—even if they seem insignificant.

You receive an e-mail from a potential new client, David. He addresses you by your first name, and says he's been referred to you by a friend (the friend happens to be a high-powered divorce professional in your town with whom you have worked before), and has heard you're a "miracle worker." He tells you he is planning to divorce, and would like to meet for a consultation as soon as possible. You respond promptly, offering several potential appointments over the next two weeks. That same day you receive an e-mail from the referring attorney: "Hey—Hope all's well. Sent an old college buddy your way. Great guy—told him you're the best of the best."

A week later David responds, saying he's been out of the country and that the times you offer don't work for him. He asks if you can fit him in the following Friday at 2 p.m. You respond that you are currently booked at that time, but that you may be able to move another client to a slot earlier in the day in order to accommodate David. You make the change and write to let him know. 24 hours later you receive a formal confirmation e-mail from his secretary with a cc: to him.

The following week David arrives 20 minutes early for his 2 p.m. appointment. You know this because your receptionist buzzes in to your office to let you know he has arrived. As you are still meeting with your previous client (your receptionist has interrupted you— something you have instructed her not to do and that she typically does not do), you tell the receptionist to offer David a beverage and to ask him to make himself comfortable—that you will fetch him at the appointed time. At 2 p.m. you walk into your reception area. Since there is only one client there, you know it is David. He is well built, handsome, tan, impeccably groomed, and expensively attired in a custom-tailored suit. On the floor near his feet is a lovingly maintained vintage leather attaché case. He seems more to inhabit than to sit on your waiting-room couch—he is semi-reclined, legs crossed loosely, one arm thrown casually along the back of the couch so that he is facing the receptionist's desk and away from the hallway through which you enter the room. As you enter, he is speaking on his cell phone in a conversational tone that he has not adjusted for the closeness of the space. After a moment he visually registers your presence and, without adjusting the tone with which he carries on his phone conversation or establishing eye contact with you, lifts his free hand a few inches from the back of the couch to hold up one finger in the universal gesture for "hang on a sec." He continues his conversation—which you now understand is with a work colleague— but has wandered into a humorous discussion about golf. A half- minute or so later he terminates his call with "Steve, look, gotta hop. Got a thing here—I'll catch you later." Tucking his phone into his pocket he turns his face to you and, still seated, locks his eyes on yours and flashes an unexpected, sudden smile so charismatic that it fills you with a destabilizing sense of warmth and excitement. He says your name in a tone you associate with reunions between old friends. You reply (in a tone as close to his as you are comfortable to muster), "David." You extend your hand; he rises laconically and shakes it firmly—holding for a beat before letting go. As you lead him down the hall toward your office he calls over his shoulder to your receptionist—"You know, sweetheart, I think maybe I will take that cup of coffee. Black, no sugar."

As we end the scene, you have not yet met with your client. On the one hand, you know nothing about him. His story is still a mystery to you. And yet, you've had thousands of responses to thousands of data points. The fact that David was referred by an influential colleague, the confusing way he communicated initial urgency then made himself unavailable for the times you offered, his entitled request for a specific appointment time and day, the fact that he arrived early for his appointment then treated you with a combina- tion of disrespect and seductive charm—these are a small fraction of the significant interactions, fleeting and easy to miss, that have passed between you before you've begun the actual "work."

David's idiosyncratic ways of relating to you have, perhaps, already triggered atypical responses in you or caused you to behave in ways that are outside your ordinary patterns. Perhaps you felt gratified by your colleague having made the referral and describing you to David in such flattering ways. On the other hand, perhaps you felt uneasy, as if the hyperbole carried an implicit pressure to give David special treatment. If you normally wouldn't change your schedule to accommodate such a specific request from a new client, or if your receptionist has never before interrupted you in session, you should ask yourself "Why now?"

From this example we can see that your relationship with your client begins, in their minds, long before they've met you—as a set of expectations based on a mix of previous experience with important figures in their lives, any factual information (or misinformation) they've gathered about you, and the nature of the interactions you have in advance of meeting. And the fantasy relationship continues to build as your client enters the building in which your office is housed ("More upscale than I expected—bet the fees are too high!"), as they enter your professional space ("Hmm, he gets *The Wall Street Journal*. Good sign."), and when they first see you in person ("He looks younger than he sounded on the phone!").

> *Your relationship with your client begins, in their minds, long before they've met you—as a set of expectations based on a mix of previous experience with important figures in their lives, any factual information (or misinformation) they've gathered about you, and the nature of the interactions you have in advance of meeting.*

Offer Curiosity without Judgment

In Chapter 3, in our discussion of the Rigidity/Flexibility Continuum and individuals' attachment styles, we looked at how a person's mental health can be measured in large part by how objectively they can assess another person's personality characteristics and by the extent to which they are able to enter into a new situation without unhelpful unconscious assumptions. We also acknowledged that we are all vulnerable to defaulting to our "presets," especially in stressful moments—such as meeting your divorce professional for the first time.

It is tempting to view David's offhand, entitled behavior as evidence of narcissistic bravado, and maybe it is. But will the tenor of David's behavior persist over the course of your work together? Will he treat you, his future ex, and other professionals with disdain? Or, as he comes to trust you, will he soften and become more "relatable?" How much volatility will he display? How much rationality? Generosity? The truth is, there is no way to know from the outset. But we do know this: Everything we have observed about David so far, especially our own reactions to him, is significant in some not-yet-understood way. It is data to be stored in our minds— not as fixed facts, but as ideas in progress. Our job is to wonder about our reactions and to use them to form working hypotheses, all in the service of building a helping relationship that can foster growth.

> *Everything we observe about our clients, especially our own reactions to them, is significant in some not-yet-understood way. It is data to be stored in our minds—not as fixed facts, but as ideas in progress.*

Remaining emotionally attuned, scanning for shifts in our client's emotional states, making informed adjustments in our responses— this process is analogous to the function of the early parent we described in Chapter 2. Not only are we learning about our client and helping them to learn about themselves, we are communicating our belief that the way our client thinks and feels is important and has meaning that can be understood. We are building the sense of basic trust in us that will make ongoing work possible.

Learn to Notice

Most of what transpires between any two or more people happens nonverbally and under the radar. There is no way to capture all the nuances of any moment—especially when you're also trying to accomplish a real task (such as gathering needed facts in an initial interview). Relax. We're not trying to turn our readers into human spectral imaging devices. We're simply suggesting you dial up your awareness of what you *already know.*

Think about it this way:

As you move through any ordinary day, you likely interact with many people—some you know well, some are strangers. Some interactions are so familiar that you barely the register them (the way your spouse grunts "good morning" before getting in the shower but emerges smiling), others are unfamiliar yet fall within the typical range of types of social interaction and, while they may leave you with a vaguely positive or negative feeling, are barely noteworthy (a group of people make room for you on a crowded elevator, the waiter at lunch is mildly surly). But occasionally something happens that falls just far enough outside our typical experience that it leaves an emotional residue. If this happens in the course of a busy day in a context that is not important to us, we may not register the experience consciously. But it will linger as a vague sense of unease.

Our interactions with clients are like our interactions with folks in our "civilian" lives in that, while there's a lot of variation, most fall within a bell curve of what, if you took time to think about it, you'd come to see as ordinary and familiar. For example, you've probably had the experience that most clients make eye contact when you say hello, shake your outstretched hand, follow you into your office, and wait to be shown where to sit.

> *As you move through any ordinary day some interactions are so familiar you barely the register them. But occasionally something happens that falls just far enough outside our typical experience that it leaves an emotional residue. We may not register the experience consciously, but it will linger as a vague sense of unease.*

In Chapter 7 we'll talk more about how we can use our minds and bodies to pick up, understand, and make sense of our emotional reactions to even minute verbal and nonverbal communications. For now, we're simply suggesting that you work at dialing up your awareness of any reaction—small or large, positive or negative—that you have in response to any interaction with your client.

Here's a metaphor we find helpful: Imagine your skin is covered with fine feathers, like a bird. Your feathers connect to nerve endings in your skin, so that you are exquisitely sensitive to shifts in the air around you. You have grown accustomed to the sensory effects of a wide range of familiar wind patterns—the way your feathers move softly in a warm breeze, the way they lie flat, cool, and smooth as you fly against a current. But occasionally your feathers move in a subtly unfamiliar way that signals a new weather pattern. You register this change—perhaps with interest (the coming of spring?), perhaps with anxiety (an approaching storm?). This atypical experience has no meaning to you yet; its significance has not yet been revealed. But you notice it.

In your next client meeting, try being a bird. Note the way your client's movements, speech patterns, and nonverbal communications do or don't ruffle your feathers. Notice the way your mind begins to generate ideas around these wisps of information—nascent hypotheses based on fragments of data.

Here are some examples of noteworthy behaviors:

- A client enters your office and sits in a chair no one ever chooses.
- A client enters your office and stops to read the titles of the books on your bookshelf, then asks if you've read them all.
- A client perches on the edge of her chair without removing her coat.
- A client removes his shoes and sits cross-legged on your couch.
- A client sits silently, waiting for you to begin the meeting.
- A client compliments your shoes and asks where you bought them.
- A client has a dry cough but refuses water.
- A client places his phone on the couch next to him and looks at it each time it vibrates, which it does frequently.
- A client begins speaking even before you sit down.
- A client comes to the meeting with no means of payment.
- A stay-at-home mom comes in dressed as if she is going to the opera.

In your next client meeting, try being a bird. Note the way your client's movements, speech patterns, and nonverbal communications do or don't ruffle your feathers. Notice the way your mind begins to generate ideas around these wisps of information—nascent hypotheses based on fragments of data.

Maintain Presence of Mind

Especially if you're a relative beginner in your field, meeting a new client may make you nervous. Will you be perceived as smart and competent? Will you be retained? And even though most of us enjoy meeting new clients and feel some excitement about embarking with them on a new journey, there are plenty of days when the work feels rote. Whether the cause is newcomer anxiety or veteran burnout, we are all at risk of becoming self-absorbed in a way that causes our attention to focus inward and away from our clients.

The truth is that even when we love our work, it's work. That means while various clients move in and out of the foreground of our thinking, they all inhabit a secondary aspect of our emotional lives. In fact, it's crucial that they do (remember our discussion of the importance of transitional space from Chapter 2). But our clients are in the tough position that while they are necessarily if temporarily dependent on us, nothing about the divorce process or us is familiar to them. Even if a given client has been through a divorce before, this one has a new story line and new cast of characters.

When a client comes to see us they are, like us, scanning the landscape for information. Because separation and divorce is intrinsically a time of intense change and many unknowns, our clients feel not only a sense of urgency about choosing their experts well, but also an enhanced sense of vulnerability and self-doubt. They are assessing whether they have found a competent expert who will care about them and in whom they can safely place their trust.

As busy professionals, it's easy to forget that for the time they are working with us (and later, in memory), we become central characters in a central drama of our clients' lives. This means they imbue our words with tremendous significance, and scrutinize our faces for information with the anxious intensity of a cancer patient studying her oncologist's expression for clues about the results of her latest CAT scan.

As busy professionals, it's easy to forget that for the time they are working with us (and later, in memory), we become central characters in a central drama of our clients' lives. This means they imbue our words with tremendous significance, and scrutinize our faces for information with the anxious intensity of a cancer patient studying her oncologist's expression for clues about the results of her latest CAT scan. In our absence, our clients call up our voices in their minds as sources of succor or guidance. Over time it will become our job to find ways to help our clients to stretch developmentally. But it doesn't matter what else we do well unless our client first feels fundamentally understood and nonjudgmentally accepted—not as we wish them to be, but as they are.

Conduct a Nondirective Interview

It's a familiar story: A hurt and frightened client seeks out a shark attorney who imposes an aggressive agenda without first listening for their client's underlying concerns, thus heightening the client's anxiety and fomenting conflict in the family. That client will always second-guess his attorney's advice (no matter how good it is) and feel mistrustful of their strategy. In the end, even if they "win," the client will remain unhappy with the outcome, because nothing their attorney did emerged from a sense of understanding between them. While there is a time and place for assertive action, leading with an aggressive agenda is a form of aggression against our clients. On the other hand, being an enlightened practitioner who prefers to keep things peaceful does not inoculate us from doing early damage to our relationship with our client or, at the very least, from missing important opportunities to build a connection.

> While there is a time and place for assertive action, leading with an aggressive agenda is a form of aggression against our clients. On the other hand, being an enlightened practitioner who prefers to keep things peaceful does not inoculate us from doing early damage to our relationship with our client or, at the very least, from missing important opportunities to build a connection.

Many divorce professionals have been trained to focus, especially during the first interview, on gathering facts of a particular kind in an ordered sequence. For attorneys (or therapists who have worked in settings where they must make quick mental health assessments and/or rapid diagnoses), there is a pressure to develop quick formulations and to offer guidance early on.

We advocate letting go of any presumed agenda, at least during the initial portion of the first interview. Again, while we believe that building a good relationship is the first order of business, we're not trying to turn lawyers and financial experts into therapists or encourage mental health professionals to do therapy in this context. We're not advocating that you relinquish your professional role, abandon the need to gather certain kinds of information, withhold basic guidance, or fail to fulfill any ethical obligations. The trick is to find the right combination of simply listening *and* gathering important data by asking questions. The balancing act between *tending* to your client and *moving* your client begins right at the beginning. Letting our clients know, explicitly and from the get-go, that we want to understand them *and* make sure we help them achieve the task at hand sends the message "You are important to me as a person, but I know you've hired me to do a job."

> *Letting our clients know, explicitly and from the get-go, that we want to understand them **and** make sure we we help them achieve the task at hand sends the message "You are important to me as a person, but I know you've hired me to do a job."*

More on the First Interview: Being Without Memory and Desire

The British psychoanalyst Wilfred Bion[1] describes the importance of meeting each new client in the psychological state of "being without memory or desire." In other words, we should strive to be free of the unhelpful, shorthand assumptions that can come from having logged a lot of hours but can inhibit our capacity to meet each client (each moment)

(Continued)

---

1. Bion, W.R. *Notes on Memory and Desire*, vol. 2, n.3, *Psycho-Analytic Forum* (pp. 271–280). [reprinted in E. Bott Spillius (Ed.) *Melanie Klein Today, Vol. 2: Mainly Practice* (pp. 17–21), Routledge, 1988.

More on the First Interview: Being Without Memory and Desire (*Continued*)

with a clear mind, fresh ears, and genuine, caring curiosity. In the ordinarily frenetic, demanding environment of our day-to-day work lives we all, from time to time, find ourselves emotionally dissociated from our work. We find Bion's concept helpful when we need an intentional reset.

Another Plug for the Nondirective Interview: Learning About Your Client

In Chapter 3 we talked about secure and insecure attachments, and how we can learn a lot about how our client is wired by paying attention to how they treat us in our role as a helping professional. Our relationship with our client is like a laboratory in which our their typical ways of relating emerge and can be studied, explored, understood, explained, and, hopefully, modified for the better.

Attachment styles are also coded in the manner in which our clients speak—their cadence, grammar, sentence structure, word choice, tone, and way of organizing spoken information. Holding back and allowing our client's personal narrative to unfold organically and without interference gives us access to a treasure trove of information. Remember the bird metaphor we used earlier? Next time you listen to a new client's story, activate your sensory feathers. Here are just a few illustrative examples of things to watch, listen, and *feel* for that suggest your client is unable to think clearly at the moment and/or has a vulnerable or disturbed sense of attachment (in other words, lacks a sense of basic trust) We've put them in the form of questions to ask yourself:

- Does your client have a story to tell you (about herself, about the divorce) that makes logical sense (a separate

(*Continued*)

Another Plug for the Nondirective Interview: Learning About Your Client (*Continued*)

question from whether or not you like the client or agree with her perspective), or do her thoughts ramble without organized direction?

- Does your client vilify his future ex completely, without insight into his own potential contributions to the failure of the marriage?
- Does your client know why they are in your office or do they claim to be there only because their spouse told them to come?
- Does your client sit passively and wait for you to ask questions?
- Does your client speak without stopping, leaving no space for you to ask even a clarifying question?
- Does your client reject your comments as being wrong, even when you are simply paraphrasing what she has said?
- Do you find yourself wanting to protect your client?
- Do you find yourself hating your client?
- Do you find yourself wanting to champion your client?
- Do you find your client "creepy" without knowing why?
- Are you sexually attracted to your client without knowing why?
- If your client is a parent, does she never mention her children?
- Is your client's narrative packed with so many details that you become lost or bored?
- Does your client keep talking even after you've told her time is up for the day?

Deciding How to Begin

We generally start off our meetings with a very brief overview of the ethical considerations we want our clients to be aware of before they tell us their story. We note that our conversation is confidential (for lawyers, "privileged") and will remain so until or unless the client gives us explicit, written permission to communicate with others. We note the length of the meeting ("We will have about an hour today, so we will finish up by noon"), since respecting time boundaries is an important aspect of the holding environment. Then we dive in.

Here are some of our favorite post-introduction openers:

- Please begin wherever you like.
- Now I can shut up and let you speak. Please start anywhere . . . . I'll be taking some notes so I can refer back to them later. Let me know if that bothers you."
- So . . . (*sitting back, putting down pencil and pad, etc.*) . . . . I'm ready to listen. Please begin anywhere you like.
- I know your story is complicated and the best we can hope for today is for me to get an initial sense of what's going on and how I can help and for you to get an initial sense of what it might be like to work with me. Don't worry about getting everything in—I'll ask enough questions for us to be able to discuss possible next steps before you leave. Why don't we start with what's brought you in?
- I know from our brief telephone conversation that there are several issues that feel pressing to you. There are lots of thing we could talk about, but there's no need to cover anything particular today. Would you like to begin with the issues that you told me are keeping you up at night?
- You and I have had a couple of phone calls, so I have a sense of the broad strokes of your situation. I know, for example, that your wife left very suddenly and very recently. There's a lot to talk about, but what I'm really wondering is "How are you doing?"

Tips for Conducting the Nondirective Interview

Although in the beginning it's important to let your client's narrative unfold organically so that you can learn about them and begin to establish a sense of trust, you'll still need to gather enough concrete information that you can begin to move into an actual *process*. Here are some tasks, emotional and practical, that you should accomplish within the first meeting or two:

- Ensure that your client feels that you are authentically present, caring, organized, and effective—that you have formed the beginnings of a good working alliance.
- Develop an initial understanding of your client's strengths and vulnerabilities.
- Understand what your client wants ("If you had a magic wand . . . ?").
- Find out why your client is in your office. Have they already decided on a process? Are they looking to you for advice in choosing a process?
- Find out if your client and their partner have already made any agreements (e.g., to mediate, or to share custody of their children).
- Find out if your client is operating on any assumptions (rational or irrational) about a potential outcome.
- If your client is unsure as to how best to proceed, educate them about process options or (if that falls outside your area of professional expertise) send them in the direction of an appropriately qualified professional.
- Before you are retained, make sure your client is fully informed about the process they have chosen and about the nature and scope of your role in it. Disabuse your client of any false or unrealistic expectations about the divorce process and your role (and document that you did so since many clients will claim false advertising later).[2]
- Develop a game plan for the next steps.

What to Do When Your Client Doesn't Say Anything

Occasionally, a client will come to us so frightened or anxious that they stare like a deer in the headlights, unable to speak. Later, when we know them better, we might let the silence build for a while before jumping in ourselves (more on that in Chapter 9). But in the beginning, it's best to put your client at ease as quickly as possible. To give you the flavor of what we mean, here are some examples of good openers to use with timid clients:

---

2. Each professional field—legal, financial, mental health—has its own code of ethics relating to these obligations. This kind of conversation is second nature to lawyers and financials, but is often new to mental health professionals.

- I'm guessing you have been dealing with really hard things for quite a while now. Maybe it's a bit hard to know where to dive in?
- Maybe it's hard to know where to start. Let's just start with your current circumstances. Are you and your husband still living in the same house?
- I'm wondering if this is the first time you've talked about what's going on? Yes? Okay, just take your time. (Client becomes tearful. Blows her nose.) I'm guessing things have been fairly awful lately. (Client is weeping and unable to talk.) I wouldn't be surprised if just putting one foot in front of the other feels like a Herculean task. (Client nods.) Would it be easier if we started by my asking a few basic questions? Are you up for that?

What to Do When Your Client Seems Overwhelmed and Disorganized

Sometimes clients enter our office emotionally flooded. We have no way of knowing if this is a chronic condition, or if it's specific to the moment. Either way, we know that while they're overwhelmed with feelings our client can't take in (or deliver) any new information. So we need to start by helping them to downshift into a calmer frame of mind. Here's an example:

Professional: *A middle-aged woman enters her divorce professional's office for the first time. She is bedraggled and gasping.*

Client: *"God, the subway was stopped for 15 minutes, and then I walked south instead of north to find your office. It's so damn confusing in this neighborhood! It's like traveling to China!"*

Professional: *"This office can be hard to find the first time, especially if you're not used to navigating downtown. Take a minute to catch your breath. How about some water or a cup of tea?"*

Sometimes disorganization manifests itself in the inability to stop talking. In this vignette you'll see a professional working with a client who fits that bill:

Lindsey, a 30-year-old woman in stiletto heels, has come to the office of her divorce professional for a first meeting. When the professional goes to collect her from the waiting room, Lindsey *is animatedly chatting up the receptionist. As she is guided down the hall to an office, she continues to jabber nonstop—about the office décor, the high rents in the neighborhood, and a friend who works in the next building. As she sits down (and without taking a breath), Lindsey launches into a barrage of bitter complaints about her "crazy husband," her inability to pay the mortgage on time, and her frustration with how long it took to get any divorce process started as she has wanted "O-U-T out for **six** excruciating months."*

As he listens, the professional realizes that if anything is going to come out of this meeting he is going to have to corral Lindsey. He says, "Sounds like you've been having a very rough time! I'm interested in what you're telling me; it's important and we'll come back to it soon and for as long as we need to. But because this is our first meeting and we both have questions, I'm going to ask you to push pause, just for now, so I can get some basic information."

Lindsey does not "push pause," but rolls over the professional's words to continue her rant.

*This time, the professional says, "Lindsey, I know how frustrating it has been waiting for this appointment; a lot has happened that you want me to know about. But if I'm really going to **get it** I'll need to start with a couple of questions. I also need to give you some important information. Once we get through that, I am all ears."*

Most clients who behave like Lindsey will, with this sort of intervention, settle down long enough to have a reciprocal conversation. On the other hand, some will be unable to stop talking, perhaps even beyond this meeting and for the entire duration of your work with them. Our task is to find a flexible balance between allowing a "Lindsey" to talk when she needs to and setting limits when the moment calls for it.

The next time you're working with a client like Lindsey, try expressing (out loud, in words) the way he or she fills up the space between the two of you and, in so doing, pushes away anything you have to offer that might be helpful. Invite *your* Lindsey to wonder with you about why they can't be quiet long enough to take anything in. Think attachment: This kind of behavior is analogous to a baby stiffening when it's mother tries to cuddle it or a school age child shrugging off a hug. Try something like, "You're here because you want my help, but I notice that every time I open my mouth you interrupt. I'm not sure why you do that. Maybe you're worried that if I don't know every detail of what's going on I won't understand your situation. But I don't know how I can help if I can't get a word in. What do you think?"

Over time, some "Lindseys" will quiet down within the calm, accepting environment you provide and will respond to your interest in finding meaning in their behavior (after all, they'll expect you to be irritated by them—everyone else is!). On the other hand, some clients will never be able to tolerate your attempts to create a transitional space for understanding, and will become disdainful or angry at your attempts to organize or redirect them. These early sessions offer an opportunity to gather initial information about where our client falls on the Rigidity/Flexibility Continuum, and to develop working hypotheses that you can test over time.

> *The next time you're working with a client who won't stop talking, try expressing (out loud, in words) the way he or she fills up the space between the two of you and, in so doing, pushes away anything you have to offer that might be helpful. Invite your client to wonder with you about why they can't be quiet long enough to take anything in. Some clients will quiet down; others will become disdainful or angry at your attempts to organize or redirect them.*

Follow the Affect, Not the Content

Conducting a nondirective interview means letting our client lead. Sometimes that means simply allowing them to talk about what's uppermost in their minds and asking open-ended questions to expand a topic of interest. But, as the previous example illustrates, it's not helpful to focus exclusively on what our client says, because words can divert our attention and obfuscate meaning just as effectively as they can illustrate and explain.

Let's return to our model of the loving parent-infant pair from Chapter 2. Remember our description of the way the parent holds their baby while gazing at them with intense focus? The parent registers shifts in the baby's muscular tension, posture, facial expressions, and voice and takes them *in* (body and mind) so as to make sense of them. The parent resists any internal pressure to become too anxious themselves, or to discharge anxiety by rushing to a premature solution (both of which would heighten the baby's distress and shift the focus of the exchange away from the baby's needs and onto the parent's). Instead, the parent offers containment; they simply allow the baby's experience to *be* and to resonate within them. This process begins to regulate the infant's distress. The parent is *with* their baby, but they don't become their baby; they hold open the increment of distance, the transitional space, that leaves room for thinking and making meaning (for metabolizing distress by changing it from raw feeling into processed experience). Then, using a body posture and tone intuitively matched to the baby's, the parent uses physical and vocal expression to communicate their understanding to the baby.

Conducting a nondirective interview means letting our client lead. But it's not helpful to focus exclusively on what our client says, because words can divert our attention or obfuscate meaning just as effectively as they can illustrate and explain. Our antennae should always be extended and vibrating—ready to hone in on the moments when our clients communicate to us without words.

From the first meeting to the last, our observational stance should be very much like that of the parent of a preverbal child. To mix metaphors, our antennae should be extended and vibrating—ready to hone in on the moments when our clients communicate to us without words.

While we're at it, let's throw in yet another metaphor (clearly we can't resist a juicy metaphor). We like the image of digging for clams: You learn where to dig by watching for the air bubbles on the surface of the sand—evidence of the treasured creature beneath. You need to dig quickly (before the clam is buried too deeply for you to reach), but not aggressively (or the clam will take evasive action).

Here are some examples of nonverbal but important "air bubbles"—clues that your client is experiencing a feeling you should follow:

- Your client stops mid-sentence, says, "never mind," and changes topic.
- Your client pauses mid-sentence, then begins to speak again without explanation.
- You notice a subtle shift in your client's body posture.
- You notice a shift in the tone of your client's voice.
- You sense your client's attention is no longer in the room.
- Your client pauses to take a sip of water.
- Your client looks at their watch.
- Your client listens silently while their partner speaks, but shakes their head almost imperceptibly.
- Your client uses a word to describe a feeling then retracts it ("I think my husband should be punished. Well, not punished, but I don't think it's fair how he treated me.").

Listen for What the Client Doesn't Say

Sometimes, especially when our client's story is emotionally fraught or compelling, we can get so swept up in the details of what they do say that we fail to note crucial missing elements. When a client omits or pays short shrift to a significant issue or dismisses your attempts to address it, that's a clue that something important lies beneath the surface. In an early session, before you have earned your client's trust and know when it's safe to apply some emotional pressure, it's not a good idea to push in sensitive areas. But, like other nonverbal clues, lapses in their narrative are hints that you've hit on an issue that you should come back to later. Later on, in Chapter 9, we'll discuss specific techniques for *how* to dig once you've identified *where* to dig. But for now, here are some common examples of the clues clients give us that there is an important hidden idea that's worthy of our attention:

> When a client omits or pays short shrift to a significant issue or dismisses your attempts to address it, that's a clue that something important lies beneath the surface.

- Your client has been treated objectively badly by his ex, but he displays no anger or grief.

- Your client tells you her father died last month, but adds no detail and moves quickly to the next topic.
- The meeting is over before you realize you don't know the name of your client's spouse.
- Your divorcing client and their spouse clearly don't have the funds to support two households (or to pay their professionals), but your client never mentions money concerns.
- You know there is a 30-year age difference between your client and her partner, but it doesn't come up.
- You get to the end of your time and realize you don't know the reason your client is separating from his spouse or who initiated the split.

Provide Structure in the Holding Environment

Fees

Lots of us have more trouble talking openly about money than we do about sex. But it's important to have fee policies, to depart from them only after careful consideration, and to discuss them explicitly either before or during your first meeting. Make sure your client has your policies in writing, so you can refer to them later if necessary. Even if they grumble at your hourly rate, clients appreciate knowing the parameters of the relationship from the get-go. No one likes to be charged for a service they didn't know was billable—surprises on an invoice undermine trust.

One of the benefits of having a consistent set of policies is that when a client acts out, you can recognize their behavior easily and, therefore, talk about it with them. If you allow your policies to sag it becomes much more difficult to know who is responsible when things get messy (and thus hard to reestablish clearer guidelines).

Still, the fact that you make your fee policies crystal clear at the outset doesn't mean your client will remember or adhere to them later. One of the benefits of having a consistent set of policies is that when a client acts out you can easily recognize their behavior and, therefore, talk about it with them. If you allow your policies to sag, say by letting your client rack up a big bill or by writing off a portion of your fee without discussing your rationale, it becomes much more difficult to know who is responsible when things get messy (and thus hard to reestablish clearer guidelines).

Deadlines

If you promise to produce a draft Agreement in a week, do. If life intervenes, let your client (and any other interested parties) know in advance that you'll need more time. Following through on your commitments to your client echoes good parenting; it reinforces the safety of the holding environment. It also communicates respect, and models the kind of behavior you expect in return. It's hard to hold your client accountable for not producing their long-awaited budget when you haven't made good on your promise to find the name of a vocational counselor.

> *Following through on your commitments to your client echoes good parenting; it reinforces the safety of the holding environment.*

Time

Set start and end times for each meeting and stick to them. When a meeting begins, remind everyone of the plan ("We've set this meeting to run two hours, so we'll be stopping at four o'clock. That means we should look at our calendars by three forty-five, to make sure we have time to schedule our next few meetings."). Setting and resetting structure in this way reinforces the sturdiness of the container.

Limits and Boundaries

As we discussed in Chapter 4, limits and boundaries are crucial components of both the Microcontainer and the Macrocontainer. They help us establish appropriate professional distance

Limits and boundaries help us establish appropriate professional distance and create a sense of safety. At the same time, there are times when doing good work requires a thoughtful departure. But, in the beginning, be clear and consistent. You'll learn a lot about your client by tracking their response to the protocols of your work. Later, if you think it makes sense, you can make adjustments.

and create a sense of safety. At the same time, there are times when doing good work requires a thoughtful departure (an occasional Sunday e-mail or off-hours telephone call). But, in the beginning, be clear and consistent. This way you'll have the opportunity to observe how your client reacts to structure. Will they push for more of you? Will they be too shy to reach out even in appropriate ways? You'll learn a lot about your client by tracking their response to the protocols of your work. Later, if you think it makes sense, you can make adjustments.

Minimize Self-Disclosure

Therapists are trained to keep information about their personal lives out of their work with clients; lawyers and financial experts are not. In fact, attorneys and financial professionals are likely to use non-work topics as a way of connecting with clients (see our discussion of "small talk" in Chapter 9). Whatever your profession, we favor a less-is-more approach to sharing information about life outside of work. Providing too much information about ourselves, especially at the start of a case before we know the landscape, is risky. Not only can it blur the lines between the professional and the personal in confusing ways, it can lead clients to imagine that our personal relationships are blissful or to idealize our successes in ways that can impede their willingness to speak freely about themselves. Consider these seemingly trivial examples:

- Your client notices your undergraduate diploma from Yale. They comment, *"Wow. Yale. Impressive."*

A socially ordinary response:

"Yeah, thanks! Great school. Very tough but I made great friends there, and my diploma opened a lot of doors."

A more professional, safer response:

Silence and a little neutral nod

- A client mentions she just has just returned from a visit to her family's home on the Delaware shore.

A socially ordinary response:

"No kidding! We own a house there too—in Bethany. Where's yours? We love it there. Time with the kids, just love the peaceful moments with my wife."

A more professional, safer response:

"Glad you had a chance to get away and recharge."

Frequently a client will throw you a curve ball by asking a direct personal question such as "Do you have children?," "Are you married?," or the ubiquitous "Have you ever been divorced?" There's no magic formula for how to respond (see our discussion of "Factors to Consider" in Chapter 8). The best advice we can offer is that you take a beat before answering. Ask yourself: "What is the most helpful response based on my understanding of this client in this moment?" You may make a bad call, but if it comes from a caring place nothing fatal will come of it.

> *When it comes to professionals sharing details of their personal lives with their clients, we favor a less-is-more approach. But sometimes a client will throw you a curve ball by asking a direct personal question such "Have you ever been divorced?" There's no magic formula for how to respond. The best advice we can offer is that you ask yourself "What is the most helpful response based on my understanding of this client in this moment?"*

Maintain a Stance of "Involved Impartiality"

The fact that we listen empathically and accept nonjudgmentally doesn't mean we should buy our client's story hook, line, and sinker. We talked about this is in Chapter 3: Becoming the standard-bearer for our client's story exactly as they tell it leads to positional thinking and problematic forms of advocacy.

The psychoanalyst Jill Scharff introduced the phrase "involved impartiality."[3] We like it because it describes a state of being empathic while remaining open to alternate perspectives. It suggests a benign skepticism in which, even as we fully accept our clients nonjudgmentally *as they are* (including their dark mucky feelings such as anger, shame, and hopelessness), we listen for clues to potential other sides of the story. The "facts" as our clients relate them are neither good nor bad—they simply are. And, as we listen and begin to assess our client's capacity to perceive nuance and to modify their opinions, we ask ourselves such questions as "In what way might my client be distorting the reality of her husband's behavior?" or "Is it really true that my client's children don't know anything about the divorce?" Questioning your client's narrative is not a betrayal. Developing a three-dimensional picture of your client in the context of her life and relationships is critical when the time comes to help her to recognize a new idea and stretch toward it.

> *We like the phrase "involved impartiality" because it describes a state of being empathic while remaining open to alternate perspectives. Questioning your client's narrative is not a betrayal; it's critical if you're going to help her to recognize a new idea and stretch toward it.*

The technical challenge to maintaining a stance of "involved impartiality" lies in making sure your client continues to feel held, even when they suspect you don't fully support their position.

Here's an example of challenging comments from a positional client. We've followed it up with an "unhelpful response" contrasted with a "helpful response."

Client: *I feel like you're not supporting me. I've told you that my husband is a liar. He says he wants time with the kids, but he's just taking them to punish me. When he has the kids, it's round-the-clock nannies. Tell me, how is this fair? On what planet does he deserve equal custody?*

---

3. Scharff, Jill. *Projective and Introjective Identification and the Use of the Therapist's Self*, 244–247 (Jason Aronson 1992).

The unhelpful response:

Professional: *I hear you. You're right. If he is going to have the kids then he has to be **with** the kids. Children should be with a parent, not a babysitter! He can't just take them to make a point. I'll e-mail his lawyer saying that you'll only agree to shared custody if your husband can prove that **he** is taking care of the kids. He won't be able to do it on his work schedule—he's probably trying to hide that fact.*

The helpful response:

Professional: *I get it. It's already painful for you to give up time with the kids, but it's doubly hard to feel that they're being cared for by a babysitter rather than by you. I also know it feels terribly unfair that even though you've been the go-to parent from the beginning, their dad is now asking to spend significant time with them. That means time away from you. But I take your point about the nanny situation. Maybe we can get some more information about how much time the kids are spending with nannies versus with their dad and go from there.*

The Irrational Client: The Benefits of Responding to Feeling Versus Content

It's never helpful to argue facts with a client who wants to enlist you as an ally in an emotional battle. Steering clear of content and speaking to deeper emotions has a lot of benefits, including:

- It slows the pace of the conversation and gives you the opportunity to create a transitional space for thinking.
- It turns a moment of controversy into a moment of opportunity for greater understanding.
- In not jumping into the fray or moving too quickly to action, you are providing containment and conveying a sense of true interest and concern.
- You are setting a shared expectation about pacing and the manner in which you and your client will work together.
- You are sending a powerful message about the importance of thinking over doing.
- You're staying clear of the trap of saying something negative about the "other side" that could come back to bite you.

Don't Say Anything You Don't Feel

Empathy is predicated on authentic curiosity—a genuine interest in "getting" another person's experience in a profound way. If you really want to know someone and you suspend preconceptions (think: "without memory and desire"), you can come as close to a shared understanding as it's possible to come—given that you are two separate human beings.

But you can't fake empathy, so don't try.

Coming from a place of deep emotional connection, the words "That must have been horrible for you!" can be powerfully comforting. Coming from a place of intellectual understanding ("A terrible thing happened to you, therefore I assume it must have been horrible for you") the same words will feel pat, patronizing, insulting, or like a form of abandonment.

> *You can't fake empathy, so don't try. Coming from a place of deep connection the words "That must have been horrible for you!" can be powerfully comforting. Coming from a place of intellectual understanding, the same words will feel pat, patronizing, insulting, or like a form of abandonment. If you don't feel empathy, don't fight it. But don't, in that moment, talk.*

How can you know the difference? You can feel empathy in your body—perhaps as a pit in your stomach or heaviness in your heart. Sympathy, on the other hand, comes from your head, as a disembodied thought. There are many moments when, try as we might, we can't find a way to feel empathy. Don't fight it—this is happening for a reason and it will take you time to sort it out. But don't, in that moment, talk.

The Malignancy of Platitudes

If you're not feeling it, don't say it. It is so, so, *so* much better to remain silent than to say something superficial and generalizing that moves the conversation away from the client's experience and leaves them feeling dropped and alone.

(Continued)

The Malignancy of Platitudes (*Continued*)

Platitudes are the worst. They are caricatures of help-fulness. We're talking about the chicken soup-y aphorisms that are well intended but, because they are generic and pat, make the recipient feel some version of horrible.
Here are some of our least favorites:

- Every cloud has a silver lining.
- What doesn't kill us makes us stronger.
- Tomorrow is another day.
- Time heals all wounds.
- There are plenty more fish in the sea.
- It's always darkest before the dawn.
- It's never to late to start again (and its evil twin: Age is just a number).
- God never gives us anything we can't handle.
- Everything happens for a reason.
- Five years from now you'll look back on this and laugh.

We could go on . . . . Use any of these with a client and our angry spirits will rise out of your conference table and rap your knuckles with a ghostly ruler.

Eschew Premature Pep Talks

Clients often come to us feeling ashamed and afraid to show their vulnerability for fear of appearing weak or pathetic. How many times has a client sheepishly told you, "I'm sure I'm not telling you anything you haven't heard before—you've probably seen every-thing by now."? What they're really saying is "I'm worried you'll see my situation as mundane and my worries as trivial. I'm afraid you'll judge me."

So if a client enters your office feeling down in the dumps and leaves an hour later saying, "Thanks so much; I feel so much bet-ter. I'll be fine this weekend," resist the urge to grin and respond with "That's so great! This is going to be easier than you think! You're so brave! I'm so proud of you!" The same client who pres-ents as chipper and upbeat on Wednesday may not be able to get out of bed when the weekend rolls around and his kids go off to their mom's. We pointed this out in Chapter 3, but it bears repeating: When we convey the idea that feeling good is better than feeling awful or that being brave is morally superior to being afraid, we set our clients up to feel they have failed us.

Your clients will take comfort in the idea that you've been around the block a few times and know how to help. At some point they may even need to hear that you've worked with other clients in similar situations who have survived the experience. But in the beginning, guard against the impulse to set your client's mind at ease by conveying that you understand the totality of their experience based on a few data points and your own years of experience. To a grieving client, the phrase "Don't worry; I've seen this a million times and I know what I'm doing" is like a dagger to the heart. If your client believes that you think you can understand their unique situation after only an hour or two of discussion, they'll never feel safe with you.

> To a grieving client, the phrase "Don't worry, I've seen this a million times and I know what I'm doing" is like a dagger to the heart. If your client believes that you think you can understand their unique situation after only an hour or two of discussion, they'll never feel safe with you.

Don't Say Anything Your Client isn't Ready to Hear (Even if it's True)

Tact and timing are more important than being right. Here's a hypothetical:

Your empty-nester client, Sandra, has taken a seemingly unshakable (if financially unrealistic) position that she must hold on to the couple's five-bedroom vacation home. What Sandra doesn't say (or perhaps fully understand) is that this home has become a symbol of safety and stasis for her, an island of the familiar in a world of frightening new changes. If you try to shake your client out of her irrationality by looking her in the eye and saying, firmly, "Sandra, you don't need a second home, and you can't afford it. Anyway, that house is your past—time to march into your future!" you may traumatize her. On the other hand, if you first spend time with Sandra, encouraging her to discuss the significance of the home ("We spent every summer there when the kids were growing up.") and her fears about losing it ("I see the same friends every summer. I'm afraid I'll fall apart without them."), she'll likely start loosening her grip.

Don't Ask Rhetorical Questions

This one can be hard for attorneys who have been trained not to ask questions to which they don't already know the answer, but therapists are by no means immune.

Leading questions are the antithesis of empathy. Trying to get your client to say something you believe to be true as a way of making a point is never a good idea—it comes across as trite, patronizing, and (sometimes) sarcastic. Ask a rhetorical question such as "Sandra, tell me: What do you think will happen to your finances if you don't sell your vacation house?" and you instantly become the first-grade teacher everybody hates.

Leading questions are the antithesis of empathy. Trying to get your client to say something you believe to be true as a way of making a point is never a good idea—it comes across as trite, patronizing, and (sometimes) sarcastic. Ask a rhetorical question and you instantly become the first-grade teacher everybody hates.

While we've offered a few concrete examples of interventions, this chapter has mainly been a lesson in how to move into a *state of mind* that supports the conditions for positive change. So if you're itching for more specifics about what to do or say in a given moment, fear not. Chapters 8 and 9 are all about technique!

Summary of Concepts from Chapter 5

- Your relationship with your client begins before you meet, both in your client's fantasies about you and in your reactions to any pre-meeting interactions.
- Enhancing your awareness of the nuances of your client's behaviors allows you to gather information that will help you to establish empathy and develop an initial working hypothesis about how to help most effectively.
- The authors describe a number of techniques for establishing the Microcontainer, including:
  - Offering curiosity without judgment
  - Learning to notice
  - Maintaining presence of mind
  - Conducting a nondirective interview
  - Deciding how to begin
  - Dealing with silent or disorganized clients in a first interview
  - Following affect, not content
  - Listening for what the client doesn't say
  - Providing structure within the holding environment
  - Minimizing self-disclosure
  - Maintaining a stance of "involved impartiality"
  - Avoiding inauthentic communications
  - Avoiding premature pep talks
  - Utilizing tact and timing
  - Avoiding rhetorical questions

Chapter 6

The Second Step in Establishing the Container:
Process Guidelines and Relationships among Colleagues

Follow your heart but take your brain with you.

—Alfred Adler

In Chapter 4 we introduced the concept of the Macrocontainer and its function in supporting the Microcontainer of you and your client. We described it as providing a warm, organized, emotional, and physical environment analogous to that provided by a second parent (plus extended family and trusted others) who supports and protects the holding environment that the on-duty parent provides for his or her infant. The quality of the Microcontainer of you and your client—the strength of your holding environment—depends

The quality of the Microcontainer of you and your client—the strength of your holding environment—depends on the concrete and psychological aspects of the Macrocontainer. In other words, how you work with your client (your process and protocols), who else you work with (opposing counsel, mental health and allied professionals), and the quality of your interactions with everyone involved are as important as your skill at tending to emotion while moving forward on the task.

on the concrete and psychological aspects of the Macrocontainer. In other words, *how* you work with your client (your process and protocols), *who else* you work with (opposing counsel, mental health and allied professionals), and the *quality of your interactions* with everyone involved—all these factors are as important as your skill at tending to emotion while moving forward on the task.

Characteristics of a Strong Macrocontainer

Like the Microcontainer, the professional Macrocontainer has some key characteristics:

- Mutually agreed-upon protocols that provide structure for the chosen process (understanding of flow of communication and confidentiality, meetings that begin and end on time, shared responsibilities, mutual expectations)
- A shared commitment that any change in protocol will be made only after careful thought and with a clear understanding of the reason for the change
- An appropriate work environment that is welcoming and professionally run
- An adequate number of strong Microcontainers (one-on-one relationships) for both professionals and clients
- A strong metabolizing function (the ability to understand and repair ruptures and to use the experience to enhance shared understanding in the service of transformation)

The Role of Microcontainers in the Macrocontainer

Some professionals are most comfortable working one on one with their clients in a traditional advocacy model. Others gravitate toward partnerships (such as in co-mediation), or teams (such as in multidisciplinary settlement negotiation or Collaborative Practice). There are also many hybrid models. For example, we know lawyers who often collaborate with mental health professionals and financial experts in litigation, and others who conduct settlement negotiation in a spirit of partnership with co-counsel.

Although the authors admit to having preferred ways of working (we did write a book about Collaborative Practice), we have come to understand that collaboration and transformative possibility are not the sole domain of any particular legal process. Rather, they stem from any given professional's attitude toward their work. If you're reading this book, you're probably already inclined to keep things as nonadversarial as is reasonably possible, even in a litigated case. But being peacefully inclined and knowing not to take a one-size-fits-all approach are not enough when it comes to establishing a good Macrocontainer.

When we are educating a client about legal processes and advising them in making a choice, most of us already consider such factors as the client's stated wishes and those of their spouse, their

Although the authors admit to having a preferred ways of working, we have come to understand that collaboration and transformative possibility are not the sole domain of any particular legal process. Rather, they stem from any given professional's attitude toward their work.

Have you ever had a seemingly calm and reasonable couple come to you for mediation but then, in the first session, become so shocked and angry at each other's stated goals that the process fell apart immediately? Your case likely failed because you didn't take the time to know your clients well enough to build a Macrocontainer that had the requisite number (or quality) of Microcontainers.

respective emotional and cognitive states, and our knowledge of and historical experience with any other professional(s) the client and his or her spouse may have already hired. But have you ever had a seemingly calm and reasonable couple come to you for mediation but then, in the first session, become so shocked and angry at each other's stated goals that the process fell apart immediately? If you did a careful postmortem on such a case you'd learn that it likely failed because you didn't take the time to know your clients well enough to build a Macrocontainer that had the requisite number (or quality) of Microcontainers.

In Chapter 3 we explained our concept of the Rigidity/Flexibility Continuum—a tool for assessing the level of conflict within each individual and between the clients as a couple. Nancy Cameron and Susan Gamache, an attorney and a psychologist from Vancouver, have developed another helpful tool for anticipating emotional challenges in cases. Their Process Intensity Evaluation (P.I.E.) provides a mechanism for professionals to gauge the levels of intensity and complexity in three areas of a case: financial issues, parenting issues, and the couple's relationship.[1] If intensity and complexity are high in even one of these areas, Cameron and Gamache suggest that attorneys should consider augmenting their team (in our parlance, "beefing up the Macrocontainer") by adding professionals who can offer expertise and support.

A case involving amicable clients with complex finances may well benefit from the addition of a financial neutral to consult with both clients and both attorneys throughout the process. A high-conflict couple raising three children while running a family-owned business might require a full team of attorneys, mental health coaches (including a child specialist), a financial neutral, and a business evaluator. In this case, many readers will understand the benefits of bringing on a coach or business evaluator simply based on the fact pattern. But sometimes the potential benefits of bringing on additional professionals are more difficult to see at first. If, early on, we can move beyond the facts of a case toward a three-dimensional study of its complexities, we can build

---

1. Nancy Cameron and Susan Gamache, article on the website of the International Academy of Collaborative Professionals (not available to the public; used with permission of the authors).

a Macrocontainer with enough Microcontainers—think of them as support beams—to set us up for success.

Consider two attorneys involved in a traditional settlement negotiation. In addition to expertise, each attorney provides her client with a good holding environment—they remain supportive without overidentifying. But let's say the husband is so angry about his wife's affair that he is unable to have rational discussions. And let's say his wife lacks both empathy and insight; she can't see her contribution to her husband's intractability and wants to push on more quickly than he is able. The attorneys have an amicable relationship and share a vision of the couple's dynamic, so they are able to support each other in doing their hard work (trying to nurture *and* nudge the husband, trying to support *and* restrain the wife). They provide each other with a strong Microcontainer that helps them both to remain centered in a state of "involved impartiality" and keeps them from becoming demoralized or burned out. But, over time, it becomes clear that the husband is currently too traumatized to participate in the process. He likes and trusts his attorney, but he doesn't trust his wife or her attorney. The Microcontainer between the husband and his attorney is strained, and so is that between the wife (who grows impatient with the slow pace of the process) and her attorney. The couple appears to be at impasse; the process sputters and seems on the verge of conking out.

This is a moment when some clients or attorneys might give up on a nonadversarial approach and begin to consider litigation. And maybe they should. Some clients are, in the end, hell-bent on getting their day in court (see our discussion of "The Terrorist" in *Navigating Emotional Currents of Collaborative Divorce*).[2] But, in our experience, very few clients are unable to reach agreement out of court if they and their professional team have adequate Microcontainers at their disposal.

In the scenario we just described our attorneys might consider bringing on a mental health neutral to provide support to both spouses. Skilled mental health professionals often provide individual Microcontainers to each member of a couple while remaining neutral and retaining the respect and trust of both. But in very

2. Kate Scharff & Lisa Herrick, *Navigating Emotional Currents in Collaborative Divorce: A Guide to Enlightened Team Practice*, 73–74 (American Bar Association 2010).

high-conflict cases, or cases when the mental health professional is less experienced or is brought on midstream (when acrimony is already at a high ebb), it's worth considering using two mental health professionals who can work cooperatively and provide a Microcontainer for each other. And if the husband and wife can be helped to trust *each other's* mental health professions—voila! Two *more* new Microcontainers and a much strengthened Macrocontainer.

Our rule of thumb: The more complex the case and the more intense the conflict, the more Microcontainers you'll need—that translates to a greater number of specialized professionals.

Theoretical Microcontainers in Various Legal Contexts

Litigation
Cast of Characters in the Macrocontainer

Two attorneys
Associate attorney(s) (working on the case)
Non-neutral experts (forensic, financial, custody)
Staff at both law firms (senior colleagues, junior
    colleagues, peers, administration)
Therapist(s) for one or both parties

Potential Microcontainers

One attorney and one client
The two attorneys
One or the other attorney and a colleague from his or her firm
One client and his or her therapist
One attorney and his or her client's therapist
One attorney and a non-neutral expert
One client and a non-neutral expert

Settlement Negotiation
Cast of Characters in the Macrocontainer

Two attorneys
Neutral and/or non-neutral experts (forensic, financial,
    custody)

(Continued)

Theoretical Microcontainers in Various Legal Contexts (*Continued*)

Associate attorney(s) (working on the case)
Staff at both law firms (senior colleagues, junior colleagues, peers, administration)
Therapist(s) for one or both parties
Neutral mental health consultant (perhaps working on parenting plan)

Potential Microcontainers

One attorney and one client
The two attorneys
One or the other attorney and a colleague from his or her firm
One client and his or her therapist
One attorney and his or her client's therapist
The mental health consultant and each client
The mental health consultant and each attorney
One attorney and a non-neutral expert
One client and a non-neutral exert
One client and a neutral expert
One attorney and a neutral expert

Mediation without Separate Attorneys
Cast of Characters in the Macrocontainer

Mediator

Potential Microcontainers

Mediator and Client 1
Mediator and Client 2

Mediation with Separate Attorneys
Cast of Characters in the Macrocontainer

Mediator
Attorney 1
Attorney 2

(*Continued*)

Theoretical Microcontainers in Various Legal Contexts (*Continued*)

Potential Microcontainers

Mediator and Client 1
Mediator and Client 2
Attorney 1 and Attorney 2
Attorney 1 and Client 1
Attorney 2 and Client 2

Co-Mediation without Separate Attorneys
Cast of Characters in the Macrocontainer

Mediator 1
Mediator 2

Potential Microcontainers

Mediator 1 and Mediator 2
Mediator 1 and Client 1
Mediator 1 and Client 2
Mediator 2 and Client 2
Mediator 2 and Client 1

Co-Mediation with Separate Attorneys
Cast of Characters in the Macrocontainer

Mediator 1
Mediator 2
Attorney 1
Attorney 2

Potential Microcontainers

Mediator 1 and Mediator 2
Attorney 1 and Attorney 2
Attorney 1 and Client 1
Attorney 2 and Client 2
Mediator 1 and Client 1
Mediator 1 and Client 2
Mediator 2 and Client 2
Mediator 2 and Client 1

(*Continued*)

Theoretical Microcontainers in Various Legal Contexts (*Continued*)

Collaborative Practice (Team Model with Sole Neutral Coach)
Cast of Characters in the Macrocontainer

Attorney 1
Attorney 2
Sole neutral coach
Financial neutral
Mortgage professional
Child specialist

Potential Microcontainers

Each professional and each client
Each professional and each teammate

Viva La Difference! Examining the Containers Across Disciplines

So far we've focused primarily on the emotional benefits of strengthening a Macrocontainer by adding Microcontainers. But let's not minimize the importance of the specialized knowledge and expertise each of us brings to the table. While there is significant overlap in the quality of Microcontainers across disciplines (all divorce professionals need to provide the same Three Conditions for Positive Change in order to be helpful), there are important differences in the function and flavor of containers offered by professionals from different fields. A client's sense of basic trust in their attorney is grounded in their confidence in that attorney's knowledge of the law, the nature of their advocacy, and the quality of their legal advice. A client's sense of basic trust in their mental health professional is grounded in that professional's ability to understand the psychological makeup of both members of the couple and to provide explanations and guidance based on that understanding. A client's sense of basic trust in their financial expert is grounded in their confidence in that expert's knowledge of the client's areas of financial interest, their ability to deliver the type of information or guidance the client wants, and the integrity of that information or guidance.

A Macrocontainer made up of two attorneys will have a different vibe than one that also contains a mental health professional or financial expert. But the difference isn't simply due to the differences in skill sets and professional roles. Not only do professionals from different disciplines have different expertise, but they also have different ethical responsibilities. In every case, some of the protocols and guidelines in the Macrocontainer will be profession specific. For example, while mental health professionals want their clients to make informed choices, they don't have an ethical duty to make sure their clients are informed about the law. Conversely, while lawyers care about the emotional safety of their clients, they are not bound by the ethical "duty to warn" that governs when a mental health professional must break confidentiality.

A world-class Macrocontainer contains both an adequate number of strong Microcontainers and the right combination of Microcontainers from different disciplines *for that particular case.* Maybe this seems obvious. But for professionals who are used to working in any particular way (e.g., lawyers who are used to flying solo, or mental health mediators who believe it's best to "keep the attorneys out of it"), it can be tough to replace well-established modes of practice with the question "What model will work best for this family?"

Strengthening the Macrocontainer

Here are two examples of ways to strengthen the Macrocontainer by adding Microcontainers from other disciplines:

- Mental health mediators working with clients on parenting issues hit an impasse when discussing a time-sharing schedule for the children. They suggest holding a meeting with the clients' attorneys present. In the presence of the Microcontainers offered by their attorneys, the clients feel safer to make compromises.

(Continued)

Strengthening the Macrocontainer (*Continued*)

- The anxious wife in a litigating couple is told by her attorney that her husband's financial settlement proposal is reasonable—better than she'd likely get in court. The wife has liked and cooperated with her attorney up to now, but begins to mistrust him when he advises her to accept the offer. She is the financially disadvantaged spouse and has had little to do with the couple's financial dealings over the years, so accepting her husband's offer frightens her. Now, when her attorney patiently tries to explain the terms of the proposal, the wife becomes overwhelmed and unable to listen.

  Rather than becoming visibly frustrated, the attorney wisely suggests that the wife consult a financial advisor with expertise in divorce. The wife meets with the financial advisor, whom she experiences as compassionate and understanding. Once they have reviewed the proposal and run cash flow and retirement projections, the wife is able to see that her husband's proposal will allow her to live comfortably without having to give up her home or return too quickly to the job market. She returns to her attorney with renewed trust in him and the process.

The Risks of an Expanded Macrocontainer

As you read the previous examples, you may have noticed that the larger the team, the greater the number of potentially helpful Microcontainers. But you also may have wondered, "But what if attorney 1 and attorney 2 can't get along?" It's true: Two people do not guarantee a Microcontainer. The more people on the team, the more complicated the emotional terrain.

In our profession it's always important to remain self-aware (more on that in Chapter 7), but the task of self-management becomes increasingly difficult as you add more personalities to the mix. Pauline Tesler made this point eloquently in her foreword to our first book:

> *The challenge in team service delivery lies in the need for divorce professionals . . . to learn how to share the sandbox. . . . Every interaction between two or more people provides banana peels to slip on, sore toes to step upon, rabbit holes to fall into . . . [adding professionals to the team] multiplies the opportunities for missteps geometrically. . . . At the same time . . . [it] also provide[s] abundant opportunities for learning together what works, what does not, and why.*[3]

Aggression Against the Macrocontainer

Think of a client who ties your hands by insisting that you do not speak to opposing counsel ("Why should I pay for you two to discuss Saturday's golf game?"), or another who wants the divorce done *yesterday* but can't clear time to meet with you. Some clients resist our attempts to help, accuse us of incompetence, rail against our limits, or try to wrest control of the process away from us. This kind of aggression isn't an attack on *us*; it's an attack on our role and on the executive functioning of the Macrocontainer.

It's hard not to take it personally when a client hurls snarky comments our way. But like a child having a temper tantrum (in emotional pain but needing his parents to remain calmly firm), aggressive clients need us to hold the line, refrain from retaliation, and avoid getting into power struggles. Our clients need us to accept their aggression nondefensively and to remain curious about it. Our Macrocontainer (and the

Our clients need us to accept their aggression nondefensively and to remain curious about it. Our Macrocontainer (and the Microcontainers within it) supports us so we can contain our client's aggression, empathize with it, and make sense of it.

---

3. Pauline Tesler, JD, foreword to *Navigating Emotional Currents in Collaborative Divorce: A Guide to Enlightened Team Practice*, Kate Scharff and Lisa Herrick (American Bar Association 2010).

Microcontainers within it) supports us so we contain our client's aggression, empathize with, and make sense of it.[4]

Rupture and Repair in the Macrocontainer

Sometimes highly rigid clients fire their professionals because their professionals are simply too *reasonable*. Other times there's a lack of fit between the client and the professional (we'll talk more about this in upcoming chapters). But it's been our experience that when a case falls out it's usually not just a matter of an "impossible" client or a client-professional mismatch. It's also not usually due to a technical mistake on the part of one or more professionals. When there's serious trouble on a professional team it's usually because a toxic dynamic between two or more professionals on the team goes unaddressed. Sometimes that dynamic is due to a personality clash between two professionals. But often, the toxic dynamic is due to some aspect of the clients' conflictual relationship that has worked its way into the relationships among team members. That idea may sound complicated, but it really isn't. Let's unpack it a bit—as we do you'll likely realize that this sort of thing happens regularly in your practice.

> *When there's serious trouble on a professional team it's usually because a toxic dynamic between two or more professionals on the team goes unaddressed. Often the toxic dynamic is due to some aspect of the clients' conflictual relationship that has worked its way into the relationships between team members.*

Mark and Roberta: Rupture and Repair in the Macrocontainer

Mark and Roberta are divorcing. Each has an attorney; they are working in a settlement negotiation model.

---

4. We want to draw a clear distinction between the ordinary kinds of frustrating, irritating, or offensive behavior we all experience from time to time and truly abusive or threatening behavior. No professional should work with any client who is verbally abusive, threatens violence (either explicitly or implicitly), or makes the professional feel physically or emotionally unsafe in any way.

*The four-way settlement meeting is set for 9 a.m., but Roberta is running late—again. Mark waits in the law firm's reception area while his attorney (Michael) and Roberta's attorney (Renee) are in the conference room looking over documents. Mark has come to the meeting already tense. He reviewed their financial spreadsheets last night. The team hasn't yet begun their discussion of asset division, so Mark isn't yet familiar with relevant aspects of the law. He also doesn't trust his wife or her attorney. So when he saw the list of marital assets arranged by title, he jumped to the false conclusion that he'd be forced to give his wife half of everything—even his premarital assets. Now, as he waits for Roberta to show up, he begins to stew. He thinks, "All that money! Money from investments I made long before I met her! And all the money I made by working my tail off so she could live a life of leisure. And she's the one who wants the divorce! Where the heck **is** she? I'm the one with the tight schedule!"*

*Meanwhile, in the conference room, Michael gets increasingly anxious. For weeks Mark has been regaling him with complaints about how Roberta's disorganization is dragging out the divorce. More than once Mark has barked at Michael: "The only reason my wife's attorney lets this continue is because she is racking up fees! So get on the phone and **do** something about this already!"*

*Presently, the receptionist comes into the room. "Michael," she whispers, "Mark would like a word; he's in the library." She gives Michael a look that says, "Your client **is** not happy!" Groaning, Michael leaves the room.*

*After ten torturous minutes of being dressed down by his client for "not getting the process under control," Michael is emotionally triggered—big time. He returns to the conference room where Renee is still awaiting her client, Roberta, and launches into an attack on Renee. "This is insane," he snarls. "You need to get on the phone with your client **right now** and find out where she is. I can't imagine what excuse she has this time, but her lateness is unacceptable. Given his work obligations, Mark has a hard time scheduling these meetings. What can Roberta be doing that is so important she'll waste everyone's time and his money?"*

Renee feels defensive at first. After all, Mark is no angel. But she knows Roberta's lateness is sabotaging the process, and Mark and

Michael have reason to be upset. She manages to stay calm. She listens to Michael, and empathizes with his and his client's frustration. She explains that she's frustrated with Roberta too. As a matter of fact, Roberta is just as late to individual meetings, often fails to complete assigned tasks, and rarely returns calls or e-mails until there's an "emergency" (at which point Roberta expects her attorney to respond pronto!). Renee has tried to address these issues many times. Roberta is incorrigible.

As he listens, Michael's anger is replaced by empathy for Renee; she has a difficult client. "You know," he says "Roberta is hard to work with. But Mark is tough too. Last night he sent Roberta a nasty e-mail accusing her of being a gold digger and saying he wasn't going to give her a penny in the divorce. He knows how to rile her up. Actually, I'm not surprised she's late."

*"Well, I'm sure it's not fun being the target of Mark's rage," offers Renee. "I know he's loaded for bear today, and Roberta really knows how to poke him with a stick. I'll try to have your back in the meeting; I'll try to keep her from riling him up too much." "Thanks," says Michael, feeling supported. "I'll have your back, too. I'll do what I can to keep Mark from going off like a grenade. Maybe it would help to diffuse things if we both find a way to express empathy for each **other's** client." "Agreed," responds Renee. "Let's think about how we can do that without pissing off our own clients!"*

Now, let's take a closer look at what happened in the above vignette by breaking it down into its component parts (represented by the below diagrams).

In Figure 6.1 we see the team: a Macrocontainer of two attorneys, and two Microcontainers (each attorney-client pair). The jagged line between the clients represents the conflict between them. In this meeting their conflict takes the form of Roberta's lateness and Mark's rage and paranoia.

In Figure 6.2 we see the conflict between Mark and Roberta leaking out into the Microcontainer of Mark and his lawyer. Mark directs the rage he feels toward his wife at Michael, angrily accusing him of "not getting the process under control." Michael has been under attack by his client for some time now. He feels frustrated and impotent.

Conflict Between Clients
Expression of Individual/Marital Dynamics

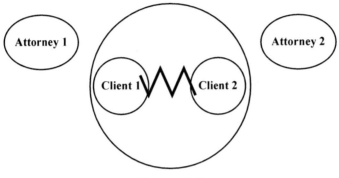

FIGURE 6.1

In Figure 6.3 we see the conflict move further into the team. Michael, upset after his exchange with Mark, directs his anger at Renee by accusing her of not having client control. The Microcontainer between the two professionals is ruptured. And since the two of them provide the Macrocontainer, it's weakened too.

In Figure 6.4 we see the beginning of repair, starting in the Microcontainer of the two attorneys. Had Renee responded defensively to Michael's attack, the two of them would have started to look a lot like their clients. They might have been caught up in a cycle of mutual accusation that would permanently damage their

Conflict Spreads to the Professionals
Rupture in One Microcontainer

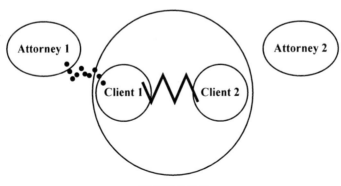

FIGURE 6.2

Ruptures Spread
Weakening of Microcontainer

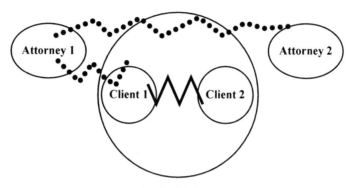

FIGURE 6.3

Microcontainer (and perhaps lead to the collapse of the Macro-container and of the whole process). Instead, Renee listens non-defensively. She offers empathy for what Michael has been through. She also makes herself vulnerable by sharing her own frustration at not being able to get her client to cooperate in the process. Both these actions diffuse Michael's anger so that he can respond in kind.

In Figure 6.5 we see how the repair of the attorney-attorney Micro-container allows the professionals to repair the individual attorney-client Microcontainers and reestablish a strong Macrocontainer. Having reconnected, Michael and Renee are able to come back

Repair Begins
Repair of One Microcontainer

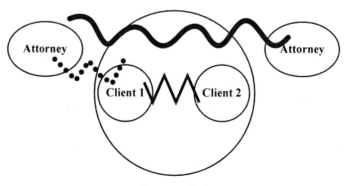

FIGURE 6.4

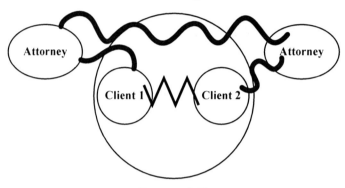

Macrocontainer is Reestablished
Metabolizes Experience

FIGURE 6.5

together as a well-functioning professional pair. Even though each is the other's "opposing counsel," they know that today's meeting (and the whole process) will go more smoothly if they collaborate. The attorneys share information about their own clients. In the process, they expand their shared understanding of the couple and enhance their ability to empathize with both spouses.

In Chapter 2 we talked about how divorce professionals can "metabolize" their clients' feelings and actions by taking them in, making sense of them, and (by adding insight) use them to move the process forward. What Michael and Renee have done is a perfect example. They've gathered up their clients' raw feelings and behavior (Mark's anger, Roberta's passive aggression), reflected on them, gained a better understanding of their clients, and used that understanding to come up with new strategies for working more effectively. Their workday started out rough, but the result has been a net gain.

Enactments: What They Are and Why They Matter

In our example, Mark (the husband) was angry with Roberta (the wife). He took that anger out on Michael (his attorney), who in turn took it out on Renee (the wife's attorney). When

(Continued)

Enactments: What They Are and Why They Matter (*Continued*)

a professional gets personally caught up in their client's dynamics and recreates them, that is an "enactment." Enactments are inevitable. But, while they are momentarily problematic, they are rich opportunities for growth. When we can think ourselves *out* of them, enactments offer us a unique opportunity to deepen our understanding of our clients. With any professional and any team the important questions are: "How often will enactments occur?," "How long will it take us to recover from an enactment?," and "What will we learn from the experience?" Handled badly, enactments can tank a process. Handled well, enactments become the gold standard for moments with transformative potential.

Summary of Concepts from Chapter 6

- The Macrocontainer is made up of the rules and protocols governing the process and the professional-to-professional Microcontainers. It provides structure and support to each Microcontainer on a case.
- High-conflict, high-intensity cases can strain a Macrocontainer. The Macrocontainer can be strengthened by the addition of one or more Microcontainers (though expanding a Macrocontainer can present new challenges).
- The Macrocontainer repairs ruptures in the Microcontainers.
- The Macrocontainer metabolizes clients' and professionals' negative feelings and behaviors by supporting professionals in gaining greater insight, enhancing empathy, and developing new ideas about how to work more effectively going forward.

Chapter 7

The Importance
of Self-Awareness

The best way to capture moments is to pay attention.
This is how we cultivate mindfulness. Mindfulness means
being awake. It means knowing what you are doing.

—Jon Kabat-Zinn, *Wherever You Go, There You*
Are: Mindfulness Meditation in Every Day Life

Being in Sync

When we are able to create a powerful container, our clients benefit in lots of ways. They feel supported when they suffer, reassured
when they're anxious, and empowered to make daunting decisions
when they're scared. We lend them our confidence and create a
zone of safety that frees them up to generate new potential options
(without feeling they are negotiating against themselves), to evalu-
ate scenarios with an open mind, and to problem-solve during discussions about specific issues that are important to them—even
when the issues are hotly disputed.

Like every other aspect of development over one's lifespan, a
divorce process is never linear. But when our relationship with our
client is solid—when the Microcontainer is in great shape—we
have the experience of being in productive sync with our client.

Our client may be paddling hard through rough water, but we are shouting encouragement from the shore, providing ballast in the back, or manning the rudder to help steer clear of a shoal. Sometimes we are the passengers and our clients are the captains, navigating solo—a developmental triumph!

Like every other aspect of development over one's lifespan, a divorce process is never linear. But when the Microcontainer is in great shape we have the experience of being in productive sync with our client.

We aim to connect with the part of our client that wants to propel their own craft forward rather than dive out and swim to safety or run it against the rocks. Think back to the Three Conditions for Positive Change: the helping relationship, the new idea, and optimal anxiety (see Chapter 2). Remember how each developmental challenge represents two emotional polarities in dynamic tension; one polarity pulling toward regression or stasis, the other pulling toward the future. Remember how a good parent supports his or her child to master a new developmental challenge by calmly containing the child's anxiety and providing the right mixture of support and encouragement for *that* child in *that* moment. Remember our description of the transitional space—how we should stand two steps ahead of our client on the path of their divorce journey, reaching our hand back across the gap to draw them toward us. All of these ideas come together to form the heart of our work: the ongoing act of honoring our clients' fears while allying with their strengths.

We aim to connect with the part of our client that wants to propel their own craft forward, rather than dive out and swim to safety or run it against the rocks. This is the heart of our work: the ongoing act of honoring our clients' fears while allying with their strengths.

Staying in Sync

To stay in sync, we need to be clearheaded. How, for example, can we read our client's emotional states or determine when to push, pull, or stand aside if we can't tell where our client's feelings end and ours begin? How can we see clearly if we're looking through a screen of our personal reactions? How can we hear well if our ears are filled with static? When we lose our equilibrium—our position of involved impartiality—we can't work effectively. If, as we're rowing down the divorce river, our boat capsizes and we become preoccupied with our own safety, we'll lose track of our client (and anyone else who was in the boat with us), and we'll have a hard time assessing the situation and figuring out how to help. And later we'll have difficulty figuring out what went wrong. Did our client, in a moment of panic, throw the boat off balance? Did we fall out of sync and yank our client along too hard, thus raising our client's anxiety out of their optimal range? Or did we hit a hidden rock beneath the surface, an emotional hotspot we didn't yet know was there? Being able to ask the right questions and suss out the answers will allow you and your client to work together to right the boat, rechart your course, and move forward with a new awareness of potential obstacles.

> *To stay in sync, we need to be clearheaded. How can we read our clients' emotional states or determine when to push, pull, or stand aside if we can't tell where our clients' feelings end and ours begin?*

You'll have lots of personal reactions to your clients and their situations. After all, we are individuals with our own histories and accumulated knowledge and skills in our own areas of expertise. We need to bring our personhoods to bear, including, from time to time, our own best judgments and opinions. And we need to draw on our past experiences and our authentic emotions in order to connect empathically. On the other hand, there's no room in our work for moral judgment, proselytizing, or personal agendas. When our biases go unchecked, they inhibit our ability to remain

> *We need to draw on our past experiences and our authentic emotions in order to connect empathically. On the other hand, there's no room in our work for moral judgment, proselytizing, or personal agendas. When our biases go unchecked, they inhibit our ability to remain present in the moment and to respond in client-focused ways. They can impede or derail the process.*

present in the moment and to respond in client-focused ways. They can impede or derail the process.

How to Stay in Sync with Our Clients

- Let go of any personal agenda or attachment to a specific outcome.
- Remain curious.
- Remain client-centered and client-focused.
- Stay attuned to emotion and affect.
- Suspend moral judgment.
- Refrain from proselytizing.
- Avoid assumptions.
- Remain as objective as is reasonably possible and professionally responsible.
- Maintain compassion.
- Maintain empathy.
- Remain self-aware so you can restabilize when your equilibrium is disturbed.
- When you become destabilized, use the experience to gain understanding about you, your client, and a possible better path forward.
- Remember that when your client treats you badly it's not personal; he or she is unconsciously repeating old trauma-based patterns.

Turning Potential Obstacles into Opportunities for Growth

Think again how a healthy parent provides a good holding environment and, within it, works hard to understand their baby's distress in a given moment. The parent's ability to do both of these things helps the growing child, over time, to develop self-esteem, empathy, and the capacity to form more healthy relationships. But the whole process is predicated on the parent's ability to keep in check his or her own needs (for sleep, to go to the movies) and his or her own anxieties ("What if I can't get this baby to stop crying?

What if I've tanked my career by taking paternity leave?"). He or she *needs* to do this; otherwise preoccupations will fill the space in his or her mind that the parent needs to hold open in order to take in and reflect on the baby's subjective, separate experience.

The parent's tasks are made even more difficult by the fact that having children always stirs up feelings about one's own childhood—both positive and negative.

The good parent just described has to manage the momentary, natural anxiety that comes from holding a crying baby while simultaneously keeping at bay any intensely painful feelings about ways his or her own parents may have fallen short in the empathy department. In order to do this, the parent has to find a strategy. For example, he might identify the areas in which his own parents were competent (even if there were also big trouble spots) and model his own parenting style on those. Or he might choose

> *Divorce is painful; the content of our work will always stir us up. It goes without saying that we need good training and lots of experience. But if we don't also have sufficient understanding of how our personalities and ways of seeing the world have been shaped by our own experiences, we can't achieve competence, let alone mastery.*

to learn to parent in different and better ways (which is tough without good mental models).

As divorce professionals, we face the same emotional challenges as a new parent. Divorce is painful; the content of our work will always stir us up. It goes without saying that we need good training and lots of experience. But if we don't also develop sufficient understanding of how our personalities and ways of seeing the world have been shaped by our own experiences, we can't achieve competence, let alone mastery.

We can't separate ourselves from who we are, and we should never try to become someone else. Understanding and accepting our whole selves, warts and all, allows us

> *Understanding and accepting our whole selves, warts and all, allows us to turn our vulnerabilities into strengths. When we have suffered and processed the experience, we can better understand the suffering of others. Metabolized pain is the basis for empathy.*

to turn our vulnerabilities into strengths. When we have suffered *and* processed the experience of suffering, we can better understand the suffering of others. Metabolized pain is the basis for empathy.

Useful Concepts for Describing and Understanding the Impact of Our Internal Obstacles to Change

Transference and Countertransference

If you become personally affronted at your client's lateness, he or she may be (rightfully) upset with you. After all, they haven't *really* treated you badly. Quite the opposite; it's their time and they're paying for it. Now they've squandered some of it. And it's their process; if they drag it out, they have to live with the consequences. You've had a misplaced reaction and you need to get a handle on it. You might need to apologize in order to reestablish harmony.

> If you become personally affronted at your client's lateness, he or she may be (rightfully) upset with you. After all, they haven't really treated you badly. Quite the opposite; it's their time and they're paying for it. Now they've squandered some of it. And it's their process; if they drag it out, they have to live with the consequences.

On the other hand, some kinds of acting out would upset *anyone*. For example, if your client refuses to pay your bill when you've been working your tail off and all the charges are legitimate, you'll be angry. No one would accuse you of taking the behavior too personally or suggest you apologize for expecting to be paid.

Transference is the mental act of treating a new relationship as if it were an old one. When your client, before getting to know you, already expects you to judge them harshly, they're imposing an old template (based in early traumatic experience) onto your relationship. They're making false assumptions about your character that feel real to them but don't match up with reality. Some transferences are negative. These can turn us off to our clients. Some are positive, even idealizing. These can push us to overfunction, violate our professional boundaries, or develop rescue fantasies.

Here are a few examples of a client's transference to a divorce professional:

- Idealizing the professional—thinking the professional has the power to "fix everything" (for example, by causing the other spouse to metamorphose into a different person!)
- Treating the professional like an incompetent pawn
- Mistrusting the professional for no good reason
- Feeling the professional only cares about the fees, not about them

Countertransference is a professional's reaction to a client (or colleague). There are two types of countertransference: professional-owned (as in the example where a professional becomes angry at a client's noncompliance) and client-induced (as in the example where a professional is upset at their client's refusal to pay their bill). Here are a few examples of professional-owned countertransference:

- Getting angry when a client doesn't take advice
- Feeling personally affronted by lateness or failure to accomplish assigned tasks
- Expressing disappointment when the client changes their mind
- Expressing frustration when the client is afraid to let go of a position

Now, some examples of client-induced countertransference:

- Becoming upset or frightened when a client speaks or behaves in a truly offensive or abusive manner
- Becoming worried or upset when your client mistreats their child

As we noted in our first book:[1]

The ubiquitous quality of professional-owned countertransference is a good argument for each of us doing the hard

---

1. Kate Scharff & Lisa Herrick, *Navigating Emotional Currents in Collaborative Divorce: A Guide to Enlightened Team Practice*, 41 (American Bar Association, 2010).

work of knowing ourselves well. Good psychotherapists know that they must undergo significant psychotherapy themselves before they can be effective clinicians. The authors of this book would go so far as to suggest that personal psychotherapy should be a prerequisite for [divorce] practice.

It's worth acknowledging that it takes a lot of emotional self-restraint not to rise to the bait when a client levels a nasty transference at you. And it takes a lot of self-awareness to exercise that restraint. Another good argument for therapy!

Personal Biases and Assumptions

Where countertransference describes a distorted reaction to a particular person or situation (in other words, an individual's actual emotional experience in a real-time moment), a bias is a persistent predisposition to view a type of person or group of people in a specific and fixed way—favorable or unfavorable—that is distinct from the way one views other people or groups of people. To be biased is to lack impartiality. All of us carry our own biases and assumptions. Especially since we work in an emotionally provocative field, biases will pop up now and then. But as with countertransference, the important questions are "Under what circumstances will biases emerge? How will they manifest themselves?" and "How will we handle them?"

> *A bias is a persistent predisposition to view a type of person or group of people in a specific and a fixed way—favorable or unfavorable—that is distinct from the way one views other people or groups of people. Especially since we work in an emotionally provocative field, biases will pop up now and then. The important questions are "Under what circumstances will biases emerge? How will they manifest themselves?" and "How will we handle them?"*

Here are some hypothetical examples of professionals' biases and assumptions in the practice of separation and divorce:

- Fathers are not as good as mothers at taking care of babies.
- Women who spend a lot of money on spa treatments are usually spoiled brats.

- Women who travel a lot for work after having children are putting their egos ahead of the kids' needs. They shouldn't be mothers.
- Gay dads aren't as good at parenting boys as they are at parenting girls.
- Stay-at-home dads are underachievers.
- Parents who watch pornography can never be trusted with their children.
- Babies can't handle overnights away from their mothers.
- People who have affairs are always in the wrong.
- There's something wrong with a woman who doesn't want to have kids.

The Authors Share Some of Their Own Biases

We have frequently talked together about our own biases— because they keep showing up in our cases! Kate, for example, is highly attuned to how parents handle the introduction of new significant others; she tends to bristle when she perceives that a stepparent is overstepping, behaving intrusively, pushing boundaries, or moving so quickly into their new role that they fail to respect the emotional pace of the ex-spouse and/or the children. This bias leaves Kate vulnerable to missing signs that the biological parent and/ or children actually *welcome* the involvement of the stepparent. Lisa, on the other hand, leads with a "more the merrier" philosophy when it comes to new parental partners. This bias leaves her vulnerable to supporting divorcing clients in establishing house-to-house boundaries that are too loose to facilitate a healthy adjustment to a new post-divorce normal.

Neither of these "presets" is problematic by default. They only cause trouble when we forget we have them or fail to keep them out of the work so we can remain in a state of being "without memory or desire." We use each other as a mutual Microcontainer in which to process the moments when our biases get in the way. That way we can reestablish equilibrium and learn from the experience.

The Interplay of Professional Experience and Bias

We talked earlier about the idea that accumulated professional experience can provide us with skill and a nuanced understanding of our work, but it can also leave us vulnerable to developing unhelpful biases. If you've worked with scores of clients who have had extramarital affairs, you may have developed assumptions about how the unfaithful client "should" behave during settlement negotiations, or how the abandoned spouse is likely to react. If these assumptions don't fit with the realities of a given case, they can cause problems. They could lead you to miss data that might otherwise have led to creative solutions, or cause you to behave in ways that clients and colleagues find aggressive, obnoxious, or off target. And since we're usually not consciously aware of our own biases or how they show up in our work, we're likely to feel baffled or defensive when they stir up bad feeling in others. Shortcuts sometimes lead to getting lost.

> *While accumulated professional experience can provide us with skill and a nuanced understanding of our work, it can also leave us vulnerable to developing unhelpful biases. False assumptions can lead us to miss data that might otherwise have led to creative solutions, or cause us to behave in ways that clients and colleagues find aggressive, obnoxious, or off target. And since we're usually not consciously aware of our own biases or how they show up in our work, we're likely to feel baffled or defensive when they stir up bad feeling in others. Shortcuts sometimes lead to getting lost.*

By contrast, less experienced professionals naturally come to each new case with fresher eyes; every scenario is new. A seasoned divorce professional might assume that a stay-at-home mother is going to balk at the idea of returning to the work force and is going to demand significant alimony (bias: stay-at-home moms are dependent on their breadwinning partners and are afraid of going back into the work force). A greener professional, on the other hand, might have an easier time remaining curious as to whether this woman feels dependent and afraid or, perhaps, impatient to regain her former professional status in her field.

Still, inexperience doesn't inoculate us from bias. If the newbie professional we just described grew up in a community where mothers *always* raised the kids while fathers *always* went to work, he or she might develop the notion that a traditional division of labor is superior to other modes of family functioning. That bias might carry over into the professional's work, and linger there until it was successfully challenged by a colleague or until the professional had run across enough successful working mothers and competent, happy stay-at-home fathers that the assumption shifted on its own.

False assumptions are usually long held, deeply engrained, and grow out of experiences in our family of origin or elsewhere in our childhoods. Once we figure out where our biases come from, we can work to sort them out from current reality. But that can be hard work, so best to get started now. Root out your biases. And if you can't diffuse them right away, at least learn to keep them under control until you can.

Being Triggered

"Being triggered" is a phrase that the authors (and others) use to describe the phenomenon of having an emotionally intense reaction that is incongruent with the content of the current moment. It's a sign that something deeper is being activated in us—we are having a problematic countertransference, or something in the present is reactivating feelings from a past traumatic experience. Our reactions in the "now" match our reactions in the past, but the circumstances of the "now" don't actually replicate the circumstances of the past.

> *"Being triggered" is a phrase that the authors (and others) use to describe the phenomenon of having an emotionally intense reaction that is incongruent with the content of the current moment.*

We like the phrase "being triggered" because it is not jargon; everyone can relate to it. But it can be used interchangeably with "having a professional-owned countertransference reaction," "imposing a bias," "or working on a false assumption."

Here are some ways to recognize that you've been triggered:

- Your state of mind shifts suddenly and dramatically (e.g., you suddenly become depressed, anxious, or angry).
- You say or do something out of character and potentially problematic.
- A client or colleague describes your behavior as scary, offensive, odd, or out of character.
- You're suddenly unable to think clearly.
- Your mind makes a seemingly random association to a past experience and lingers there, distracting you from what's happening in the moment.

Issues That Commonly Trigger Divorce Professionals

Situations
- A client grieves the loss of their spouse.
- A client reels in the wake of a spouse's infidelity.
- A client faces financial reversal or the loss of their home.
- The children are in pain about their parents' divorce.
- The divorcing couple is pregnant or has an infant or toddler.

Client Behaviors
- Lateness
- Disorganization
- Clinging to entrenched positions
- Refusal to settle even when the terms are fair
- Interrupting
- Passivity
- Noncompliance
- Changing their minds frequently
- Aggressive comments
- Passive-aggressive comments
- Sarcasm
- Contempt for spouse

(Continued)

Issues That Commonly Trigger Divorce Professionals (*Continued*)

- Contempt for professionals and/or the process
- Playing the victim
- Playing the martyr
- Insisting on having their "day in court"—even if it means mutually assured destruction

Mindfulness: The Key to Staying in Sync

Mindfulness is a state of being conscious and aware in a given moment. Jon Kabat-Zinn, emeritus professor of medicine; creator of the Stress Reduction Clinic and the Center for Mindfulness in Medicine, Health Care, and Society at the University of Massachusetts Medical School; and author of *Wherever You Go, There You Are: Mindfulness Meditation in Everyday Life*, wrote:[2]

Mindfulness practice means that we commit fully in each moment to be present; inviting ourselves to interface with this moment in full awareness, with the intention to embody as best we can an orientation of calmness, mindfulness, and equanimity right here and right now.

Mindfulness Means . . .

- Maintaining an acute awareness of being here, now.
- Maintaining awareness of the totality of ourselves in this moment—what we are feeling in our bodies, and what we are thinking.
- Having a sense of the connectedness between our physical sensation, our emotions, and our thoughts.

(*Continued*)

---

2. Jon Kabat-Zinn, *Wherever You Go, There You Are: Mindfulness Meditation in Everyday Life* (1994) Hyperion, New York, New York.

Mindfulness Means . . . (*Continued*)

- Feeling simultaneously engaged and relaxed.
- Maintaining an openness to new sensations and ideas.
- Connecting with the subjective experiences of others.
- Bringing emotional authenticity to our work.

Especially if the concept is new to you, or if you're under stress in your personal life, mindfulness can be difficult to achieve. But without it, your work will lack depth. In calm moments you'll only read the surface of things. In difficult moments the experiences of other people in the room with you, the qualities of interpersonal interactions—everything significant—will flow past you unnoticed. You'll be preoccupied with yourself—with your own emotional state, your own intrusive thoughts, and your own physical discomfort. At best you'll be partly there. Learning to bring presence of mind to each interaction and being fully alive and tuned in to both ourselves and others is the key to making sense of all the big questions, such as:

- "Why am I feeling this way?"
- "Does the source of my feeling originate in this room?"
- "If not, how can I make use of it?"
- "What is my client or colleague trying to communicate to me?"
- "What does my client or colleague need from me?"
- "How can I stay in sync with my client or colleague?"

Mindfulness as a Navigational Tool

Mindfulness, in the way we are describing it, means bringing your authentic self into the work of the immediate moment. Remember the bird metaphor from Chapter 5, the way in which paying attention to how a particular client ruffles our feathers offers important clues about his or her state of mind? The same capacity turned inward, the ability to notice subtle shifts in our own internal states of being, is what allows us to pick up on these subtle shifts in body posture, tone, and rhythm of speech in other people. It keeps the fibers of our being (our "instrument") vibrating in "receive mode." Mindfulness makes it possible for us to resonate with others; it lets us know when something important is going on that requires our attention.

Mindlessness

The opposite of mindfulness is mindlessness—a state of focusing on the past, the future, or a place or time other than the one you presently inhabit. Mindlessness causes us to miss everything important. It's like walking through a spring meadow while reading your text messages. We've all had long periods of mindlessness. We rush through weeks, forgetting to be grateful for our loved ones and other blessings. Instead, we focus on our fears or obsess about what we feel is missing in our lives. In our work with people in pain, this sort of emotional absence leaves our clients feeling dropped or abandoned. It leads to missed opportunities and mistakes that will slow, impede, or even derail our client's process.

Finally, Make Friends with Your Ghosts

If your takeaway from this chapter is that there are parts of yourself that you should ignore, suppress, purge, or avoid engaging with, we've sent the wrong message.

Make friends with your ghosts. Go exploring in the darker forests of your nature. Hate your client? Ask yourself why. Find yourself agreeing to meet your client on a Sunday when you'd rather be at church? Do some soul searching. Your personal and professional vulnerabilities are the result of emotional conflicts you haven't fully faced and

> *Make friends with your ghosts. Go exploring in the darker forests of your nature. Your personal and professional vulnerabilities are the result of emotional conflicts you haven't fully faced and worked through. They're like pieces of furniture in a dark room; you're going to knock your shins on them until you turn on the light so you can navigate better.*

worked through. They're like pieces of furniture in a dark room; you're going to knock your shins on them until you turn on the light so you can navigate better.

When You Feel Alone in the Work

Imagine you're an attorney in a litigated case. You have a difficult client who demands a lot of time and attention. Opposing counsel is aggressive and uninterested in settling. You've tried discussing the case with colleagues, but they're busy and preoccupied. You're exhausted and alone. After one particularly nasty e-mail from the other side falsely accusing you and your client of unethical behavior, you sit in your office alone, door closed, and fantasize about a career change. Maybe you *should* reconsider that journalism degree. But the real problem of the moment: You're missing a Microcontainer.

From time to time, at work and in our personal lives, we find ourselves feeling overwhelmed and out of our depths, with no one to understand, to tether us to the earth. These are moments to turn our attention inward, to listen for our inner voices. Some voices will be critical ("You're incompetent, you shouldn't be a lawyer!"). Ignore those. In the cacophony, try to identify at least one voice that induces a sense of safety and well-being. Find the one that broadcasts empathic, supportive messages such as "You are a good person" or "You are competent." This is the voice of a strong internal Microcontainer. Perhaps you can associate it with a particular person (your grandmother, your first-grade teacher, your partner, a colleague). Or perhaps somewhere along the line, through self-reflection (by yourself or with a therapist), you've constructed a sturdy Microcontainer on your own.

When we take good aspects of outside relationships *inside* ourselves, they can become portable Microcontainers, transitional objects from which we can draw strength even

(*Continued*)

When You Feel Alone in the Work (*Continued*)

in the absence of a supportive other. Learn to tune to their frequencies. After all, that's what we're asking of our clients. While we are flesh and blood Microcontainers now, we hope that over time our clients will learn to carry us in their minds and into their futures.

Summary of Concepts from Chapter 7

- To the authors, being in sync means maintaining focus on the client so we can read shifts in their emotional state and make adjustments to our own behavior that will protect the integrity of our Microcontainer.
- Being in sync means knowing our client well enough to be able to gauge, in a given moment, what they need from us so we can maintain the Three Conditions for Positive Change.
- Being in sync means knowing how to honor our client's fears while siding with the part of them that wants to move forward. It means knowing how best to help our client navigate polarities—the part of them that wants to stay still or move backward and the part that wants to take a leap of faith.
- We all have opinions, but there is no room in our work for moral judgment, proselytizing, or personal agendas.
- Our personal reactions to clients are both powerful tools and potential obstacles to effective work. They allow us to connect empathically, but (when they arise from our unresolved inner conflicts) they can drive us to behave in unprofessional and destructive ways.
- Transference is the mental act of treating a current situation as if it were an old one. When our clients treat us in ways that don't resonate with our true characters, that's transference at work.
- Countertransference is transference from the professional to the client. It can be client-induced or professional-owned.

- Our countertransferences, biases and assumptions, trigger points, and historical relationships to conflict are potential obstacles to maintaining a client-focused stance. Handled well, they also offer rich opportunities for enhanced understanding.
- Mindfulness, the state of being present and aware in the current moment, is the key to staying in sync, that is, attuned to our clients' thoughts, feelings, and needs.
- Under stress, and in the absence of a person with whom we can establish a helpful Microcontainer, we can listen to the voices of internalized Microcontainers that represent the good aspects of supportive relationships in our past.

Chapter 8

What Should I Do? What Should I Say? Factors to Consider in the Moment

The key to good decision making is not knowledge. It is understanding.

—Malcolm Gladwell, *Blink: The Power of Thinking Without Thinking*

Here are two short vignettes. As you read, consider such questions as:

- What should happen now?
- Who should speak?
- What should they say?
- If I were present in this moment, what might I be feeling and/or doing?

Vignette #1

David and Becka are in a four-way meeting with their attorneys. As the couple discusses child support, the question emerges of whether or not to buy their 17-year-old son a car. Becka says, "He has to get to hockey practice by 5 a.m., then to school. If he had a car my life would be **so** much easier." David responds sharply, "Then you can pay for it. I'm not a walking wallet." David's attorney is startled; in a prior one-on-one meeting David had already raised the issue of buying his son a car. He had even started shopping online for a used Honda.

Vignette #2

Jaden is meeting alone with his attorney, Anton. They're working on a time-sensitive response to a financial settlement proposal from his wife Eleanor and her attorney. Both Jaden and Anton feel it's important to send their response **that day,** while the proposal is still fresh. They have scheduled two hours for their meeting. They are making progress, but as they come to the end of their time they're far from finished. With ten minutes remaining (and seemingly out of the blue), Jaden says to Anton, "On another note, the kids were with me last Saturday night. Our youngest, Ella, woke up in the middle of the night and came into my room. My girlfriend Melinda was in the bed with me. Melinda wasn't going to spend the night, but she hadn't left yet. I don't think Ella has told her mom about this, or I'd have caught hell from Eleanor by now. But I don't know what to do. I know I agreed not to have my lady friends anywhere near the kids. I screwed up, I guess. I told Ella not to tell her mom and I think that was probably a mistake too."

The question of how to respond to a given client in a given situation is often complicated and tough to navigate. Should David's attorney ask him directly, in front of his wife, why he changed his mind about buying his son a car? Maybe—but only if David has a very trusting and sturdy relationship with his attorney. Should Jaden's attorney move into an in-depth discussion about why Jaden made the choices he made regarding his girlfriend and his daughter? Probably not, given that the meeting is nearly over and there is another important task to complete. We're often in a position of needing to respond in important ways in real time and under pressure. Mindfulness in the moment is essential to making good choices.

But pre-meeting preparation is important too. Let's start by looking at how the process of figuring out what to do and say can be made easier through forethought, then work our way into a closer examination of the moments in which we must think quickly on our feet.

Anticipating the Moment

On any given day, how do *you* prepare for a meeting with a client? Do you review your notes or other documents in the case file? Do you take time to reflect on the upcoming meeting's agenda, and consider any steps you or other professionals might take to maximize efficiency? Do you wonder about the emotional state of your client, or worry about any interactions he or she may have had with their spouse since your last meeting? Perhaps you telephone or meet with your client in advance—to reconnect, contain anxiety, and help them anticipate what to expect. Perhaps you have advance contact with opposing counsel, or a pre-brief telephone call with colleagues on a Collaborative team. On the other hand, you may have risen predawn, thrown breakfast at your kids, careened through the carpool line, and been going full tilt at work for six hours without a moment to breathe, so that by the time your meeting starts it takes you ten minutes to get your head in the game. We've all been there.

Generally, though, the more experienced we are, the more likely we are to have a metaphorical file cabinet in our heads—a stash of information that we flip through in advance to access relevant pieces of information about *this* client, *this* case, and *this* meeting. We want to be mentally teed up, ready to interact with clients and other professionals in ways that will be most effective.

> *The more experienced we are, the more likely we are to have a metaphorical file cabinet in our heads—a stash of information that we flip through in advance to access relevant pieces of information about* **this** *client,* **this** *case, and* **this** *meeting. We want to be mentally teed up, ready to interact in ways that will be most effective.*

A lot of this happens without effort, almost unconsciously. As you walk down the hall toward your office or conference room, you might find yourself recalling the nasty phone call you had with your client the night before. Has he calmed down, or is he still furious about your bill? Or you might find yourself worrying that the agenda for the meeting is overly ambitious. Will two hours be enough time to cover everything? Perhaps you'll find yourself reflecting on the imminent challenge of helping a highly conflictual couple to reach an interim custody arrangement by the end of the week—since they're due to deliver their third child in ten days. Maybe you'll notice that you've developed a headache and wonder if it's because the other attorney in the case has a tendency speak to you in a patronizing tone that makes you want to slap him.

What we've just described are examples of a process in which you've mentally reviewed various potentially relevant facts that might inform your sense of how best to intervene. These inner monologues make great fodder for real life dialogues. They can serve as helpful conversation starters among peers (common practice on Collaborative teams, but useful whenever collegial relationships allow). It's helpful when you can prepare for a meeting by, for example, offering your colleague a "heads up" that your client is coming in with a chip or her shoulder, or that she has suffered a recent loss or has been fired from a job. Sometimes the important information relates to *you*—perhaps you need some special consideration for your own fatigue or stress level, or want your colleague to know that you aren't operating at the top of your game because you're feeling triggered or befuddled by your own client. On other occasions you might suggest to colleagues (as you enter the conference room but before the clients arrive) that the team focus on a particular topic first, because your client is so preoccupied with that issue that he won't be able to focus on anything else until it is resolved.

> If you're feeling uneasy, the chances are your colleague is too. Even a brief pre-meeting air clearing can decrease the odds that old difficulties will resurface, and can set both your minds at ease so you can be emotionally present for your clients.

Less commonly (but importantly) you might choose to have a conversation with a colleague about a difficult exchange that occurred between the two of you that's left you feeling upset. If you don't know your colleague well it might not make sense to try this just before a meeting. It might be better to pick a time well in advance, or to save the conversation for later. But if you're feeling uneasy, the chances are your colleague is too. If you trust your colleague and know him or her well, even a brief pre-meeting air clearing can decrease the odds that old difficulties will resurface, and can set both your minds at ease so you can be emotionally present for your clients.

Choosing an Intervention in "Ordinary Moments"

Each moment of interaction in a case is important in a couple of ways. First, the moment may contain data that, while not obviously significant, may actually *be* significant (we discussed the importance of heightening our sensitivity to our clients' verbal and nonverbal communications in Chapter 5). Second, every moment requires us to behave in ways that maintain the Micro- and Macrocontainers. The effort of keeping those containers sturdy while you do your ongoing work is analogous to the effort of keeping the muscles of your body's core engaged while you do a cardiovascular workout. The dual exertion can be tough at first but the tasks complement each other. And over time, as your muscles get stronger and you become more practiced, it all gets easier and eventually becomes reflexive. As we gain experience, we get better at remaining mindful on multiple levels while performing the tasks associated with our jobs.

Choosing an Intervention in Developmentally Important Moments

Not all moments in a case are fraught with emotion or present us with complex technical challenges. Some moments are *particularly* loaded and difficult—sometimes because the subject matter is painful, sometimes because one or more clients are faced with

Some moments are particularly loaded and difficult. These are moments in which we feel affected, activated, and alive with a sense that there is something to be addressed. We sense that the stakes are high. These are the toughest moments of our work, and they are pregnant with transformative potential.

a difficult choice, sometimes because one or more people in the room is triggered—usually for multiple reasons. These are the moments in which polarities are in stark relief—with multiple tensions operating in the clients' minds (Should I agree to this proposal or go to court? Should I let my wife know how angry I am, or suck it up and stay on task?). These are moments in which *we* feel affected, activated, and alive with a sense that there is something to be addressed. We sense that the stakes are high. These are the toughest moments of our work, and they are pregnant with transformative potential.

What to do? What to say? How to decide?

The process of choosing a technique in a developmentally important moment is fundamentally the same as in any ordinary moment; peer in the file cabinet, flip through the contents, pull out the relevant information, and sort through it to see how it all adds up. But the task is harder in a difficult moment. For one thing, there are more metaphorical files to choose from, and more information in each of them. Also, it's likely that emotions will be running hot and things will be moving quickly—not conditions under which any of us can do our best thinking. And, if there are a lot of people in the room, it can feel like we're sitting on an emotional billiard table. It's tough to know what to say or do while dodging balls and tracking angles.

We know you can't possibly think about or even be aware of all the Factors in any given moment. But you can dial up your awareness of the importance of them and, over time, get increasingly proficient at recognizing and holding in mind a greater number at the same time.

In order to make our task more manageable, the authors have developed a list of what we call "Factors"—seven significant categories of issues to consider when deciding how to intervene in a pressured moment. (We'll dig into specific techniques for doing so in the next chapter). As you read through our list, bear in mind that we know you can't possibly think about or even be aware of all the Factors in any given moment. But you can dial up your awareness of the importance of them and, over time, get increasingly proficient at recognizing and holding in mind a greater number at the same time.

The Factors are described here in a manner that suggests they are to be considered only when choosing an intervention in a face-to-face meeting. However, they are applicable in every context in which you are interacting with a client or colleague, including e-mail, over the phone, or in your own mind (e.g., when you find yourself acting or feeling in an uncharacteristic manner and need a tool to help you reset).

At the opening of the chapter we discussed ways you are likely already getting ready for meetings (and the moments they contain) by thinking about various aspects of your case and having a variety of preparatory conversations with clients and other professionals. The Factors can be useful in that context, too. Try using the list of Factors as a personal road map when preparing for an individual client meeting, or as springboard for a pre- or post-meeting conversation among colleagues in a cooperative, Collaborative, or co-mediated case.

By the way, these Factors are listed in no particular order of importance. And you may come up with some new ones of your own. How much weight to give any Factor or Factors in any given moment will become a more comfortable and confident decision as you become more familiar with their use.

Seven Factors to Consider When Choosing What to Do or Say in a Given Moment

Factor 1: Topical Context

- What are the primary tasks for this meeting?
- Which team members and clients are present for this meeting and what are their roles in this context?
- How much time has been allotted for this meeting and for each task on the agenda for this meeting and why?

- In what (if any) sequence do you plan to approach each task and why?
- How pressing or emotionally fraught is the topic at hand?
- Does the topic at hand relate to the goal of the meeting?

Factor 2: Temporal Context

- Where are you in the time trajectory of the case as a whole? First meeting? Final meeting?
- Where are you in the time trajectory of this meeting? Beginning? Middle? Final 30 seconds? The meeting is over? The meeting should have ended 10 minutes ago, but you've run over?
- How well or badly has the case been flowing? Has it followed a reasonable pattern of meetings at a reasonable pace. Is anyone frustrated with the pattern or pacing of the case?

Factor 3: Intrapersonal Context

Note: The word "intrapersonal" refers to issues within an individual personality; the "Intrapersonal Context" refers to an analysis of the individual dynamics of all clients and professionals.

- Where do each client and each professional fall on the Rigidity-Flexibility Continuum *at this moment* and *in general*?
- What is each client's and each professional's level of cognitive functioning *at this moment* and *in general*?
- What is each client's and each professional's typical attachment style?
- Are there any topics or situations that tend to trigger any of the clients or professionals in the room in problematic ways?

Factor 4: Interpersonal Context

Note: The word "interpersonal" refers to interactions between individuals; the "Interpersonal Context" refers to an analysis of the relationship dynamics between clients and professionals.

- Who is present at this meeting? How many clients? How many professionals?

- Is anyone present (clients and/or professionals) who is/are particularly emotionally provocative to anyone else (positively or negatively)?
- Is anyone present who *everyone else* experiences as destructive to the process?
- What is the *general* nature of the relationship between the clients? High conflict with lots of negative interaction between meetings and entrenched positions? Low conflict with little need for interaction between meetings and flexible stances?
- How well does each professional understand each client and the marital dynamic between the clients?
- How much agreement/disagreement is there between the professionals about the nature of the marital dynamic and the relative rigidity and flexibility of each client?
- How collaborative (versus adversarial) are the professional-to-professional relationships on this case?

Factor 5: Recent or Impending Occurrence Context

Note: This one is closely related to the State of the Two-Part Container and the Interpersonal Context, since upsetting occurrences (in the life of any individual or between two or more individuals on a case) can cause ruptures in one-on-one or group relationships.

- Has any event occurred recently (in the life of a client or professional or between two or more clients and/or professionals) that is likely to have a strong impact on either or both clients or on any of the professionals?
- Is the event related to the case or unrelated to the case?
- When did the event occur? At the end of the last meeting? Between meetings? As you were walking into the present meeting?
- If the event involved either or both clients and/or any of the professionals, have the people involved discussed the event in advance of this meeting?

- Is there an *impending* event that will have a strong impact on either client or both clients or on any of the professionals?
- If there has been or will be a significant occurrence, who knows about it at this moment? One or both clients? One professional? More than one professional?

Factor 6: The State of the "Two-Part" Container

THE STATE OF THE MICROCONTAINERS

- How well can each professional empathize with each client?
- What are the levels of trust and respect between each professional and each client?
- What is the nature and quality of the attachment between each professional and client? Between each professional and each other professional?
- Has the nature and quality of any of the Microcontainers strengthened since the last meeting?
- Have there been any difficult interactions or ruptures of trust between any of the professionals and clients since the last meeting or team discussion? If so, what is the status of any repair work? Has the strength of any Microcontainer been affected (positively or negatively)?
- How experienced and skilled is each professional on the case?

THE STATE OF THE MACROCONTAINER

- How well do each of the professionals know each other?
- What is the general nature and quality of the relationship(s) among the professionals?
- What is the level of trust and respect among the professionals?
- Have there been any difficult interactions or ruptures of trust between any of the professionals since the last meeting or team discussion? If so, what is the status of any repair work being done? Has the strength of the Macrocontainer been affected (positively or negatively)?

- Have there been any particularly positive interactions among professionals that have resulted in an improvement in the strength of the Macrocontainer?
- How much agreement or disagreement is there among the professionals about how the case should be conducted?

Factor 7: The Developmental Task Context

Note: the Developmental Task Context differs from the Topical Context in that while the latter refers to the observable and concrete, the former describes the abstract and emotional. For example, the Topical Context of a meeting might include the practical task of dividing a couple's assets. The Developmental Task Context for that same meeting might include the need for each spouse to develop empathy for and generosity toward the other.

- How would you define the developmental tasks of each client in the room?
- How would you define the polarities associated with each client's developmental tasks?
- Is either client able to recognize their own developmental tasks and the attendant challenges?
- Which polarity is dominant in this moment for each client?
- Is either client facing a developmental crisis (with respect to a particular developmental task)?
- With which polarity do you think it is most important to primarily align (in this moment for each client)?

Factor 7: The Developmental Task Context: A "Cheat Sheet"

"Developmental phase," "developmental task," "developmental crisis," "polarities". . . . We've given you a lot chew on. Because we know the distinctions between these terms can be confusing, we thought it might be helpful to throw in a cheat sheet—an easy-to-find list of short definitions you can

(Continued)

Factor 7: The Developmental Task Context: A "Cheat Sheet" (*Continued*)

refer to when you're thinking about the Developmental Task Context of a moment in a case. You'll find these definitions again (along with those of other important concepts from this and other chapters) in the glossary.

Developmental Phase

A developmental phase is a point in the life of an individual in which he or she must master new emotional, cognitive, and perhaps physical challenges in order to evolve to a new level of maturity. Some developmental phases are universal (such as adolescence); some are not universal but are common and contain universal themes (such as divorce). The successful navigation of any developmental phase requires an individual to let go of the familiar and embrace the new. When an individual successfully navigates a developmental phase, he or she strengthens the foundation on which they can build future successes.

Developmental Task (or Developmental Challenge)

A developmental task is an emotional challenge that, when mastered, leads to emotional growth. An example of a developmental task is when a formerly financially dependent wife is faced with the shift from thinking of herself as dependent toward thinking of herself as strong enough to provide for herself. A developmental task may be something an individual wants to do from the outset (perhaps the wife in our example desires to become more independent from her husband because it will enhance her self-esteem), or it can be driven by outside realities (perhaps there will not be enough money to support two households post-divorce, so both spouses will have to work).

(Continued)

Factor 7: The Developmental Task Context: A "Cheat Sheet" (*Continued*)

Developmental Crisis

A developmental crisis occurs when an individual, couple, or family is unable, over time, to master a new developmental challenge (or challenges) and the result is stasis, regression, or breakdown. All divorcing couples and families are in developmental crisis; the divorce itself is evidence that their capacity to foster development has failed. Within the divorce process individuals face many discrete developmental challenges. When a client is unable, even with our support, to successfully navigate one of these challenges (which happens frequently, since divorce is hard and our clients are already in a compromised state), they face a discrete developmental crisis. For example: A grieving, divorcing client persistently refuses (over many months) to participate in his divorce process because he can't face the fact that his marriage is really over and that he will have to move on without his wife by his side.

Polarities

Polarities are two competing emotional urges that are alive within us when we face a developmental challenge. One pole represents the pull toward stasis or regression; the other pole represents the desire to relinquish the past (or the safe and known) and move forward into the future (toward the "new idea").

Example of Competing Polarities

A client struggles to forgive his wife for her infidelity, yet knows that his sustained anger is slowing his own emotional recovery.

Polarity 1: If he holds on to his anger he can stave off the pain of accepting that the marriage is really over. Polarity 2: If he forgives her he can then move on and find happiness of his own.

Summary of Concepts from Chapter 8

- Preparing for client meetings by taking a mental inventory of potentially relevant or problematic issues can help professionals be more centered and, when there is a threat of disruption, can point the professional toward a helpful preemptive action.
- While most moments in a case seem "ordinary" and don't pose obvious technical challenges, every moment contains potentially important data and requires us to be mindful of the state of the Microcontainers and Macrocontainer.
- Developmentally important moments contain transformative potential. They tend to be fraught and confusing. Choosing what to do or say in these moments is difficult and at the core of our work.
- The authors offer a model of "Seven Factors" to consider when choosing how to intervene in fraught moments in a case.
- The Factors are also useful as a tool for preparing for individual client meetings, or as a road map for team discussions (either in advance of or after a client meeting).

Chapter 9

Facilitating Positive Change:
The Essence of Technique

*Rather than being your thoughts and emotions,
be the awareness behind them.*

—Eckhart Tolle, *A New Earth:
Awakening to Your Life's Purpose*

In Chapter 8 we laid out a roadmap for deciding what to do or say in a specific moment of our work, in the form of seven "Factors" to consider. Now it's time to get concrete; we're ready to move from "what to do or say" to the nuts and bolts of "how to do or say it."

We use the word "techniques" to describe the variety of interventions we all need to learn to become effective divorce professionals. Teaching technique is challenging; the word itself doesn't capture the nuance and complexity of what we do in our offices and conference rooms every day. It's not just that there are so many good techniques that even if the authors knew them all (we don't, but we hope we know many of the important ones) we couldn't describe them comprehensively. It's also that techniques are difficult to separate into categories, since professionals often employ more than one simultaneously and in a style that is personal to *them* (hence difficult for someone else to re-create).

In order to make this broad and deep topic accessible to our readers without skimping on content, we've carefully divided this chapter into sections. In the first section we'll introduce "The Tending/Moving Continuum," a new, overarching concept the authors developed with our colleague, Barbara Burr, that captures our understanding of the general nature of good technique in divorce work and grounds it in the theoretical ideas we've presented in this book. In the second section we'll describe four broad categories of technique. Finally, in the third section, we'll define many specific techniques from each of the four categories and describe what these techniques look and sound like in the real moments of our work.

Linking Developmental Theory to Technique: The Tending/Moving Continuum

Think about what it's like to be with a seasoned and highly effective professional. As they interact with clients and colleagues, do they stop to discuss Factors? Do they seem to be carefully picking and choosing from within a mental toolbox? No. Most of the time they appear natural and unselfconscious; they seem to be working spontaneously and organically—simply "going with the flow." Even when they're stumped, they maintain their emotional equilibrium. It can be inspiring, but also intimidating.

Flip through your mental files and call up the memory of a meeting in which you experienced a difficult moment. Maybe the clients were overwhelmed or aggressive. Maybe the professionals were paralyzed or argued over what should happen next. Perhaps you began to wonder: "Okay, what the heck do we all do *now*?" Then a colleague had the presence of mind to do or say something that relaxed tensions, unlocked a dilemma, or illuminated the previously invisible white elephant that had lumbered into the room. And you thought, "Wow. That was perfect; a beautiful thing. And I never would have thought of it." It's true: you wouldn't have. Because you're you, not them.

Although we can and should learn from and model the effective techniques of others, we'll never be able to replicate their interventions. The best professionals *are* the best because they've learned to implement sound techniques using their own authentic styles.

Working with seasoned and highly skilled colleagues can be both inspiring and intimidating. Although we can and should learn from and model the effective techniques of others, we'll never be able to replicate their interventions. The best professionals are the best because they've learned to implement sound techniques using their own authentic styles.

The central thesis of this book is that divorce is a developmental crisis and that as helping professionals our goal is to create the conditions under which our clients can successfully navigate the challenges associated with that crisis, restructure their families and their lives, and get back on developmental track—hopefully with an even better emotional trajectory than they had before the marital breakdown. Our discussion of technique is really a discussion of how best to interact with our clients and our colleagues in order to accomplish that goal. The authors and Barb Burr (mentioned above) have developed a model for organizing the

Our discussion of technique is really a discussion of how best to interact with our clients and our colleagues in order to accomplish the goal of helping our clients get back on developmental track—hopefully with an even better emotional trajectory than they had before the marital breakdown.

myriad ways we can work with our clients to help them face and master the challenges they encounter in the divorce process. We call it the Tending/Moving Continuum.

We've explained that a fraught moment in any case is one in which our client grapples with two polarities—the part of them that wants to cling to the familiar and the part that wants to take a leap of faith. We've explored how, within the Microcontainer, we help our client to take that leap—simultaneously honoring their fears and encouraging them to move beyond them. No grieving, divorcing parent could be coached into giving up custodial time if they didn't believe that (1) we understood the pain that they would incur in doing so, that (2) we believed in their ability to tolerate that pain, and that (3) we believed their pain served a greater good for them and for their children.

"Tending" is our catchall word for everything we do to make a client feel understood, supported, and emotionally held. "Tending" describes the act of leaning into emotion; it is predicated on our capacity to empathize and contain.

To the naked eye (and ear), the act of tending can appear to be a break in the action, a moment of wandering off task into the emotional weeds. But when it's done well, tending improves the efficiency of our work by removing psychological impediments to resolution. We tend to clients so they can focus on the job at hand; we do it in the service of the task.

"Moving," on the other hand, is our word for everything we do that stretches a client forward by leaning away from emotion and redirecting our client toward the concrete task(s) of the moment. To the naked eye (and ear), the act of moving can appear insensitive. But tact and timing are everything. You can't move a client who doesn't already feel tended to. But if leaning into emotion with a particular client has already proven to be counterproductive, a firm move can be the best form of a tend.

It's really a false distinction: a well-timed tend is also a move; a good move is often the best way to tend. We tend in order to move, and vice versa. For our purposes these words describe *where we put the emphasis in a given moment.* Some moments are more overtly focused on emotion, others are more overtly active. Most moments are a visible blend of tending and moving. More on this in a bit.

We feel the model of the Tending/Moving Continuum is helpful because it captures the dynamic quality of the thousands of tiny moments when we choose to say or do one thing rather than another.

Tending and moving are not, in themselves, techniques. They describe the very heart of our work. Together they form the essence of our ongoing effort to meet our clients where they are while helping them get where they want to go.

But tending and moving are not, in themselves, techniques. They describe the very heart of our work. Together they form the essence of our ongoing effort to meet our clients where they are while helping them get where they want to go.

Navigating the Tension between Tending and Moving: Four Categories of Technique

To make it easier to think about (and choose among) the myriad ways we can help clients navigate the fraught moments in our work, we've created four categories of technique. As you read, note that we begin by describing a category of techniques that occur only *within* the mind of the professional (Category 1). We then move outward, describing techniques that involve increasing inter-personal activity. We describe techniques that involve tending to, or opening up, our client's emotion (Categories 2 and 3), then techniques that involve moving, or putting a cap on emotion, in order to stick close to the task at hand (Category 4).

Remember: These are *general ways to approach any given moment.* We'll look at the four categories now, along with a few illustrative examples. After that we'll explore, in depth, *specific techniques that might be used within any of the approaches.*

Category 1: Acknowledge Emotions Internally (to Yourself)

In this category of techniques you (the professional) make note of and mentally file your emotional observations away and use them (1) to develop hypotheses about yourself, your clients, and your colleagues, (2) to later reflect on whether the clients/colleague/ situation is/are evoking the emotion or whether it is coming more from your own problematic countertransference and therefore needs to be managed separately.

Example: During a team meeting your client looks out the window, apparently not paying attention to the discussion. You read your client as overwhelmed by the content of the conversation. You are aware of some anxiety in yourself, a pressure to comfort and re-engage your client, but you carry on as you were—without comment and without changing anything about your tone or pacing. However, you remember this moment and remain watchful to see if your client re-engages, or appears to withdraw further, in which case a verbal technique may be called for.

Category 2: Acknowledge Emotions Nonverbally (to Another Person)

There are a number of ways to acknowledge emotion without using words. Nonverbal communications are crucial tools that comprise about 90 percent of our interpersonal exchanges.

Examples:

- Seek out eye contact with a client or a colleague; note his or her response and attempt to have a "silent conversation."
- Convey interest, concern, and empathy through subtle adjustments of your facial expression or posture while remaining silent or continuing the current line of discussion.
- Use physical touch, e.g., a pat on the shoulder.
- Make a connecting gesture, e.g., passing a tissue box to a client who is tearing up.
- Scan the room—connect to each person with a facial expression that conveys authentic curiosity and creates a sense of connection.
- Use your body to create space without using words, e.g., raise a finger in a gesture that says, "Let's keep quiet for a bit, folks," when one client or colleague is struggling to find words or to maintain composure.

Category 3: Acknowledge Emotions Verbally and Open a Space to Explore

Examples:

- "I see that you're tearing up a bit. What just happened that triggered you?"
- "I just saw a shift in your facial expression—not sure how to read it, but I'm interested to know what may have just happened for you."

- "You've mentioned many times that this topic makes you anxious. Please tell me if I've got it wrong, but from the look on your face I'm guessing you're having one of those moments. Let's just push pause for a minute so we can talk a bit and see how you're doing with this."

Consider complementing your words with nonverbal techniques such as those described in Category 3.

Category 4: Acknowledge Emotions Verbally, then Move On

Sometimes clients need us to acknowledge emotions verbally before they can allow us to steer them back toward practical matters.

Example: "This is tough stuff. I can see you're struggling. But I know you wanted to get this issue resolved today . . . so are you okay to keep going?"

The Well-Equipped Divorce Professional's Toolbox of Essential Techniques

Time to get practical. We'll start with techniques that work with a broad range of character types then end with techniques that, while they won't work with more limited clients, can help more flexible clients grow in important and exciting ways.

Techniques that are Effective with Every Client

The following techniques are useful when working with clients and colleagues of all stripes, including folks whose personalities fall at the more rigid end of the Flexibility/Rigidity Continuum.

STAYING IN ROLE

Because clients often come to us fragile and emotionally needy, they are never going to get quite as much *of* us or *from* us as they want. And, actually, it's important that they don't. As we've said a few times now, our capacity to empathize with our clients in ways that foster growth is predicated on our maintaining professional boundaries. Of course we want to remain in a state of empathic connectedness, but some distance allows us to reach across the divide and help regulate our client's anxiety when necessary (think back to our discussion of "transitional space" from Chapter 2).

Staying in role means wearing one hat. You're a divorce professional. Don't morph. Don't become your client's friend, don't hire them to design your webpage, and don't offer to fix their son up with your newly single daughter. If you cross the professional boundary and enter the sphere of social interaction, you've already lost your capacity to see your client and their situation with the measure of professional detachment you'll need in order to be truly helpful.

Staying in role also means maintaining professional boundaries. If you've ever raised a teenager, you know the dangers of becoming the "cool parent" with the "cool house" in which kids want to congregate because the rules are relaxed. If, as a parent, you minimize your role as an authority figure you might become more popular among the high school set, but you won't be respected by them (or their parents) because no one will trust you to provide emotional and physical safety. In Chapter 2, we described the way well-functioning families are captained by loving parents who set and maintain appropriate expectations, limits, and routines. In the same way, maintaining our professional stance by setting firm, predictable (but not punitive or inflexible) boundaries from which we depart only after thoughtful consideration makes it possible for us to invite clients out of fixed positions so they can achieve their own highest transformative potential.

The more traumatized or anxious a client, the more likely it is that he or she will push against our boundaries. Healthier clients (who have developed a measure of basic trust in the world and in their own capacities to tolerate painful feelings) may express frustration when we set limits, but they are likely to respect (or at least accept) them. But think about the clients who pressure us to return their calls on Sunday, to depart from our ordinary billing practices, or to attend their son's bar mitzvah. When working with these clients, those of us who are vulnerable to overfunctioning (or overfunctioning with respect to certain character types) may find ourselves temporarily pulled out of our own professional orbit and tempted to make unusual or inappropriate concessions.

If you've ever found yourself scheduling a meeting with a client outside of your own office hours without asking yourself whether the client really needs it, then you know what we mean. Maintaining sturdy Micro- and Macrocontainers requires that we alter our ordinary way of working only after thoroughly thinking things through with our client(s) and the other professionals involved, and coming to a shared understanding of and agreement on the scope of and reason for the alteration. Holding to well-defined, predictable, reliable boundaries and resisting the urge to move too quickly to accommodate (especially when you feel under pressure) reinforces the crucial notion that you are a safe base who not only empathizes with your client but also has faith in their capacity to tolerate anxiety and become more independent.

Holding to your boundaries also mitigates professional burnout by minimizing the risk that you'll become angry or frustrated with your client, or come to dislike them. (it happens to the best of us.) This is important, because if your patience with your client wears thin he or she will sense it immediately and will feel (and be) let down by you. By failing to set limits and allowing your client to wear you down, you'll unintentionally allow your client to create the scenario they most feared and expected—one in which you're yet another person who will abandon them. So if you have trouble striking a healthy work-life balance or find yourself on a team with a culture of overfunctioning, remind yourself and your colleagues that not only are we *allowed* to take off our work hats at the end of the day and to enjoy our own families and personal lives, we owe it to our clients to do so.

> *Holding to your boundaries mitigates professional burnout by minimizing the risk that you'll become angry or frustrated with your client, or come to dislike them. Not only are we allowed to take off our work hats at the end of the day and to enjoy our own families and personal lives, we owe it to our clients to do so.*

Minimizing Small Talk

We've already talked about the fact that for the time they are working with us we are centrally important figures in the central drama of our clients' lives. In fact, because they rely on us for so much and spend so much time with us, their relationship to us is quite intimate. As a result, our clients often idealize or devalue us in ways of which we might not be aware.

How we conduct ourselves and what we talk about when we are in with our clients makes an enormous difference to them. Follow your client's lead. Clues as to what they need from you are embedded in the nature of their moods (which will likely vary from meeting to meeting). If they feel like chatting about their vacation, let them. But don't walk into the room exchanging news about your grandchildren with your colleague or open a meeting by announcing to the room that you just returned from a fabulous vacation. Even when our clients joke, it's often a way of managing more painful feelings. Ours is a serious business, and should be treated as such. Small talk that is not initiated by our clients can cause them real pain. It's also disrespectful of their time, effort, and money.

Never forget that our clients carry us in their minds when they are not with us, listen for our internalized voices when they feel unmoored, and, when in our presence, often scan our faces with the anxious intensity of a cancer patient analyzing their oncologist's expression for clues about the results of their latest CAT scan.

Not Acting Celebratory

When we work with colleagues who are also our friends or in a process we feel passionately about, it's easy to put a happy spin on things. But statements like "I'm so glad you chose a Collaborative Divorce" or "congratulations on opting for mediation" can often be upsetting or offensive to clients who, while putting on a brave face, feel their world is collapsing around them. Divorce is not a cause for celebration. Especially at the beginning (before you and your client know each other well), find a way to support your client's higher order choices without offering up any emotional high fives.

PRACTICE NONJUDGMENTAL LISTENING

In Chapter 5 we talked about the state of being "without memory or desire," in other words meeting each new client fresh and listening to their story without imposing our own assumptions, biases, or agendas. Especially if you've been practicing your profession for many years, it's impossible not to recognize certain character types or to project the trajectory of a given case. But that type of professional shorthand can get in the way. We may be technically talented, but until our clients feel deeply understood and accepted—not as we imagine them to be, but as they are—nothing else we do will matter. Our job is to accept the whole person— quite a different process from attempting to like everything about them or agreeing with their positions.

Effective, nonjudgmental listening involves (1) keeping steady eye contact, (2) maintaining an open, caring facial expression that changes appropriately but does not reflect surprise or exaggerated emotion (positive or negative), (3) adopting an emotional or physical "leaning in" posture, and (4) exercising self-restraint in allowing the client plenty of time for their narrative to unfold organically (without too much direction from you).

ASKING CURIOUS QUESTIONS[1]

Authentically curious questions are nonrhetorical and not rote. They carry no assumptions, biases, or judgment and so invite vulnerability—the precursor for empathy and intimacy. They convey a genuine interest in the reply, even if the reply may contain painful truth. In order to be effective, a curious question must convey the sense that the speaker can be trusted, so when we ask one, our tone and nonverbal behavior should convey sensitivity to our client's style of communication and their emotional state in the moment. Often a curious question requires us to invite our conversation partner's aggression toward us, rather than deflecting it, countering with aggression of our own, or fleeing into another topic.

---

1. The concept of the "curious question" comes from Sharon Ellison's *Taking the War Out of Words: The Power of Non-Defensive Communication* (Wyatt-MacKenzie Publishing, January 2009). If you haven't read it yet, we highly recommend that you do.

Examples:

- "I can hear in your voice that you're frustrated with me, but I'm not sure why. Can you help me understand?"
- "My bookkeeper let me know today that you're several months behind in paying my fee. I'm interested to know if there's anything on your end that might be making it difficult to stay current, or if you have any questions or concerns about my bill that we haven't discussed?"

Offering Empathy Versus Sympathy

You've probably noticed in your own life that the phrase, "That must have been so terrible for you," can sometimes make you feel worse and sometimes make you feel better. Assuming the speaker is someone whose good intentions you're inclined to trust, what accounts for the difference?

Any words offered to you in a moment of powerful feeling that do not give you a sense that the person speaking has a true grasp of your emotional experience will fall flat. On the other hand, those same words, spoken from a place of deep understanding and emotional connection, can have the power to sustain you through your darkest moments.

Generally speaking, sympathetic words are not only unhelpful, they can be destructive. These words are spoken from a position of distance. They are often self-referential ("Sorry you're sick! I hope you don't have what I had last week! Gosh, it was the worst.") or are born out of an anxiety in the speaker that conveys that he or she is overwhelmed by your experience ("I'm sure your biopsy will come back negative. I just have a feeling."). Some of the most problematic sympathetic responses involve the speaker moving too quickly to advice or action ("I'm so sorry you got laid off. I know a great vocational coach—I'll e-mail you his contact info right away!") or dismissing the importance of a loss ("She did you a favor by breaking up with you! She didn't deserve you anyway!").

Empathic responses require restraint, self-management, and the ability to tolerate painful feelings without trying to discharge them in any of the ways we just described. Consider the way a good parent focuses on her baby's expressions of distress without becoming too anxious, takes the baby's communications inside herself, and lets them resonate within her until she develops an understanding of the problem and can offer the right solution. This can be tough. Listening to a baby's cry is painful, and not rushing in too quickly to "solve" the problem requires emotional maturity. An empathic listener doesn't rush to fill silence with platitudes. He or she sits in silence until they have a sense that they should speak.

> *The true expression of empathy is the emotional equivalent of saying, "Though I can't take your pain away, I am right here with you. I understand what it's like to walk in your shoes."*

If the moment is right, an empathic listener asks as many curious questions as it takes to learn enough about the speaker's experience that they can feel it on a gut level. The true expression of empathy is the emotional equivalent of saying, "I can't know everything about what it's like to be you, and, though I can't take your pain away, I am right here with you. I understand what it's like to walk in your shoes. And if the most helpful thing is for us to simply *be* together, that's what we'll do."

FRAMING THE ISSUE

To frame an issue is to pull the core meaning of the current discussion, dilemma, or task from the chaos of a moment and to articulate it in a way that facilitates understanding. Framing the issue might involve clarifying which topic should be the focus of discussion versus which topics are really repackaged versions of overworked discussions that could easily lead a team into the weeds. Framing an issue might also take the form of unpacking the elements of a quandary or conflict. The more clearly we are able to frame the issue at hand, the more likely we, our clients, and our colleagues will be able to navigate it efficiently and move forward in the process.

Examples:

- "I think this discussion is not so much about the duration of spousal support as it is about when Lynn will be able to go back to work. Lynn, can we talk about your plans and what a realistic time frame might be for getting your degree and finding your first job?"

- "In the last ten minutes both of you have raised questions about which of you will have the kids for Thanksgiving this year, which neighborhood they'll trick-or-treat in, which of you will bring cupcakes to school on their birthdays, and how you'll handle Christmas Eve and Christmas morning. I think we need to zero in on one holiday at a time, and move through them sequentially."

PARAPHRASING

Paraphrasing is the verbal equivalent of standing very close to a client—as close as we can without standing directly in their shoes. Repeating something someone says, sticking close to his or her own words without sounding (or feeling) like a parrot, is the goal of this technique. Leading into a paraphrase with a comment like "Just to make sure I am tracking you . . . " can be helpful. It can also be useful to summarize a bit, because to do so requires you to organize and condense your clients' thoughts. But be sure to let your client know you're keenly aware that you may get it wrong and that you are open to feedback. ("Let me know if I'm off base, but I think the heart of what you're saying is . . . .") The more fragile or rigid your client, the less deviation from their original wording they'll be able to tolerate. Paraphrasing is an important way to convey empathy, so it has to be accurate and authentic. Worried about sounding pat? If you *feel* the truth of what you are saying, it will "*go in*"; if you don't, it won't. It's better to be silent than to talk simply because you think it's your turn.

Example:

Client: "My husband's house is such a mess. I'm worried the kids will flunk out of school if they have to study there. No way are they staying with him during school days!"

Professional: "So you're saying that Karl's house is so chaotic and messy that the kids won't be able to work there, and we should keep that fact in mind when negotiating a time-sharing schedule."

SETTING LIMITS

As we've said previously, some clients come to the divorce process frightened and insecure, and have difficulty building trust. It may be counterintuitive, but more fragile clients need clearer limits and boundaries because those limits represent reliability and predictability—the linchpins of a good holding environment. Even if they rail against you, rigid clients will experience your calm resolve in sticking to your guns as a sign that you can be trusted and are strong enough to withstand their aggression (a sign that you can help). Pushing limits might take the form of disrespecting protocols, refusing to do homework, or behaving toward you or your colleagues in a blatantly inappropriate way. But being firm is not the same as being punitive, so don't retaliate or become patronizing. Be respectful, don't apologize, and stay the course.

Example 1:

Client: "I know we're supposed to stop at noon, but I have just a couple more things I need to talk about. Can we go until 12:30?"

Professional: "I do need to stop at noon. But let's set up a time to talk tomorrow so we can run through those other issues."

Example 2:

Client (to her attorney): "I'm firing my divorce coach. Can you give me the names of other coaches I can call?"

ProfessionaL: "Wow. Sounds like we have a lot to talk about. I want to understand your concerns about your coach. Have you spoken with her about this?"

Client: "No. I'll tell her later, after I retain someone new. I've made up my mind. Done deal. It's my divorce. Move on."

Professional: "You really must have had a negative experience; I want to hear about it. Maybe replacing your coach will turn out to be the right decision, I don't know. But this is an important cross-road in your process, and we both care about your success. Tell me more about why you feel the way you do. Then let's talk about what makes the most sense as a next step."

Example 3:

Client: (*Yelling and rising from his chair*) "I'm really pissed at you! You're not advocating for me!"

Professional: (*Seated, using a calmly firm tone and gesturing to the client's chair*) "I want to hear what I've done that upset you, Jon, but I can't listen while you're yelling. Please have a seat and tell me more."

TAKING A BREAK

Sometimes, when a client or professional in a meeting becomes visibly upset, someone in the room will suggest everyone "take a break" (e.g., pause the meeting to take a short walk, sit in another office for a while, use the restroom). There are times when diffusing the intensity by taking a break makes sense, such as

- When two or more professionals or clients are incapable (at least in that moment) of not fighting. The hope is that by taking a break the parties involved will calm down and be able to return to the work in more reasonable frames of mind.
- When an overwhelmed, flooded client is unable to recover in your presence (or the presence of others in the room).
- When an overwhelmed client feels unbearably humiliated that his or her emotions are so starkly in evidence.

Generally, though, we suggest not moving too quickly to taking a break. Here's why:

Most breaks occur because the professionals are overwhelmed or anxious—not because the clients require it. And even when a client asks for a break, it doesn't necessarily mean it's the best thing for that client in that moment.

If you're tempted to take a break, we suggest that you sit on the impulse for a while. Reflect with the client and whoever else is in the room about what is happening and what might be helpful. Let a little silence develop. Check in with yourself and make sure you don't want a break because of your **own** discomfort.

Think back to the parent and child paradigm. When a parent can tolerate the anxiety of a child, she can detoxify the anxiety through her ability to bear it. Moving too quickly away from a client's emotion can convey the idea that we find the emotions unacceptable, or that we can't bear them, work with them, or help in the face of them. Taking a break can momentarily break the container, so the decision should be made thoughtfully and with a shared understanding between the professionals and the clients about *why a break is needed.* Remember: fraught moments in a case are moments of opportunity for growth.

> *If you're tempted to take a break, we suggest that you sit on the impulse for a while. Remember: fraught moments in a case are moments of opportunity for growth.*

Caucusing

There are times when breaking up larger meetings into caucusing groups can be helpful, particularly for moving past an impasse.
Examples:

- A client who is really ready to relinquish a position feels humiliated by doing so in the presence of their partner (i.e., feels they will "lose face").
- One or more overwhelmed clients needs to "reset" within the safer Microcontainer provided by their own professional(s).

Using Tropes

As we get to know a client over time, we inevitably develop an awareness of unhelpful, idiosyncratic patterns in their ways of perceiving and relating to us, to their future ex, and to their divorce process. Sometimes these patterns echo dynamics from our client's family of origin or from their failed marriage. Usually these patterns reveal themselves most strongly when our client is under stress. A healthier client can usually be helped to see these patterns fairly quickly and can work to change them. A more rigid client may be able to see the patterns when you point them out, but have great difficulty modifying their behavior in any real or lasting way.

A trope is a well-developed metaphor—a simple way of representing a complicated pattern or idea. It's a recurring theme or set of ideas condensed into and represented by a symbol. This symbol can be a word, an expression, or even a sound or image. In our work, a trope is like a special secret language you develop with your client. A trope can only emerge from a deep understanding; it reinforces a sense of intimate connection.

Think of how much fun it is to have "in-jokes" with your friends, or to sing a spoof at an office party that puts your co-workers in stitches but would mean nothing to an outsider. There is something exhilarating about a shared, nuanced body of ideas that can be expressed simply but understood by a select few. Because tropes are inherently bonding and inherently *fun*, the construction of a shared trope that calls up the moments in which you've successfully helped your client to relinquish distorted perceptions and ways of acting that could otherwise impede their divorce process is one of our most important tools.

How and why does a trope work? Think of the way that a beloved object—a teddy bear or security blanket—represents to a child the safety and nurturance of their parents' love. A child's "lovie" is a metaphor so powerful that, when stuffed into a backpack and carried along, it can empower a frightened child to go on their first sleepover away from home. In our context, a trope is an adult version of a transitional object. For your client, a trope comes to represent you and the containing function that you provide. A trope (whether it takes the form of a brief verbal exchange that occurs in real time or is an idea your client can hold in mind and conjure up as needed) is like an icon on the computer screen of his or her mind. If they click on it, the image expands and allows them emotional access to all the good feelings they have about you. A trope is a soothing agent. The use of one can obviate the need for long conversations or between-meeting, real-time communication.

Example of a trope:

Years ago, Kate worked on a Collaborative Divorce with a client we'll call Millie. Millie had a compulsive need to rant about the evils of her soon-to-be ex-husband. Her ruminations distracted her to the point that she often forgot or was late for meetings, and inhibited her ability to think clearly when she did attend. Millie wanted to protect her young children from the conflict between herself and her husband, but her unbridled anxiety about the divorce (and the internal pressure to express that anxiety) undermined her own efforts.

During a meeting in which Millie was chastising herself for failing to protect her children from her anger and worry related to the divorce, Kate asked Millie if she remembered the song from Sesame Street called "Put Down the Ducky." It was a song that Bert—and an entire cast of stars—sang to Ernie when he wanted to learn to play the saxophone but couldn't because he was unable to bring himself to put down his rubber duck. It had popped unbidden into Kate's mind; it was a song about managing anxiety in the service of positive change.

Millie recalled the song and was intrigued by Kate's reference to it. The two shared a few silly moments humming the old tune and clumsily trying to recall the verses. Kate suggested that from then on whenever Millie started to feel her anxiety ramp up she should call up the image of herself "putting down the ducky" so that she could "learn to play the saxophone"—in other words, Millie should consciously lay aside her irrational fears so she could finish her divorce and move on with the rest of her life!

Millie had a good sense of humor and loved the idea. From then on, whenever Millie attempted to hijack meetings by cataloguing her husband's flaws, Kate would whisper something like, "Girl, put that ducky down" or would simply look at Millie and mouth the word "ducky." These interventions were highly effective. In one meeting, as Millie's voice started to rise in response to a perceived provocation by her husband, Kate quickly and surreptitiously mimed playing a sax. Millie stifled a laugh and stopped talking immediately. Occasionally, Millie sent Kate text messages along the lines of, "Having a rough night. Trying to peel my white-knuckled fingers off the ducky." This represented light-years of progress, since up to then Millie had had a regular habit of inundating Kate with "urgent" calls and e-mails to which she expected speedy responses but from which she took little comfort.

Millie's case reached a successful settlement. At their last meeting, Millie presented Kate with a small gift-wrapped package. Inside? A rubber ducky, of course.

Techniques that are Effective with Flexible Clients

Now we're entering the territory of techniques that work best with clients who have a solid sense of you as a trustworthy, competent helping professional, and whose feelings and behaviors cluster at the flexible end of the Rigidity/Flexiblity Continuum. In employing these techniques you are asking a client to stretch, perhaps by challenging their perspective or by helping them to identify a new idea. Use one of these techniques with a rigid client and your words will either fall flat, cause a flap, or do damage. But use one with a more flexible client in the right way at the right moment, and the sky's the limit.

REFRAMING

If paraphrasing is the verbal equivalent of standing right with a client, reframing is the verbal equivalent of standing one tiny step ahead of them. The trick to a good reframe is that it is different enough from what the client has just expressed to stretch the client in a helpful direction, but not so different that it elicits anxiety or annoyance. Attempting a reframe is risky when a client is in a highly agitated state, since they are likely flooded, unable to process new information, and vulnerable to feeling emotionally "dropped" by you. Reframing works best when a client is calm enough to be receptive (which, depending on your client, may be possible even when they are also significantly anxious). Reframing is effective only if and when your client already trusts that you are on their side, and that you understand and accept the complexity of their often-conflicting feelings. A badly timed reframe can, at best, fail to land and, at worst, cause a rupture in your relationship with your client.

Example (this is the same exchange we used to illustrate paraphrasing, but with an added twist at the end to illustrate the difference between the two techniques):

> *Reframing is effective only if and when your client already trusts that you are on their side, and you understand and accept the complexity of their often-conflicting feelings.*

Client: "My husband's house is such a mess. I'm worried the kids will flunk out of school if they have to study there. No way are they staying with him during school days!"

Professional: "Yeah I understand. You have a lot of concerns about the kids, including their ability to stay organized and do well in school when they have to go back and forth. It's hard to imagine that Karl is ever going to get it together, or that the kids could ever adjust, and yet that is what we might hope for."

The last sentence is the reframe: It offers understanding of where the client "is" yet suggests a possible view of a future in which the client's husband might change and her children might adjust.

REALITY TESTING

Reality testing is a technique to help your client to expand their worldview in a way that will open up possibilities for growth. The first step of this technique involves conveying your sense of respect for your client's feelings and opinions *as expressed*. The second step involves you (gently) offering a new opinion, perception, or perspective. Before attempting this technique, be sure to reassure your client—especially if they look worried—that you are not feeling critical. Find a way to share your confidence that your client is ready to be challenged a bit. And as with every "stretching" technique, use this one only if you know your client well and you have a strong working alliance.

Example:

Client: "My husband's house is such a mess. I'm worried the kids will flunk out of school if they have to study there. No way are they staying with him during school days!"

Professional: "I know how worried you have been about Karl's failure to organize his home. I can see how chaotic his life is sometimes—it's pretty apparent to me. I wonder if you would be interested, though, in hearing a slightly different take on the situation that I've been thinking about. I know you want to find a way forward in sharing parenting time with him. I have a perspective that might help us move forward—but it does contrast a bit with your perceptions of him."

Client: "Yeah, I do want to hear your thoughts. But I want you to know how worried this makes me. It's a big deal."

Professional: "It **is** a big deal. Your children's adjustment is a **huge** deal. But here's the thing I've been thinking. You've told me how much Karl loves the kids—and how much the boys miss him when they don't see him. Right?"

Client: "Yeah. True."

Professional: "So, I've just been thinking about what a learning curve Karl has. He has lived for ten years as part of a couple, and you were really the one who kept the trains running on time. You were the one who thought ahead, and who made sure the boys had clean soccer uniforms. Karl is a slob. But . . . I think he might be trying to get better at day-to-day organization. I think he is motivated to learn how to do some of the things you have always done so well. Do you think it's possible that he could get better at this, that he could learn to create enough of a clean home that the boys could spend some time with him during school nights and still be okay—if we give Karl time to practice and [here with bit of a wry smile] maybe the name of a great house cleaner?"

Making Links

To make a link is to draw a helpful connection between a client's past experience (either earlier in their life or earlier in their divorce process) and what they are feeling or perceiving in the current moment. Making a link highlights dysfunctional emotional and behavioral patterns, diffuses anxiety, and broadens perspective. It can help a relatively flexible client to weather a difficult moment, get unstuck, come back from a regressive position, or develop insight.

Example of a link between an experience in a client's earlier life and the current moment.

Professional speaking to their client:

"You're saying that you are concerned that your husband wants to leave you with no retirement. You have that worry, even though you also know that he has made it clear that he wants to ensure your financial security into the future. I'm remembering you told me that your father left your family when you were young, and that your mother had no way to care for you and your siblings. That was terrifying for all of you. I'm wondering if some of your current worry might be related to that earlier experience?"

Example of a link between an experience earlier in the divorce process and the current moment.

Professional speaking to client:

"This is the first time your husband has been away with the children for a whole week since you've been separated, and you're worried that he won't be able to care for them and that they'll miss you. But I'm remembering that you felt this way the first time he took them for a long weekend. Then later, you were able to say he had managed well and the kids had had a great time. I'm wondering if it's just difficult every time you face an increased separation from the kids. That would certainly be understandable!"

Using Silence

Tolerating silence is sometimes hard for divorce professionals. We tend to make the

> *Sitting with silence is sometimes hard for divorce professionals. We tend to make the mistake of thinking that when we're quiet we're not doing anything. Actually, exercising verbal restraint is an active process and a powerful tool.*

mistake of thinking that when we're quiet we're not *doing* anything. Actually, exercising verbal restraint is an active process and a powerful tool. Sitting with clients in the silence that follows a particularly painful interaction can convey respect for the feelings in the room at a time when words would seem inadequate or pat. Allowing silence to build in order to leave space for clients to struggle through a tough moment on their own facilitates their emotional growth.

And no two silences are alike. Don't assume clients are silent because they don't know what to say. It may be that they are working actively within the silence, mulling ideas over in their heads. Moving in too quickly to fill a silence may alleviate our own growing anxiety, but it shuts down the opportunity to learn. Remember: If you intrude into the silence by saying "Okay, maybe we should move on to a different topic and come back to this one later," you'll lose the opportunity to learn what the silence may contain.

On the other hand, in the context of a meeting, even one minute of silence feels much longer. So if a silence stretches on beyond what feels reasonable, you *will* need to say something. But don't dive in. Put your toe in the water by leading with an open-ended, inviting, curious question or comment, such as:

- "I'm not sure what's in this silence."
- "I'm wondering if this is an uncomfortable silence, or if folks are busy thinking things through."
- "I'm looking at everyone's faces. I'm not sure how to read what's happening in this silence."
- "I'm wondering if folks are comfortable in this silence, or feel worried to speak? Maybe a bit of both? Maybe each of us feels differently?"
- "I'm struggling with whether to ask if anyone feels able to share what they're feeling, or to hold back and wait."

Though we're big fans of silence, we offer two caveats:

1. When using silence, consider the question "Where does my client fall on the Rigidity/Flexibility Continuum, both generally and at this moment in the case?" Rigid clients

don't tolerate silence well; they may interpret it as reflecting indifference or incompetence on your part. As with any other technique, you'll need to apply an analysis of the Factors in determining how and when to use silence in your work.

2. As we described earlier, maintaining a thoughtful silence by actively holding our own anxieties at bay is difficult. It's an advanced-level technique. It is highly active, and bears no relation to being quietly passive in silence or failing to participate in a discussion. Sitting back too much, failing to offer your own ideas and observations, not only deprives others of your contribution, but (if there's another professional in the room) it can also create a sense of making others nervous—particularly your own client. If you're at the table and you don't add, you subtract.

There are many reasons why even a competent professional might fail to put their own perceptions into words during a fraught moment. Here are a few:

- Lack of confidence in one's skills
- Shyness or social anxiety
- Feeling uncertain that one's perceptions are accurate
- Feeling uncertain that one's thought will be experienced as helpful
- Feeling unfamiliar with the other professionals and how they'll react
- Feeling that one should defer to more seasoned colleagues
- Feeling worried that in articulating one's thought one will be stepping out of role (in a multidisciplinary model)
- Feeling uncomfortable with the subject matter or the emotional intensity in the room
- Being tired, bored, or distracted
- Being angry with a client or colleague

If you are aware, or have been told by others, that you tend to hold back too much (or if your client has complained), try to hold this in mind: Assuming they are well-timed and tactfully delivered, your perceptions, thoughts, and ideas are likely to be helpful in *some* way. If your idea is good, others will pick it up and run with it. If your idea doesn't resonate, it may stimulate other, better ideas. If you're having a reaction to an interaction in the room, others likely are too. If they're having a different reaction, they'll talk about *that*. The willingness to be wrong is a valuable aspect of our work. Participate. Use your voice. And if you're feeling intimidated, shy, or worried about how your idea will be received, say *that*. Others will be curious, and will support you in speaking up.

ARTICULATING POLARITIES

As we discussed in Chapter 2, polarities are two competing emotional urges that are alive within us when we face a developmental challenge. One pole represents the pull toward stasis or regression; the other pole represents the desire to relinquish the past (or the safe and known) and move forward into the future (the new idea). Our work is replete with polarities and their manifestations as positions related to a given issue. As a matter of fact, navigating polarities is exactly what we're doing in the ongoing balancing act of tending and moving. If a client is ready, our articulation of the polarities they struggle with *in a way that sides with the part of that client that wants to make a developmental step forward* is a powerfully helpful intervention.

Example 1:

Client: "I have to move out of this damn house, but I'm afraid to move! I'm going in circles."

Professional: "It makes sense that you're torn. You know your house is a financial drain, but it represents stability for you and the kids at a time when so much is changing. As scary as it feels to imagine moving, there may also be something appealing about selling the house and having more disposable income. And I remember you saying you're tired of the suburbs and would like to be in the city—closer to theaters and museums. Why don't we talk about both sides? What might it feel like to postpone the move? What might it feel like to look at some apartments downtown?

Example 2:

Client: "I hate the idea of needing him and his money! I'm the original feminist! But I just don't know how I'm going to get back into the work force. I don't know if I can support myself at this age!"

Professional: "You are in a tough spot. I hear you rebelling against the notion of continuing to lean on Barry for financial support. You are fiercely independent; being able to take care of yourself is an important part of your identity. But you're coming to see that you may have no choice but to accept spousal support for a few years until you get back into teaching. It's difficult to reconcile these competing truths. It's also hard for you to shift your way of thinking about the money. You feel shame in accepting it. Yet it's not a gift, it's a marital asset. And you call alimony a crutch, but what is a crutch if not something you lean on temporarily so that you can learn to walk on your own two feet?"

Polarities in Our Work: A Few Examples

- A client's wish to stay connected versus their wish to differentiate
- A client's wish for dependence versus their wish for autonomy
- A client's wish to cling to anger versus their wish to forgive
- A client's hopelessness about their prospects versus their hope for a brighter future
- A client's anxiety about taking a risk versus their yearning for new experiences

Taking time to sort out the source of our confusion not only helps us figure out the most helpful way to intervene, but it also sends powerful messages about our trust in the team, our trust in the process, our willingness to be vulnerable, and our belief that meaning can be made from chaotic experience.

ARTICULATING UNCERTAINTY

There are many moments in our work when we lose the ability to "track." We can't tell what we're feeling, let alone what our clients or colleagues are feeling. We might be temporarily confused by a cacophony of voices speaking without unity or focus. Or we might be able to follow the sense of the discussion but feel confused because the content doesn't match up with the feelings in the room.

When we're lost or confused, sometimes the best we can do is name it. There's nothing wrong—in fact there's a lot right—with saying out loud "I'm perplexed!" If you're lost, chances are others are too. Or, they may think they know what's going on, but have misjudged things. Also, assuming you articulate your confusion in a calm tone that communicates authentic curiosity, the act of admitting you're momentarily destabilized humanizes you (after all, you're copping to a vulnerability) and communicates your confidence that, together, you and whoever else is in the room can navigate the chaos to find the meaning on the other side.

Example 1:

Professional: (*to a client*) "I'm having a hard time reading you. . . . I'm not sure what might be most helpful right now."

Example 2:

Professional: (*to colleagues and clients in the room*) "So we all went from talking about one thing to talking about a totally different thing. I'm wondering if I'm the only one who is having trouble tracking. Can we push pause for a moment to figure out where we are?"

Example 3:

Professional: (*to another professional in the room*) "I'm not sure how to be most helpful right now. Do you have any thoughts about what we should do with our last 15 minutes?"

Playing Chutes and Ladders: When Our Techniques Seem to Fail Us

See if anything about this scenario sounds familiar:

You have been working with a client—a father of two small children—for several months. He has been pushing for primary physical custody of the children, in large part because his wife had an affair and plans to continue the relationship. Both parents have historically been involved and engaged with their kids, and you have repeatedly explained to your client that a judge is not likely to award him primary custody simply because his wife was unfaithful. Finally, he seems to

(*Continued*)

Playing Chutes and Ladders: When Our Techniques Seem to Fail Us (*Continued*)

come to terms with the situation. During a face-to-face meeting he tells you, "I hate that my wife can treat me so badly with no repercussions. But I get it—there's nothing I can do about it. And I really don't want to drag the kids through a court battle. Let's go ahead and send the proposal you worked up for me with the 50/50 schedule. I think it will be for the best."

You feel great. It's a leap forward. But at midnight that night you get an e-mail from your client: "I found an old AOL account full of messages from that jerk of a boyfriend of hers! Screw it! We're taking this thing to court! I don't care what it costs! *This is about justice!*"

How about this one?

In the fourth hour of a four-way settlement conference your client and her partner reach a compromise on how to divide responsibility for paying their kids' expenses. There is relief all around. As everyone prepares to leave, your client asks to speak to you alone. In an adjoining room she turns to you: "I'm sorry, I just can't do it. I know I said I could live with paying for half of everything kid-related, but given that I didn't want this divorce I'm simply not going to do it. She makes three times what I do, so she needs to step up and pay at least two-thirds." You have seen this "buyer's remorse" reaction with this client before. She often makes agreements and backs off from them later. You empathize with her feeling, gently remind her of her goal of reaching an amicable settlement, and suggest she sleep on it and talk with you the next day. "Nope," she says. "I'm just not gonna do it. We need to go back to square one on this issue."

One of the reasons our work is so technically difficult is that what is effective with a given client in one meeting might get us nowhere in the next. Remember the children's game Chutes and Ladders? Sometimes we're climbing steadily forward (up a ladder toward successful resolution),

(Continued)

Playing Chutes and Ladders: When Our Techniques Seem to Fail Us (*Continued*)

then, suddenly, our client does an unanticipated about-face and—whoops! We've slid down a shoot and we're back on the bottom rung. In these moments it's hard not to become discouraged, and even harder to figure out why we fell so far so fast. The good news is that while these moments feel like failures, they're not. Here's why.

In Chapter 3 we explained that development isn't linear, it's usually a matter of two steps forward and one step back. Often, the biggest step back is the one right before the biggest step forward. If, in their heart, your client knows they're finally ready to let go of a long-held position (because they've been working toward that moment within the Microcontainer you've provided), it makes sense that they'll recoil at the last minute. So even though it looks like they're back at the beginning of the Chutes and Ladders game board, they're really not. Positive change involves loss. Your client is having a natural response to the end of an important phase in their divorce, and to the sense of finality associated with it.

This phenomenon of falling back immediately in advance of a leap forward is so common that the authors have a name for it: We call it "the eleventh-hour regression."[2] When your client backslides at seemingly inopportune moments, it's hard not to panic or go into action mode by trying to talk him or her back into line. But if our ordinary strategies don't work it's best to say, "Okay, you're entitled to feel the way you do. Let's talk again tomorrow to see where you are and consider next steps." Keep the Microcontainer solid (don't judge, don't impose an agenda, continue to empathize while allying with the healthiest part of your client) *A, unless your client is dead set on sabotaging their process, it's very likely be back up the ladder very soon.*

---

2. Kate Scharff & Lisa Herrick, *Navigating Emotional Currents in Collaborative Divorce: A Guide to Enlightened Team Practice*, 151 (American Bar Association 2010).

A Word About Mistakes

None of us can get it right every time. And that's okay. We like to distinguish between ordinary mistakes and "mistakes of the heart." Ordinary mistakes may be technical (such as a math error), irritating but relatively minor (such as being ten minutes late to one meeting), or can reflect temporary lapses in judgment (like the enactments we discussed in Chapter 6). Ordinary mistakes are the ones from which everyone can recover and, because we learn from them, they can actually further the process.

Mistakes of the heart, on the other hand, are rare but potentially fatal to a process. They grow out of a sustained lack of self-awareness and take the form of personal bias, intrusive agendas, or the repeated expression of anger, frustration, or ill will. Mistakes of the heart reveal an underlying lack of empathy.

Finally, We Want to Leave You with this . . .

Don't be a harsh self-critic.

As a helping divorce professional you are engaged in the ongoing attempt to understand your client, to empathically convey that understanding back to them, and to use it in the service of helping them to reach their own best outcomes. Your belief in that process, your commitment to it, is far more important and powerful than hitting the sweet spot in any given moment by choosing the perfect technique and executing it flawlessly.

Summary of Concepts from Chapter 9

- The essence of our work is helping clients navigate the polarities of stasis and change.
- The foundation of technique is learning to balance the need to tend to emotion while moving forward on the task.
- Tending and moving may look and feel quite different from each other in a given moment, but they are inextricably connected.

- We tend and move simultaneously; making decisions about how much to lean into emotion versus sticking to concrete tasks is the ongoing essence of our work (as opposed to a technique in and of itself).
- The authors offer a conceptual hierarchy of four overarching categories of techniques for tending and moving, as well as several specific techniques for use in the moments of our work.
- There are two kinds of mistakes: ordinary mistakes (from which we can recover and learn) and mistakes of the heart (which are rare but destructive).
- The ongoing act of attempting to understand our clients is more important than choosing the perfect technique in a given moment.

Conclusion

Beyond Competence: Tuning Our Professional Instrument

You've got to learn your instrument. Then, you practice, practice, practice. And then, when you finally get up there on the bandstand, forget all that and just wail.

—Charlie Parker

If you've gotten this far you know the authors' thoughts on what it takes to be a good divorce professional. Here's the formula, distilled to its essential components:

- Learn the craft of your own discipline (law, mental heath, finance, an allied profession).
- Learn how to create and maintain the Three Conditions for Positive Change: a new idea, a helping relationship, and optimal anxiety.
- Be self-aware and mindful.
- When deciding what to do or say in a given moment, weigh the Factors.
- When choosing a specific intervention, consider the general hierarchy of techniques, then make an educated choice (again, considering the Factors) from within your toolbox of essential techniques.

Simple, right? Hardly. In our field, the question "How can I be really good at the work?" is complicated.

One of the manifestations of this complexity is the amount of thought we put into making professional referrals.

Competence and the "Right" Professional for the Job

When it comes to pairing clients and professionals, some considerations are just common sense. If you're looking for a child specialist for a family with a severely learning-disabled child, you should find a mental health professional with expertise in working with special needs kids. If you're looking for a lawyer to represent the nonbiological, never-married parent in a custody dispute with a same-sex partner, you'll need an attorney who knows that terrain. And very high-conflict couples usually fare best when their professionals have at least a few years of experience under their belts.

Other factors are perhaps more cynical, but whether we like it or not, many professionals take them into account. Consider, for example, a case in which an attorney strategically recommends that his client hire a particular mediator because he believes the mediator has a personal bias that will benefit his client. We've all heard comments like "Steer clear of him, he's all about fathers!," "She doesn't believe in indefinite alimony!" and "He's perfect for you; he can't resist a damsel in distress!"

Then there's the age-old question: Go with the tried and true, or take a chance by working with someone new? If you're reading this book, it's because you want more for your clients than simply "winning" the biggest piece of the marital pie or the most custodial time with their kids. But as we've been discussing all along, achieving higher order outcomes requires conditions for change that are predicated on professionals pulling together in an atmosphere of mutual support. Building a sturdy container is hard work; once you have one, you want to hold on to it. We all gravitate toward working colleagues with whom we have an established track record of success. And that's good for clients; they're getting a well-oiled machine. On the other hand, working with new people offers new opportunities for learning and for building new strong containers. It's a tough balance.

But let's assume your new case doesn't call for a specific kind of expertise, that you're not strategizing to find a professional with a personal axe to grind, and that you're not hung up on the question of tried and true versus someone new. What *does* make for a good professional-client duo?

We're fascinated by the question of how clients get paired up with their divorce professionals, and we've been tracking and thinking about it for a long time. Our interest in the topic was initially piqued a few years ago when we were both asked to serve as coaches on a Collaborative team. The referring attorneys told us, "We're asking Kate to work with the wife, because the wife is really quiet and needs someone strong. And Lisa, you're really good at getting angry spouses to calm down. This guy is furious at his wife for dragging things out. He can be pretty abrasive!"

The conversation left us both unsettled. What did it mean that Kate was "strong," or that Lisa was "good at getting angry spouses to calm down?" In this instance, the attorneys seemed to be implying that Kate had an assertive personality, a trait they felt would be helpful to the timid wife. And they seemed to be saying that Lisa had special patience for clients who wanted to speed things up beyond what their spouse could manage. We knew the referring attorneys to be skilled and caring. They had made considered, well-intentioned choices. But we saw a problem in their thinking.

The problem related to the way our colleagues were defining success and the conditions under which it could be achieved. Let's say for a moment that Kate *is* assertive and her potential client *was* timid. Were the attorneys imagining a scenario in which Kate would speak for her client when the client couldn't speak for herself? Were they thinking Kate would push her client to speak up? And let's say for the moment that Lisa *does* have a soothing touch. Were the attorneys imagining that she would be willing to spend countless hours soothing her potential client when he became impatient in the process, or holding him back when he chomped at the bit?

Think about the conditions for change. Our job as helping professionals isn't to become our client's mouthpiece, nor is it to lobby, cajole, or coddle them. It's not that the attorneys in our scenario were *wrong*. It would be disingenuous to say that they hadn't picked up on truths about our characters as they play out in our personal lives. But even so, those truths are partial and static—like a single frame in a movie. Kate is not a shrinking violet; neither is Lisa. Lisa is patient, and has a maternal, accepting energy that is effective when working with clients who feel unheard or disrespected. But so does Kate. We thought it likely that these attorneys had made generalizations about us based on certain technical and stylistic choices we had made in working with specific clients in one or more past cases. And we knew that whatever technical or stylistic choices we had made would have been based on what we felt worked best for the clients in *those* cases.

If, when making a referral, we seek a professional whose personality traits we hope will compensate for or shore up a particular vulnerability in a particular client, we're forgetting an important point about the conditions for change. As we've now said many times, our job is to honor the part of our client that wants to continue to do things in the same old way while siding with the part of the client that wants to do the next hard, right thing *so the client can become empowered to do it themselves.*

Let's assume Kate takes the case involving the timid woman in our example. If Kate speaks up for her client in a given moment (or even pushes her to speak), she'll be robbing the woman of a developmental opportunity. Better for Kate to work with the client over time by allowing her to experience what happens when she fails to speak, talking about the reasons for her silence, discussing the consequences of her silence, and supporting her in finding the courage to speak up next time.

> *Our job is to empower our clients. If, when making a referral, we seek a professional whose personality traits we hope will compensate for or shore up a particular vulnerability in a particular client, we are robbing that client of a developmental opportunity.*

Now let's think about the impatient husband. In the beginning, he will need Lisa to listen nonjudgmentally when he complains about all the ways his wife is dragging her feet. But what she does after that will depend on her assessment of the situation—overall and in particular moments. There will likely be times when she'll need to empathize with the husband's frustration over his wife's slower pace. In those moments, she may have to encourage him to take a longer view, reminding him that pushing his wife too hard will backfire and that, after all, while he has moved on his wife is still grieving. But, what if the wife turns out to have a passive-aggressive nature, and *does* slow things down unreasonably? And, what if the husband has a history of capitulating to his wife's wishes and later expressing his anger in destructive ways? Rather than trying to hold him back, it would then make more sense for Lisa to point out the pattern and its negative impact, support him in resisting the urge to resentfully capitulate, and help him to find more direct ways to communicate his feelings. Patience, for this man, might not be a virtue.

When our attorney colleagues asked us to take on this couple we already knew our professional community was thinking hard and working to tailor each team to fit the needs of each client in each case. That's a pretty high level of concern. But, once we dialed up our awareness, we saw many more iterations of the type of professional-client matchmaking strategy. Although making a certain kind of intuitive sense, these strategies didn't fit with our emerging understanding of how to create conditions for positive change. For example, it's easy to understand the instinct to pair a misogynistic husband with a male professional (out of concern that the husband wouldn't respect a female professional). But would that strategy help that husband to grow emotionally? Would it help him to get in touch with the insecurity beneath his disdain for women so he could become less judgmental of his wife? No. But the problem wouldn't be that a male professional *couldn't* stretch the husband—that could be accomplished by any skilled professional. The problem would be in mistakenly thinking that by sidestepping or accommodating the husband's disrespect of women he could be helped to behave more flexibly. And that mistake in thinking—if it weren't examined and corrected—could cause problems for that team over the course of the entire case.

After more consideration, here's where we landed:

In Chapter 3 we described the Rigidity/Flexibility Continuum, a concept we introduced in our first cowritten book in 2010. The Continuum offers us a way of understanding an individual's capacity to interact effectively with a broad range of people and situations. A healthy, high-functioning person is able to make good connections with most new people and, in new settings, is able to behave in ways that are both authentic to their own character *and* appropriate to the moment. A less healthy, lower-functioning person has trouble with most new people and new settings, because he or she sees nearly everything and everyone through the distorting lens of past negative experience.

It's the same for us. The best divorce professionals are flexible. They meet each new client with fresh eyes and ears—in a state of being "without memory and desire." They behave toward each client in a variety of ways that are both authentic to themselves (each of us has our own stylistic range) and effective in meeting the developmental needs of *that* client. A competent professional is one about whom there's no need to ask, "Will this person be able to relate to and help my client?" or "Will my client be able to relate to and accept help from this person—at least as well as my client seems able to relate to and accept help from *anyone*?"

> *The best divorce professionals are flexible. They meet each new client with fresh eyes and ears. A competent professional is one about whom there's no need to ask "Will this personal be able to relate to and help my client?" or "Will my client be able to relate to or accept help from this person—at least as well as my client seems able to relate to and accept help from anyone?"*

But there has to be more to competence than flexibility. What about the role of good old-fashioned hard work?

In his book *Outliers: The Story of Success*, Malcolm Gladwell writes:

> *Once a musician has enough ability to get into a top music school, the thing that distinguishes one performer from another is how hard he or she works. That's it. And what's more, the people at the very top don't work just harder or*

even much harder than everyone else. They work much, much harder.[1]

There's no question. The first step toward achieving competence in our work is reading everything you can, taking lots of good training, seeking good mentors, accepting helpful feedback, and logging lots and lots of hours.

So should we discount the notion that some talents are innate, and perhaps not teachable? No. Some people are born with an exceptional capacity to intuitively solve complex mathematical equations or to create stunning works of art, and some are clearly born with what Pauline Tesler calls " the peacemaker gene." But the same writer whose argument for the importance of hard work over innate talent we just quoted also makes a crucial and encouraging point about the plasticity of intuition. In *Blink: The Power of Thinking Without Thinking*, Gladwell writes:

> *Our first impressions are generated by our experiences and our environment, which means that we can change our first impressions . . . by changing the experiences that comprise those impressions.*[2]

For divorce professionals, the important implication of Gladwell's thesis is that if we change our working environment we can change our own experience of our work, and thus the ways we perceive our clients. In other words, if we shift our professional stance to one that's in line with the conditions for positive change, we can improve our intuition in important ways that will allow us to get very good at our work.

> *If we shift our professional stance to one that's in line with the conditions for positive change, we can improve our intuition in important ways that will allow us to get very good at our work.*

---

1. Gladwell, Malcolm, *Outliers: The Story of Success*, Back Bay Books Reprint Edition, 2011.
2. Gladwell, Malcolm, *Blink: The Power of Thinking Without Thinking*, Little, Brown, and Company, 2005.

Intuition, Attunement, and "Matching"

Intuition is crucial in learning what we consider to be the most interesting and powerfully effective technique available to us as divorce professionals. It's an advanced technique, it's our favorite, and we saved it for last. We call it "matching."

Think back to our parent-baby paradigm. An attuned mother registers subtle shifts in her baby's vocalizations, facial expressions, and muscular movements, and uses her observations to help her understand her baby's shifting states of mind. The mother then uses her understanding to meet the baby's changing needs.

There's no formula for this; it's intuitive. Without being aware she's doing it, the mother does what's required of her *in that moment*. If the baby is seeking recognition, perhaps the mother smiles and mimics the baby's facial expression. If the baby is seeking stimulation, perhaps the mother makes silly faces and watches for the baby's reaction. If the baby is fussy, perhaps the mother rocks him gently and uses a low soothing voice. If the mother is successful in making the baby feel seen, entertained, or soothed, it's because she has remained attuned and is able to respond intuitively in the ways the baby needed.

In Chapter 5 we talked about the importance of "learning to notice." We're talking about that again, but now on a deeper level. For us, "matching" is the highest expression of "noticing" in divorce work. It is the unconscious or semiconscious process of taking the measure of our client—reading their traits, their mannerisms, their personalities, their speech patterns—then finding an authentic aspect of ourselves that will allow us to sync up with them.

"Matching" is the highest expression of "noticing" in divorce work. It is the unconscious or semiconscious process of taking the measure of our client—reading their traits, their mannerisms, their personalities, their speech patterns—then finding an authentic aspect of ourselves that will allow us to sync up with them.

Here's what we're suggesting. Conjure an image of yourself meeting with a client.

Now: Imagine yourself as a musical instrument (pick your favorite). Next, tune yourself: Put yourself in a state of awake, engaged mindfulness. Now: Think of your client's personality as a complex piece of music with one or more melodic themes expressed in an endlessly shifting variety of rhythms, tones, forms, tempos, and pitches. Listen. Allow your client's music to enter you and to find your resonant frequency. Somewhere inside you a string will begin to vibrate, or air will pass through a valve. A sound will emerge. Go with it; let it build. Find the harmony between you and your client. And when their tempo slows down or speeds up, or when they play louder or softer, follow in whatever way allows you to stay in harmony.

> *Imagine yourself as a musical instrument and your client's personality as a complex piece of music with one or more melodic themes expressed in an endlessly shifting variety of rhythms, tones, forms, tempos, and pitches. Find the harmony between you and your client. And when their tempo slows down or speeds up, or when they play louder or softer, follow in whatever way allows you to stay in harmony.*

What Does "Matching" Look Like in the Room?

In each of the following vignettes, you are the divorce professional. As we enter each scene you are halfway through a first meeting with a new client.

Vignette #1

Your new client is a birdlike woman in a black designer suit, pearls, and delicate high-heeled shoes. Her body remains still, her posture erect, her legs crossed and her hands folded neatly in her lap. Her accent is heavily French. She speaks in a controlled manner, slowly and with purpose. She often pauses for a brief moment between sentences, as if to consider her phrasing. She enunciates each word with care. Eyes slightly downcast, she says,

"I am very angry with my husband. He is behaving in a poor way. It is, ah . . . how should I say? Terrible? It is making me very frightened. I do not know if he will make sure the house check is paid. You know what I mean? The . . . ah . . . the payment for the home?"

You, too, have been sitting with your legs crossed and your hands in your lap (a rather prim position for you). Though you normally take copious notes in a first meeting, at some point in the last half hour you seem to have placed your notepad and pen down on the side table by your chair. You are aware of a softening in your muscles. Taking care to move slowly and to otherwise hold the position of your body still, you bend slightly at the waist so you are leaning in toward your client. You hold her gaze. After a quiet moment, you speak calmly in a kind, nonpatronizing tone. You choose simple words, and pause briefly between sentences— falling into a halting cadence that matches hers.

"Yes, the mortgage, the monthly payment for your home. Your husband has always paid it, but now you don't know if he will pay it? At the beginning of our meeting today you told me you thought you had married 'a gentleman.' Perhaps you have never seen your husband behave in this way before. I can understand why this makes you frightened and angry."

Your client nods. Her eyes fill with tears. The two of you sit in silence for a moment or two. She takes a tissue from her purse to wipe her eyes. You maintain your posture and keep your eyes on her face. Presently you continue, still choosing words thoughtfully and speaking in a rhythm that echoes your client's own expressive pattern.

"It is important to you to feel your home is secure, that your husband will continue to pay the monthly mortgage. I believe I can help with that. We still have three weeks before the next payment is due, so we have enough time to work things out. Perhaps I should call your husband's attorney to discuss the matter. Would you like me to do that?

Vignette #2

Your client is an athletically toned, tan woman in pressed jeans, a sweater with a bright floral pattern, and neon-lime sneakers.

She perches on the edge of your couch—muscles taut, elbows on knees, leaning forward. The intensity of her gaze carries an implication of need. She speaks quickly and with great energy—gesticulating emphatically with her hands when she wants to underscore a point. Her words come in a pressured rush.

*"**I am Totally** pissed off with the guy at this point. He's being a major dick—excuse my French. He hasn't paid the mortgage out of his account, even though the a-hole said he would. And checks are bouncing out of our joint account like crazy. The electric bill? Boing! The cable bill? Boing! I mean, it's ridiculous! I'm ready to strangle him! I don't have a friggin' clue what to do, but I'll tell you what–I want to do **Something**, and I want to do it **Now**. How can you help?"*

You have been sitting in your ordinary default position, legs crossed, arms by your side, your notebook and pen perched on your lap. You've kept your face mostly still, nodding empathically or smiling slightly in the moments in which she became most agitated. You've maintained a relaxed steady composure, despite a growing tautness in your muscles. Your heart rate has become slightly elevated. You feel alive and alert. Still holding your client's eyes in a clear, direct gaze, you speak in a tone of calm, cool assurance. You don't raise the decibel level of your voice, but you infuse it with authoritative energy.

"Okay, none of that sounds like any fun. It must seem like your husband has chucked the playbook! I'm not surprised you're feeling freaked out. Of course you need help—this is all scary new territory. I'm sure we can noodle this through, but first things first. I think you'll feel calmer if we start by listing the things you're most worried about, like the mortgage and other bills—along with their due dates. Does that make sense? I promise to time our discussion so that by the time you leave today we'll have a game plan."

You may now be thinking some version of: "It's clear that the 'me' in these situations stayed attuned and intuitively 'matched' the client. But I live in the real world where things are messy and confusing and happen in real time. There's no way I can do that!" Well, good news.

In the introduction we talked about the work of attorney Pauline Tesler, and how it offers empirical evidence for the fact that we are all wired to connect with other people in ways that promote growth. It's really true.

Each of us is born with a genetic endowment that allows us to learn, very early in our lives, how to form strong relationships characterized by containment, empathy, and attunement. And while this capacity evolved (in the Darwinian sense) so we could carry on as a species, one needn't be a parent to learn to harness one's innate capacity to form a helping relationship—a container—with the power to support healthy development, promote positive change, and facilitate transformative experience.

Beyond Competence

We'd like to end where we began, with the question "How does one achieve excellence in the field of separation and divorce?" We think that's the question we should all spend our careers trying to answer. And if a day comes when we think we've cracked the code, well, there won't be anywhere interesting to go from there. But here is our best thinking on the subject, at least for now.

If you want to achieve your own highest level of mastery in the field of separation and divorce you should do three things:

1. *Work really hard.* Assuming you've already mastered your own professional discipline, go about learning how to create and maintain the conditions for positive change. Practice, practice, practice. Make a lot of mistakes and learn from them. Attend a wide range of professional trainings and case consultations. Read books and journals. Join listservs and keep up on what your colleagues are thinking about. Find a supervisor, consultant, or mentor. Ask for and accept helpful feedback—both positive and negative. Learn enough that you move from feeling overwhelmed by how much there is to know to feeling appreciative that you'll never know the half of it.

2. *Get out of your own way.* Get to know yourself. Well. If you haven't done it before (or for a while), consider trying therapy. Therapists engaged in advanced clinical training are often required to be in therapy themselves, and for

good reason. If you have an inappropriate or disproportionate response to a particular client, that's a flat key, a snapped string, or a cracked reed. Leave it unattended, and no matter how well you can read music, you'll never be able to play a duet with that client. But if you listen for the moments you're out of tune, seek out the source, and make the necessary adjustments, you'll be able to refind the harmony.

Okay, you're past tasks 1 and 2.

You know the science of your work so well that you're free to practice it as an art.

3. *Now, let go.* Be. Play jazz.

Appendix A

Glossary of Helpful Terms and Phrases

Acting Out

To act out is to perform an action as a way of discharging uncomfortable feelings, rather than bearing the feelings or discussing them in productive ways. Acting out is usually self-destructive and/or destructive to the divorce process. *Example: A client is chronically late to meetings rather than telling his professionals that he feels his voice is not being heard.*

Affect

Affect is the external, observable expression of emotion, as in "the client had a flat affect; she sat motionless with no expression on her face." Sometimes affect does not match emotion, as when a client is depressed but appears cheerful.

Ambivalent Attachment

A person with an ambivalent attachment style seeks out and then rejects emotional connection. This behavior is the expression of anger and helplessness, and is the result of having had an inconsistently available/responsive early caregiver. *Example: A client calls you on the weekend desperate for advice, but then ignores your advice and doesn't return your calls for a week.*

Assumption

An assumption is something one believes to be true or that one believes will happen, absent any supporting evidence and/or in the presence of evidence to the contrary. *Example: A divorce professional assumes that a stay-at-home mother is going to resist the idea of going back to work before the issue has come up for discussion.* This concept is closely linked to that of a professional-owned countertransference, and will become one if the assumption is directed toward a *particular* stay-at-home mother (so that the professional prematurely views the mother as resistant to going back to work).

Attunement

Attunement is the measure of how responsive one is to the needs and moods of another. A well-attuned professional is adept at reading their client's emotional state, and responding in accordance with their client's needs in a given moment.

Avoidant Attachment

A person with an avoidant attachment style ignores or shows little regard for a caring other—often seeming not to care if the other comes or goes. This behavior is the result of an individual having had, as an infant, an early caregiver who rebuffed their needs for attachment. It reflects the individual's having "given up" due to their expectation of rejection. *Example: A client is unresponsive to your attempts to empathize with their pain and resists scheduling meetings to discuss their goals and objectives or to develop a game plan for their process.*

Basic Trust

Basic trust is an individual's sense that the world is essentially a reliable and predictable place in which people can be counted on. Basic trust is the result of an individual having had at least one loving and responsive early caregiver. *Example: A client comes to the process predisposed to think of you as a competent professional who has their best interests in mind, and is able to hold on to that feeling even when he or she disagrees with you or you make an inadvertent mistake.*

Benign Skepticism

Benign skepticism is the state of mind in which one is able to listen empathically and without judgment while simultaneously being curious about ways the speaker may be distorting their own narrative or failing to consider alternate, potentially valid perspectives. *Example: As a divorce professional you "take in" your client's narrative in which she describes her cheating husband as "remorseless and a terrible father." You empathize with her pain, but you hold space (in your own mind) for the possibility that the husband's cheating didn't happen in a vacuum and that he might be a loving, competent parent.*

Bias

A bias is a persistent predisposition to view a type of person or group of people in a specific and fixed way—favorable or unfavorable—that is distinct from the way one views other people or groups of people. *Example: A divorce professional believes that women are inherently better parents than are men.*

Boundaries, Professional

Professional boundaries are structures (implicit or explicit) that support the ethical, legal, practical, and emotional aspects of our work with clients and ensure that the work remains client-focused. *Example: Your client, a sports talent agent, offers you coveted Super Bowl tickets. Tough as it is, you refuse—because to accept the tickets would violate professional boundaries by converting the relationship from one that is solely focused on the needs of the client into one that gratifies you.*

Conditions for Positive Change, Three

The Three Conditions for Positive Change are the authors' conceptualization, drawn from psychotherapeutic and attachment theory, of the essential elements that must be present in order for an individual to master a developmental challenge. The Three Conditions for Change are (1) a new idea, (2) a helping relationship, and (3) optimal anxiety.

Conscious Mind (or one's consciousness)

The conscious mind is the part of our psyche that contains the thoughts, ideas, feelings, and memories of which we are aware (or which we can call easily into awareness). *Example: A client is aware (his conscious mind knows) that his tendency to be critical of his wife's parenting style doesn't reflect reality (she is, in fact, a good mother), but instead stems from his resentment toward her for initiating their divorce.*

Container, The Professional

The professional container is the safe emotional space we create in which our clients can do the hard work of getting divorced at their own highest level of transformative capacity. It is composed of the Macrocontainer (the protocols of our work and the relationships between professionals) and the Microcontainer (the one-on-one relationship between a professional and his or her client).

Containment (or To Contain)

Containment is the mental act of receiving and taking into oneself the experience of another person, in order to make sense of and empathize with it. Containment is often difficult, because it requires us to *simply be* with our client in their moments of intense pain and to refrain from moving too quickly to giving advice or offering unhelpfully pat responses. Containment is one of the most powerful tools in our toolbox, because it communicates to our clients that we value their feelings, can understand them, and can tolerate them without becoming overwhelmed by them.

Corrective Emotional Experience

A corrective emotional experience is one in which a person is re-exposed to a previously traumatic situation under new and better circumstances. Corrective emotional experiences offer an individual the opportunity to replace outdated thoughts, feelings, and patterns of behavior with new and better ones. This transformation occurs on both the intrapsychic (emotional) and neurological levels (through rewiring of pathways in the brain). *Example: A client whose early caregivers gave her the consistent message that her need for emotional connection indicated that she was "needy and greedy," comes to the divorce process expecting her professionals to view her desire for reassurance as annoying and inappropriate. When the client finds that, on the contrary, her professionals solicit her feelings and empathize with them, her sense of herself as needy and greedy is challenged. She emerges from the process with better self-esteem and with the new hope of building more mutually supportive relationships.*

Countertransference

Countertransference is a professional's positive or negative reaction to a client (or colleague).

Countertransference, Client-Driven

Client-Induced countertransference is a professional's reaction to an aspect of a client's personality or behavior that is merited and within the realm of expectable, ordinary responses. *Example: A client who is relentlessly critical and frequently questions the competence of his divorce professional induces a countertransference in which that professional feels frustrated and unappreciated.*

Countertransference, Professional-Owned

Professional-owned countertransferences are not merited by the traits or behaviors of the client, but emerge from biases, assumptions, or trigger points within the character of the professional. *Example: A divorce professional whose father had an affair and left the family when the professional was a young boy takes an instant dislike to his client's unfaithful husband.*

Defense (or Defense Mechanism)

An emotional defense (often referred to as a defense mechanism) is an unconscious psychological strategy through which we protect ourselves from painful thoughts, feelings, or memories by keeping them outside of our conscious awareness. *Example: A client who has decided to leave her marriage of 20 years defends against the pain of loss by repressing it—pushing it out of her awareness and experiencing only relief and excitement.*

Denial

Denial is a defense (or defense mechanism) in which someone refuses to acknowledge or accept a reality by simply failing to acknowledge that it exists. *Example: A client who behaves vindictively toward his wife (e.g., unreasonably insists that she is unfit to care for their children or deserving of any financial support) denies that he is angry with her for leaving the marriage.*

Development, Human

Human development is the process of growth and change over the course of an individual's life.

Developmental Crisis

A developmental crisis occurs when an individual, couple, or family is unable to master a new developmental challenge (or challenges). All divorcing couples and families are in a global developmental crisis (the divorce itself is evidence that their capacity to foster development has broken down). Within the divorce process individuals face many developmental challenges. When a client is unable to successfully navigate one of these challenges (which happens frequently, since divorce is hard and our clients are already in a compromised state), they face a new developmental crisis. *Example: A grieving divorcing client persistently refuses (over many months) to participate in his divorce process because he can't face the fact that his marriage is really over and that he will have to move on without his wife by his side.*

Developmental Phase

A developmental phase is a time in the life of an individual when he or she must master new emotional, cognitive, and perhaps physical challenges in order to evolve to a new level of maturity. Some developmental phases are universal (such as adolescence); some are not universal but are common and contain universal themes (such as divorce). The successful navigation of any developmental phase requires an individual to let go of the familiar and embrace the new. When an individual successfully navigates a developmental phase, he or she strengthens the foundation on which they can build future successes.

Developmental Task

A developmental task is a challenge, which, if mastered, leads to emotional growth. *Example: A formerly financially dependent wife is faced with the shift from thinking of herself as dependent toward thinking of herself as strong enough to provide for herself. A developmental task may be something an individual wants to do from the outset (perhaps the wife in our example desires to become more independent from her husband because it will enhance her self-esteem) or it can be driven by outside realities (perhaps there will not be enough money to support two households post-divorce, so both spouses will have to work).*

Disorganized Attachment

A person with a disorganized attachment style has trouble trusting or opening up to others. They struggle to self-soothe and to regulate their emotions. They have trouble expressing themselves clearly, so their narratives are often fragmented and don't make sense. People with disorganized attachments struggle to form relationships, and can often behave in unpredictable, bizarre, frightening, and destructive ways. Disorganized attachments are the result of childhood abuse, neglect, and unresolved trauma. *Example: In a first meeting you ask your new client what has brought her to your office. After an hour (and many attempts at clarification), you are completely confused as to who your client is, why they are getting divorced (or if they even want to), and what they want from you. You feel destabilized; you have the sense there is something "off" with your client.*

Eleventh-Hour Regression

This is a term the authors coined to describe the common phenomenon in which a client does something surprisingly irrational, uncharacteristic, or unhelpful just before or *as* a single meeting or entire divorce process is about to conclude. An eleventh-hour regression is usually relatively easy to work with and to reverse if the professional(s) at the table is able to articulate the fear and pain driving it. *Example: After months of working toward a financial settlement a husband and wife have agreed on mutually acceptable terms. With ten minutes to go in the final meeting the husband turns to his attorney and says, "I've been thinking—I actually don't agree that my wife should have any claim to my bonus this year."*

Emotional Dynamics

Emotional dynamics are the blend of experiences, thoughts, and feelings that drive an individual's behavior, largely in ways the individual is not aware of. Emotional dynamics are the manifest expression of our unconscious mind's strategy for dealing with painful experiences (and the memories and feelings associated with them), so that we can maintain our emotional equilibrium. Unfortunately, when these dynamics go unexamined, they can cause trouble in an individual's life and relationships. *Example: Your male client grew up craving approval from a harsh, critical father. Because it is too painful for this man to be consciously aware of how much he still longs for approval that will never come, he represses his pain in favor of idealizing his father. Now the man's attitude is "Sure, my dad was hard on me. But he toughened me up and made me the successful man I am today!" This strategy helps your client to maintain his emotional equilibrium. But, not surprisingly, he is now a harsh, critical father and husband. His own wife and children feel they can do no good in **his** eyes.*

Emotional Growth (Positive Change)

Emotional growth is the psychological result of an individual's having mastered the tasks associated with a particular developmental phase or challenge. It refers to a state in which that individual's capacity to flexibly navigate intrapersonal and interpersonal challenges is enhanced. *Examples include improvement in an individual's capacity to regulate their own emotional states, to be empathic toward others, to develop perspective on their own contribution to their relationship difficulties, to appreciate the "blessings" in their life, to love themselves and others, and to get in touch with optimism and ambition.*

Empathy

Empathy is the ability to deeply understand, on a gut level, the emotional experience of another person. Where sympathy is to feel *for*, empathy is to feel *with*.

Enactment

An enactment is the unconscious acting out, by a professional(s), of a client's emotional dynamic. *Example: A lawyer under relentless pressure from her client to get his wife "to produce her budget already!" feels anxious, under the gun, and powerless. Reflexively, she telephones the attorney for the wife and berates him for his lack of client control. She and the wife's attorney begin to argue over whose client is in the right. The conflict (which had begun with the husband's attorney's countertransference to her own client) now takes the form of an enactment in which the lawyers act out the emotional dynamic of their clients.*

Factors, Seven to Consider When Deciding What to Do or Say

The Factors are the authors' conceptualization of seven categories of observable and non-observable phenomena that intersect, change constantly, and are at play in every moment of our work. When deciding that to do or say, we must make a split-second analysis of the state and relative importance of each of these Factors, and choose our technique accordingly. The seven Factors are Topical Context, Temporal Context, Intrapersonal Context, Interpersonal Context, Recent or Impending Occurrence Context, State of the Two-Part Container, and Developmental Task Context.

Flooded (or Emotionally Flooded)

The term flooded refers to a state of mind in which a person is emotionally overwhelmed and unable to assimilate new information or to think rationally. This state of mind occurs in response to a physical state in which an upsetting stimulus has resulted in a literal flooding of the individual's nervous system with stress hormones, thus activating the individual's primitive brain and inducing a fight, flight, or play dead response.

Following the Affect (or Leaning into Emotion)

Following the affect refers to the act of tracking manifestations of (or clues to) a client's emotions, and directing one's attention accordingly. *Example: After discussing the painful topic of her husband's new girlfriend, a wife says she is "fine" and ready to move on. However, you notice that her eyes are tearing up and she appears distraught. Rather than moving on, you gently comment on her affect, saying: "You say you're ready to move on, and maybe you are. But I can't help noticing that you seem upset."*

Framing an Issue

To frame an issue is to identify and articulate the essence of a conflict, conversation, or complex interaction in a way that brings the core underlying issue into focus. *Example: Your clients have been arguing vociferously over the number of years the husband will pay alimony to the wife. You offer: "I think this discussion is not so much about length of spousal support as it is about when Lynn will be able to go back to work. Lynn, what are your thoughts about a realistic time frame for finding a job?*

Helping Relationship

A helping relationship is one that facilitates emotional growth (positive change). It is characterized by the provision of a holding environment, containment, empathy, and attunement.

Holding Environment

A holding environment is a safe, responsive, nurturing milieu that exists within the context of a helping relationship. It has observable, structural components (e.g., a comfortable and appropriate office space, regular fee policies, predictable meeting times) *and* emotional components (e.g., the caring qualities of the helping relationship itself).

Human Development (see Development, Human)

Identification

To identify with someone is to feel you are like him or her and therefore can understand them. In our professional context, identification is potentially problematic because it can lead to over-identification, a psychological "joining," or a state of mind in which a professional feels personally connected with a client and/or invested in the outcome of their process. *Example: A divorce professional is a single mother whose ex-husband remains underemployed as a means of avoiding child support. When this professional represents single parents, she views them as victims (even when they're not), and advocates fiercely on their financial behalves.*

In Sync

"In sync" is a shortened form of the phrase "in synchronization with." It refers to a state in which two events, forces, or people are working well together in time and function (e.g., the sound track of a movie *and* the picture). The authors use the phrase here to refer to a state in which a professional and client are emotionally and intellectually connected—working together effectively in a coordinated and cooperative way with a sense of shared mission and mutual understanding.

Insecure Attachment

A person with an insecure attachment style never developed a sense of basic trust in early caregivers, and thus, as an adult, has difficulty forming trusting relationships with others. There are three forms of insecure attachment: avoidant, ambivalent, and disorganized.

Insight

An insight is an accurate and deep understanding of an idea, person, or situation. The development of insight (particularly about oneself) is an important aspect of emotional growth. *Example: Your client comes into his divorce process convinced that he is the victim and his wife is the perpetrator of his injuries. Over the course of your work together, he comes to realize that while his wife initiated the divorce, he has been unhappy for years. In fact, without being aware of it, he's been pushing her away in the hope that she'd be the one to "call the game."*

Involved Impartiality

Involved impartiality is a state of being empathic and nonjudgmental while remaining open to alternative perspectives. If we are in a state of involved impartiality, we can listen to our client's story, accept it as their reality, and offer empathy without becoming over-identified with them and thus unable to imagine another side of the story. Being open to the idea that our client's way of seeing things is only one of many and that they may, for example, be distorting or mischaracterizing their spouse's behavior, is crucial when it comes to "stretching" our client along their developmental path.

Leaning into Emotion (see Following the Affect)

Limits, Professional

In our context, a limit is a point beyond which we have made an educated choice to not gratify a client's desire *because to do otherwise would not serve our client's best interest.* A limit is not arbitrary, but rather based on a thoughtful blend of (1) a clear understanding of our professional role, (2) our own style and comfort zone, and (3) an understanding of our client's developmental needs. It is based on a good parenting paradigm. So, in the same way that a parent who is trying to help their five-year-old learn to self-soothe might say "no" to a third glass of water at bedtime, a divorce professional who is trying to help their client to learn to manage anxiety might say "no" to responding to e-mails over the weekend.

Macrocontainer

The Macrocontainer is the safe psychological space that supports the work of each Microcontainer in a case. The authors describe it as providing an "arms around" experience for the one-on-one relationships among colleagues and between professionals and their individual clients. It is also the place in which interactions (positive and negative), enactments, and ruptures that arise in the Microcontainers are made sense of (metabolized) and are used to move a case forward. The Macrocontainer is composed of the guidelines/protocols of a given case and modality (e.g., mediation, settlement negotiation), as well as all the Microcontainers among professionals involved in the case.

Making Links

In our context, "making a link" is a technique we can use with a relatively flexible client when we want to help them weather a difficult moment, get unstuck, come back from a regressive position, or develop insight. In making a link we draw a connection between past experience (either in the client's earlier life or within their divorce process) and the current moment. These links highlight dysfunctional emotional and behavioral patterns, diffuse anxiety, and broaden our client's perspective. *Example of a link between an experience in a client's earlier life and the current moment (professional speaking to their client): "You're saying that you are concerned that your husband wants to leave you with no retirement. You have that worry, even though you also know that he has made it clear that he wants to ensure your financial security into the future. I'm remembering you told me that your father left your family when you were young, and that your mother had no way to care for you and your siblings. That was terrifying for all of you. I'm wondering if some of your current worry might be related to that earlier experience?"* *Example of a link between an experience earlier in the divorce process and the current moment (professional speaking to client): "This is the first time your husband has been away with the children for a whole week since you've been separated, and you're worried that he won't be able to care for them and that they'll miss you. But I'm remembering that you felt this way the first time he took them for a long weekend. Then later, you were able to say he had managed well and the kids had had a great time. I'm wondering if it's just difficult every time you face an increased separation from the kids. That would certainly be understandable!"*

Marital Dynamics

A couple's "marital dynamics" are their unique emotional and behavioral "dance," the patterns of feeling, communicating, and behaving that have characterized their relationship in repeating and predictable ways. Dysfunctional marital dynamics are difficult to modify because there are driven by largely unconscious factors. Marital dynamics do not end with the decision to separate or divorce. In fact, they often become temporarily more intense, and can create difficulties between clients and professionals and among professionals on a team.

Matching

Matching is the authors' term for the professional technique of (1) being in a state of emotional attunement with a client such that we can intuitively "read" their traits, mannerisms, personalities, interpersonal styles, and speech patterns, and (2) finding an authentic aspect of our own characters from which we can connect with that client in harmonious synchronicity.

Metabolize

When we metabolize a client's idea or feeling we empathize with it, enrich it through self-reflection, and elevate it from its raw form to a higher order concept that includes new insight and perspective. *Example (professional speaking to client): "You are angry, and you want to lash our at your wife—to punish her by not letting her take the kids to her family reunion. You don't want this divorce; it must be painful not to be included in the reunion this year. Maybe it's easier to feel angry than to let in all that pain. On the other hand, I also know you don't want to punish your kids by keeping them from seeing their cousins. It's so hard to do the right thing when you're hurting."*

Microcontainer

The Microcontainer is the holding environment provided by the intimate one-on-one relationship between a professional and his or her client that allows the client to do the hard work of getting divorced at their own highest level of transformative capacity. A Microcontainer is analogous to the early parent-baby relationship, in that within it a helping professional is entirely focused on taking in, tolerating, and helping their client to make sense of his or her experience in the service of developmental growth. A professional team may also include Microcontainers composed of other supportive one-on-one relationships among colleagues.

Mindfulness

Mindfulness is a state of active, open attention to the present moment. It describes a psychological presence and nonjudgmental receptivity to stimuli that are picked up by any or all of your senses. These stimuli may originate within you (in your mind and body) or outside of you (in your physical environment and in other people).

Mistakes, Professional (see Ordinary Mistakes and Mistakes of the Heart)

Mistakes of the Heart

Professional mistakes of the heart are rare but potentially fatal to a process. They grow out of a sustained lack of self-awareness, and take the form of personal bias, intrusive agendas, or the repeated expression of anger, frustration, or ill will. Mistakes of the heart reveal an underlying lack of empathy.

New Idea, Higher and Lower Order

In the context of our work, a new idea is a goal that can only be achieved by mastering the tasks associated with a new developmental challenge. A new idea must be compelling enough that the anticipated achievement of it is greater than the fear associated with mastering any potential obstacles. Lower order new ideas provide opportunities for small increments of emotional growth; higher order new ideas provide opportunities for large increments of emotional growth.

Optimal Anxiety

Optimal anxiety is the increment of emotional discomfort that incentivizes an individual to work toward the mastery of a developmental task (suboptimal anxiety does not create sufficient incentive; too much anxiety floods the individual and temporarily incapacitates them).

Ordinary Mistakes

Ordinary mistakes may be technical (such as a math error), irritating but relatively minor (such as being ten minutes late to one meeting), or can reflect temporary lapses in judgment. Ordinary mistakes are the ones from which everyone can recover and, because we learn from them, can actually further the process.

Overidentification (see Identification)

Paraphrase

To paraphrase is to mirror a client's words back to them without shifting their meaning in any way. *Example (client speaking to professional): "I can't believe this is happening to me. I wish I were dead." Professional (in response): "This is completely surreal. You wish you were dead so you wouldn't have to experience this pain."*

Platitude

A platitude is a phrase that is intended to convey understanding or to offer comfort but is empty of authentic emotion, banal, hackneyed, or used too often to be of real value to the recipient. Platitudes, because they do not convey empathy, can often cause unintentional emotional harm. *Example: "Oh well, every cloud as a silver lining—at least you'll never have to see your mother-in-law again!"*

Polarities

In our context, polarities are two competing emotional urges that are alive within us when we face a developmental challenge. One pole represents the pull toward stasis or regression; the other pole represents the desire to relinquish the past (or the safe and known) and move forward into the future (toward the new idea). *Example: A client struggles to forgive his wife for her infidelity, yet knows that his sustained anger is slowing his own emotional recovery. Polarity 1: If he holds on to his anger he can stave off the pain of accepting that the marriage is really over. Polarity 2: If he forgives her he can move on and find happiness of his own.*

Positive Change (see Emotional Growth)

Primary Parental Preoccupation

Primary parental preoccupation describes the phenomenon in which the parent (or other primary caregiver) of a newborn baby withdraws the locus of their attention from other concerns and focuses their mind and body on the task of caring for their infant.

Process Task, Concrete and Emotional

Concrete and emotional process tasks are the very real challenges that our clients face within their divorce process. Accomplishing concrete and emotional tasks help a client to successfully navigate their developmental task. For a financially dependent wife, an example of a concrete process task might be making an appointment with a vocational counselor. For the same wife, an example of an emotional process task might be facing the possibility of reentering the job market. Both concrete and emotional process tasks are psychologically challenging; the main difference is that while concrete process tasks require the doing of something in the real world, emotional process tasks require wrestling with internal conflict.

Reality Testing

Reality testing is a technique for use with relatively flexible clients in which we attempt to help them to see a situation for what it really is, rather than what they hope or fear it to be based on past experience. *Example (professional to client): "I know you feel your wife wants to keep the children from you. But actually I'm remembering that at the last meeting she talked about her wish that you could travel less and spend more time with the children."*

Reframing

Reframing is a technique in which a professional restates a client's idea in such a way that they extract the essence of the client's underlying concern and fortify it with an added increment of understanding—in an attempt to move the client off a position and "stretch" them along their developmental trajectory. *Example (client to professional): "My husband is a chaotic mess. The kids have to live with me during the school week." Professional (in response): "You know your kids do best when they have regular, predictable routines—especially during the school week when their schedules are complicated, they have homework, and they really need enough sleep. You're worried that your husband can't provide enough organized structure to keep them on track."*

Repression

Repression is an emotional defense (or defense mechanism) in which an individual suppresses their memory of an event or series of events and/or their conscious awareness of the thoughts and feelings associated with that event or series of events.

Rigidity

A rigid client views and reacts to people and situations based in predictably distorted ways based on past negative experiences (usually from their early childhood). Very rigid clients often hold tight to irrational positions, lack insight, blame others for their difficulties, and adopt a victimized stance.

Rigidity/Flexibility Continuum

The Rigidity/Flexibility Continuum is the authors' model for assessing an individual's emotional health (both under conditions of stress and in general) and for developing strategies for working with that individual to achieve their best divorce outcome. The model is based on the notion that an individual's level of emotional health can be defined by how well he or she can relate realistically to a broad range of new people and situations.

Safe Base

When a child forms a strong attachment with a loving and predictably available caregiver, that caregiver becomes a safe base—a source of succor that gives the child the confidence to explore the world. In our work, within the holding environment of the Microcontainer, we can become our client's safe base—someone who gives them confidence in their own abilities to take risks and to whom they can return for refueling when they experience fear and self-doubt.

Secure Attachment

A person with a secure attachment was able to form strong bonds with nurturing early caregivers and has developed a sense of basic trust. As an adult, he or she is capable of forming trusting relationships with others and has the sense that the world is essentially a safe place in which his or her needs can be met.

Sympathy

Sympathy is a sense of pity or sadness for the suffering or misfortune of another.

Tending/Moving Continuum

The Tending/Moving Continuum is the authors' model (developed with colleague Barbara Burr) for describing the techniques we employ when making moment-to-moment decisions about how much to explore emotion (tend) and how much to focus on the practical tasks at hand (move). In any given moment we must do some measure of both; the continuum is an exploration of where we put our technical emphasis in any given moment of the work.

Three Conditions for Positive Change (see Conditions for Positive Change, Three)

Transference

Transference is the unconscious mental act of treating a new relationship as if it were an old one. It is the process of misdirecting (or projecting) the qualities, motivations, or behaviors from a person or relationship from one's childhood onto someone in the present.

Transformation (see Emotional Growth)

Transitional Object

A transitional object is something that provides comfort because it has come to stand for an attachment figure. A transitional object is a bridge between a safe base and the outer world; it is a tangible representation of the psychological support provided by a real person or people (or the memory of that person or people).

Transitional Space

In our context, the transitional space is the increment of emotional distance between a professional and his or her client that allows that professional to empathize with their client without *taking on* their client's experience. It is also the psychological space into which the professional invites their client as the client moves along their developmental path, and the creative space in which new ideas are generated.

Trigger

A trigger is a category of experience (perhaps a topic, personality type, or type of behavior in another person) that stimulates an emotional reaction that is incongruent with the content and context of the current moment. Someone who is "triggered" is unconsciously experiencing the reactivation of a repressed trauma and is misdirecting (projecting) the feelings associated with that trauma onto a person or situation in the present.

Trope

In our work, a trope is a well-developed metaphor—a simple way of representing a client's recurring anxiety along with the insights they have developed around it and the strategies they have developed for dealing with it. The construction of a shared trope is a way of offering our clients a transitional object—a metaphorical stand-in for us (their safe base). *Example: A client who perseverates endlessly about the many decisions she must make in her divorce process describes the experience as being "like juggling a million balls at a time." She says, "I'm worn out from all the juggling, but I'm afraid if I put one ball down they'll all fall and my world will come crashing down." She and her divorce professional talk about how "juggling" gives her a false sense of control in a scary situation (her divorce), but leaves her emotionally exhausted. After that, whenever the client finds herself unable to stoped ruminating on all the decisions she must make and all the potential negative implications of those decisions, she imagines her professional whispering "Put down the balls; stop juggling. Everything will be ok."*

Unconscious Mind (or One's Subconscious)

Our unconscious mind consists of all our memories, thoughts, and feelings of which we are not, in any given moment, aware.

Without Memory or Desire, Being

In our context, to be without memory and desire is to be in an openly receptive mode in which we do not impose assumptions based on past experience onto the present moment. From this stance we can meet and learn about our client with a clear mind, fresh ears, and a sense of authentic curiosity.

Appendix B

Using This Book for Ongoing Learning Supplemental Study Modules

Supplemental Study Modules

Since the publication of our first coauthored book for divorce professionals (*Navigating Emotional Currents in Collaborative Divorce: A Guide for Enlightened Team Practice*), many professionals across the country have told us that they've read it not only on their own, but also along with colleagues, in reading groups, peer-supervision groups, and practice groups. Many folks use the book as a kind of structuring curriculum—a springboard for discussions that further ongoing learning. Together they grapple with new concepts, and share how they've been integrating their new understanding into their work. We are always gratified and excited to hear the range of ways in which colleagues actively engage with our material.

That got us thinking: We know that many of the ideas we offer will be new and strange for some readers (especially the non-mental-health professionals). Some concepts will be difficult to understand, at least at first. So why not make things easier this time around (and more fun!) by offering "study modules"— discussion topics and/or experiential exercises to accompany many of the chapters? Our thought is that any reader who wants to augment their learning (either solo or with study buddies) and bring the written material to life by thinking about it in the context of their own life and practice can dip into these modules. So use them if a particular topic confuses or interests you, or if you sense you could benefit from thinking more directly about a particular area of the work. Use them in whatever ways you like, with whomever you like. Make up some new exercises; add new fact patterns. Be creative! And let us know how it goes—we'd love to hear!

Modules

Chapter 1: Divorce Reimagined as a Developmental Experience

In Chapter 1 we described the way human beings "grow up" by facing and mastering a series of developmental phases, moments in which we are challenged to master new tasks in the service of growth. Some of these phases are predictable (like learning to talk); others are not (like getting divorced). Well-functioning couples, parents, and families support each other in navigating these phases, with each success setting the stage for further successes. But eventually we all run up against a developmental moment that we can't easily move through. There are lots of reasons this could be true; perhaps the content is painful (someone close to us dies and we have trouble moving beyond our grief), sometimes we are under stress (it's time to leave for college but our parents are getting divorced), and sometimes we simply don't have adequate emotional supports at our disposal.

Having a sense of our own developmental trajectory (the phases we've experienced so far, and which ones went well and which didn't) not only enhances our self-awareness, it also enhances our capacity for empathy with our clients (who are struggling with the developmental crisis of divorce). It can also make us better parents, friends, partners, and colleagues.

Exercise: Mapping Your Own Developmental Trajectory

On a piece of paper, list all the developmental milestones you have faced in your life. Some you won't remember (e.g., learning to sleep through the night). If you like, write them down anyway. If you prefer, start with the ones you remember (e.g., going to preschool or sleeping away from home for the first time). Don't think too hard. Don't worry if the events or accomplishments you're writing technically qualify as developmental phases. That part doesn't matter. What's important is that they occur to you.

Here's the beginning of an abbreviated hypothetical list to get you started:

1. Learned to walk
2. Learned to talk
3 Stayed with my grandparents when my parents went away
4. Stood up to a bully
5. Learned to live with my dyslexia
6. Joined a soccer team even though I sucked
7. Asked a boy to a dance, got turned down, survived
8. Conquered my fear of flying

We could continue, but you get the idea. Make your list as long or as short as you like.

Now, review your list while considering the following questions:

- Which of these tasks were relatively easy to navigate?
- Which were more difficult?
- Are there any tasks that I only partially mastered? (e.g., "I was able to sleep away from my parents, but I was anxious the whole night and I still don't like being away from home.")
- Are there any tasks that I was unable to navigate? (e.g., "I have never been able to speak in front of an audience.")
- What developmental challenges am I currently facing? How do I feel about them?
- What developmental challenges will I inevitably face in the future? Which do I look forward to? Which do I fear?
- What unpredictable developmental challenges MIGHT I face in the future? As I imagine them, how do I feel?

Chapter 2: Conditions for Positive Change
EXERCISE 1: EXPLORING THE THREE CONDITIONS FOR POSITIVE CHANGE

Get a piece of paper and something to write with.

1. Identify a developmental achievement.

In your mind, conjure up the memory of something significant that you have accomplished. Make it something you'd been thinking about and working up to for a long time, and that was difficult to achieve. It can relate to any area of your life—a physical challenge, an academic challenge, a professional challenge, a social challenge, an emotional challenge, a parenting challenge—or any combination. It need not be something you've discussed with anyone else, though it could be. It needn't be something that brought you lots of kudos from others (such as running a marathon). It could be a quieter internal triumph (such as conquering a fear of speaking up in meetings). *This accomplishment represents a developmental achievement.*

Write the accomplishment down on your paper.

2. Describe the polarities associated with your developmental achievement.

In order for you to have mastered your developmental task, you had to navigate two internal polarities: One part of you said, "Hey, this is too hard," while another replied, "Yeah, but I really want to do this!"

Turn back to the paper on which you've written your accomplishment. Underneath it, create two columns by writing the words "Polarity 1: Stasis" on the left side of the paper and the words "Polarity 2: Positive Change" in the center. Under each Polarity write every thought or feeling that comes to your mind. Don't censor or edit your thoughts, just let them flow in a stream of consciousness. To illustrate, here's a hypothetical example:

ACCOMPLISHMENT: GETTING IN AN ELEVATOR
FOR THE FIRST TIME IN 15 YEARS

Polarity 1: Stasis	**Polarity 2: Positive Change**
Elevators are terrifying; I want to stay out of them! I get nauseated just thinking about it.	I want to conquer my fear so I can live a normal life! I am so tired of walking up the seventeen floors to my office every day.
I heard a story about someone who got stuck in an elevator for two days and died trying to escape.	I am embarrassed when others get into the elevator and I have to take the stairs.
I'm not unusual; lots of people are afraid of elevators.	I'm sending a bad message to my kids.

What if I have a panic attack in front of other people?

I bet if I can conquer this I'll be less of afraid of other things, like being in tight spaces, or flying in planes.

Not being able to do this makes me feel weak and ashamed.

Being able to do this would make me feel strong and proud.

3. Identify and analyze your helping relationship.

Now consider whether there was anyone who was particularly helpful to you in mastering the tasks associated with *your* accomplishment, your developmental achievement. This might have been someone in your current life, or someone from your past whose "voice" lives on in your mind. Who is (or was) your primary go-to person when you were struggling or when you wanted to share your pleasure in your accomplishment? This may or may not have been someone who taught you specific skills or strategies. But either way, focus on the emotional aspects of your relationship. If more than one person comes to mind, great. Consider the differences and similarities in their styles. What did each have to offer? Where were they lacking in their ability to offer support? Did they complement each other?

Under your analysis of polarities, write down the name of that person (or people).

Holding this special person in mind (as well as the four elements of the helping relationship: a holding environment, empathy, containment, and attunement), consider and jot down whatever ideas you have about the following:

- How would you describe that person's listening skills and style?
- What kinds of questions did that person ask?
- Did that person offer any advice? If so, what kind?
- What did that person say or do that you found helpful?
- Did that person say or do anything unhelpful? If so, did you point it out? How did they react?

- In what ways was (is) that person different from other people in your life to whom you did not turn for support (or didn't in this instance)?
- What traits did that person possess that made him or her an especially helpful source of support, encouragement, and/or comfort?
- If you had failed to reach your goal, how might this person have reacted?
- What did (does) it feel like to be discussing your dilemma with that person?
- Are there any situations in which you would choose not to seek support from that person? If so, why not?
- When you think about that person now, how does it make you feel?
- When you face a new challenge, do you ever find yourself wondering what it would be like to discuss it with that person? Do you ever have imaginary conversations with them?

4. *How did you reach optimal anxiety?*

Now you've identified the polarities associated with your accomplishment and all the feelings that accompanied them. You can see that everything in your left-hand column (under Polarity 1) carries a lot of negative feelings (e.g., fear, humiliation, shame, anger, frustration, self-doubt). They all add up to a sense of overwhelming anxiety that scream "I can't do it!" The ideas in your right-hand column (under Polarity 2) carry positive feelings ("I can do this," "If I do this I'll feel great," "If I do this, many new things will be possible"). But these positive feelings are also imbued with anxiety. Success in our context means mastering new challenges *in the face of anxiety*. As we discussed in Chapter 2, the trick is in finding the sweet spot between overwhelming anxiety (which paralyzes us) and just the right amount of anxiety (which motivates us).

Write the words "Optimal Anxiety" on your paper. Think back to the helping relationship you identified and analyzed in the last portion of this exercise. As you consider the following questions, jot down whatever ideas occur to you:

- Describe what it felt like to be stuck in Polarity 1. Include not only thoughts and emotions but also physical sensations (e.g., "When I thought about getting in an elevator I got lightheaded and I had to lie down.").

- Describe what it felt like when you took baby steps toward your goal, or when you attempted to take steps toward your goal but were unsuccessful.
- Describe what it felt like when you were able to accomplish your goal. Again, include thoughts, emotions, and physical sensations.
- Can you identify anything about your helping relationship that helped regulate your anxiety to an optimal level? If it had been too low (because you'd felt temporarily hopeless and given up), did your helping person do anything to raise your anxiety a bit (e.g., reminding you of a potential downside to not mastering your task or a benefit of mastering it)? If you'd been flooded, did they do anything to bring your anxiety down (e.g., reminding you that there was no particular timetable for mastering your task, or pointing out all the good progress you'd already made)?
- When you have imaginary conversations with this person, what are the qualities of that conversation? What is the tone of their "voice?" What messages about yourself do you receive?

Exercise 2

This exercise is essentially a repeat of Exercise 1, but is applied to your work with a particular client. Consider trying this exercise with a colleague who works with the client's spouse. Each of you can work through the steps as they apply to your own member of the couple, then compare notes. See what emerges!

Again, rustle up a piece of paper and something to write with.

1. Identify a developmental achievement.

Identify a client who either (1) is struggling with a particular issue in their divorce or (2) has managed, with lots of work and help from you, to successfully navigate a difficult issue.

On your paper, describe your client's goal or accomplishment (or desired goal or accomplishment).

2. Describe the polarities associated with your client's developmental achievement.

Again, make columns for Polarity 1 and Polarity 2. Then describe each of them in words. Under each column, write your understanding of your client's thoughts and feelings about each polarity. In doing this, pretend you *are* your client; imagine what they would write if they were doing this exercise themselves. Here's a brief example; your client's columns will likely contain many more entries:

ACCOMPLISHMENT: LETTING GO
OF THE MARITAL HOME

Polarity 1: Stasis	**Polarity 2: Positive Change**
I can't live without the house.	I'll be broke if I keep the house.
My kids won't visit me if I'm in an apartment.	Maybe what my lawyer told me is true; maybe it's *me* that my kids think of as "home" and not the actual house.
I'll be depressed if I leave the house.	A fresh start sounds exciting.

3. Analyze your helping relationship

Think about the things you did to help your client master the tasks associated with his or her developmental task. Again, think about the four components of the helping relationship: a holding environment, empathy, containment, and attunement. Write down some ideas about the following:

- What did it feel like to be with this client as they struggled?
- Did you notice any particular thoughts or behaviors in yourself that you don't often feel but did feel when you're with this client?
- How well did you feel you knew your client—their personal narrative and where they fell on the Rigidity/Flexibility Continuum?
- How well did you do in providing a holding environment, containment, empathy, and attunement?
- Did you struggle in providing one or more of those components? If so, consider whether providing one or more qualities of the helping relationship is difficult for you in general, or whether there is something about this client's personality that you found challenging.

- If you had difficulty staying in a helping stance toward this particular client, try to unpack the problem. Did you have a client-induced countertransference, or is the problem coming from inside you and stemming from a personal area of sensitivity (trigger) or bias?

4. How did you help your client to reach and maintain optimal anxiety?

Think of a meeting or moment in a meeting with your client when they were actively grappling with their developmental task. Maybe it turned out to be a transformative moment in which Polarity 2: Positive Change won the day. Maybe it was a moment of entrenchment or backsliding; the client remained connected to Polarity 1: Stasis.

Record your reactions, including to such questions as:

- What did it feel like to be with your client in this moment?
- Were you aware of the desire for a particular outcome?
- Were you connected to what your client was feeling?
- What factors did you consider when choosing how to intervene?
- Were you able to hold your client's polarities in mind?
- Was your intervention successful in moving your client forward? If so, why?
- Was your intervention unhelpful? If so, why?
- What might you have done differently or better in this moment or in future moments with this client?

Chapter 3: Understanding Our Clients

EXERCISE: GATHERING DATA, FORMING HYPOTHESES, AND DEVELOPING STRATEGIES ABOUT HOW TO HELP

Below is a vignette from the opening of Chapter 5. It describes interactions with David, a new client. Let's read it again, this time with an eye toward gathering data points that might help us to understand him and to form hypotheses about how we might work most effectively with him over time.

You receive an e-mail from a potential new client, David. He addresses you by your first name, and says he's been referred to you by a friend (the friend happens to be a high-powered divorce professional in your town with whom you have worked before) and has heard you're a "miracle worker." He tells you he is planning to divorce, and would like to meet for a consultation as soon as possible. You respond promptly, offering several potential appointments over the next two weeks. That same day you receive an e-mail from the referring attorney: "Hey—hope all's well. Sent an old college buddy your way. Great guy—told him he'd be in good hands with you."

A week later David responds, saying that he's been out of the country and that the times you offer don't work for him. He asks if you could fit him in the following Friday at 2 p.m. You respond that you are currently booked at that time, but that you may be able to move another client to a slot a bit earlier in the day in order to accommodate David. You make the accommodation and write to let him know. 24 hours later you receive a formal confirmation e-mail from his secretary with a cc: to him.

The following week David arrives 20 minutes early for his 2 p.m. You know this because your receptionist buzzes in to your office to let you know David has arrived. As you are still meeting with your previous client (your receptionist has interrupted you—something you have instructed her not to do and that she typically does not do) you instruct the receptionist to offer David a beverage and to tell him to make himself comfortable—that you will fetch him at the appointed time. At 2 p.m. you walk into your reception area. Since there is only one client there, you know it is David.

He is well built, handsome, tan, impeccably groomed and expensively attired in a custom-tailored suit. On the floor near his feet is a lovingly maintained vintage leather attaché case. He seems more to inhabit than to sit on your waiting-room couch—he is semi-reclined, legs crossed loosely, one arm thrown casually along the back of the couch so that he is facing the receptionist's desk and away from the hallway through which you enter the room. As you enter, he is speaking on his cell phone in a conversational tone that he has not adjusted for the closeness of the space. After a moment he visually registers your presence and, without adjusting the tone with which he carries on his phone conversation or establishing eye contact with you, lifts his free hand a few inches from the back of the couch to hold up one finger in the universal gesture for "hang on a sec."

He continues his conversation—which you now understand is with a work colleague—but has wandered into a humorous discussion about golf. A half-minute or so later he terminates his call with "Steve, look, gotta hop. Got a thing here—I'll catch you later." Tucking his phone into his pocket he turns his face to you and, still seated, locks his eyes on yours and flashes an unexpected, sudden smile so charismatic that it fills you with a destabilizing sense of warmth and excitement. He says your name in a tone you associate with reunions between old friends. You reply (in a tone as close to his as you are comfortable to muster), "David." You extend your hand. He rises laconically and shakes it firmly—holding for a beat before letting go. As you lead him down the hall towards your office he calls over his shoulder to your receptionist—"You know, sweetheart, I think maybe I will take that cup of coffee. Black, no sugar."

Based on your early experience of David, what working hypotheses might you begin to develop? What initial feelings or ideas might you have in response to questions such as:

- What reactions does David stir up in you? What is their level of intensity? Are they familiar to you? Unfamiliar?
- If you were asked to come up with a hypothetical story about David's childhood and his relationship with his parents, what would it be?
- What type of attachment style does David seem to have?
- Does David remind you of anyone you know? If so, in what way?
- If you were the divorce professional in the vignette, is there anything you imagine you would have done or said differently from what our hypothetical divorce professional did and said? In what ways?
- Do you feel empathy for David? Would you feel relaxed around him? Do you feel you could easily provide him with a sturdy Microcontainer? Why or why not? How can you understand your answer in the context of your own upbringing and experience?
- What do you know about yourself in relation to people like David that might become strengths or vulnerabilities in your work with him?

EXERCISE 2: THE RIGIDITY/FLEXIBILITY CONTINUUM: A LOOK INWARD

Here, again, is our diagram of the Rigidity/Flexibility Continuum.

<u>The Rigidity/Flexibility Continuum</u>

Rigidity <———————————————> Flexibility

Significant Pathology <———————————> Relative Health

Less Transformative <———————> More Transformative
Capacity   Capacity

<u>Common Emotional and Behavioral Manifestations</u>
<u>of Rigidity and Flexibility</u>

Positionality <————————> Willingness to Consider
                                              Options

Lack of Insight <———————> Self-Reflection/Insight

Blame/Projection <——————> Ownership/Perspective

Anger/Vengefulness <——————> Forgiveness

Entitlement/Self-Absorption <————> Generosity

Victimization/<————————> Volition/
Passivity   Empowerment

Catastrophizing <—————————————> Hope

As you study the diagram, start to think about yourself and your own capacities. As you do, hold these ideas in mind:

- Everyone's personality contains aspects of rigidity and flexibility.
- We are all vulnerable to being more rigid when under stress or if a situation is particularly triggering to us.
- The important questions are "Under what conditions do we become rigid?," "How often does it happen?," "Are we able to recover?," and "How long does it take us to recover?"
- The way to assess our own rigidity or flexibility is by analyzing where our behaviors tend to cluster over time.
- If we frequently view others and situations in stereotypical ways or have emotional reactions that others find

inappropriately intense, that's a sign that our character falls on the rigid end of the continuum.

- If we meet most new situations and people with fresh eyes and have reactions that jibe with those of others, that's a sign that our character falls on the flexible end of the continuum.

Now, think of a client or colleague you dislike.

- Why do you dislike this person?
- Does this person display specific behaviors, attitudes, or qualities that you find distasteful?
- Do you often encounter people with these qualities? If so, do you typically dislike them?
- Do you rarely encounter people with these qualities?
- Do you avoid people with these qualities?
- Does anyone in your family or past experience have these qualities?
- What feelings does this person engender in you?
- How are you likely to behave toward that person?
- How do you imagine others are impacted by your reactions and behaviors?
- Do you find that your negative feelings about this person remain consistent, or do they fluctuate across different situations? If so, what factors influence these shifts?
- Are you likely to hold on to your negative feelings about this person, or are they likely to dissipate over time?
- Do others tend to share your dislike of this person?

Let's do this again. This time, think of a client or colleague you like.

- Why do you like this person?
- Does this person display specific behaviors, attitudes, or qualities that you find likeable?
- Do you often encounter people with these qualities? If so, do you typically like them?
- Do you rarely encounter people with these qualities?
- Do you seek out people with these qualities?
- Does anyone in your family or past experience have these qualities?

- What feelings does this person engender in you?
- How are you likely to behave toward that person?
- How do you imagine others are impacted by your reactions and behaviors?
- Do you find that your positive feelings about this person remain consistent, or do they fluctuate across different situations? If so, what factors influence these shifts?
- Are you likely to hold on to your positive feelings about this person, or are they likely to dissipate over time?
- Do others tend to share your positive view of this person?

Once you've answered some or all of the above questions, consider the following:

- Can you identify any patterns in the way you relate to the clients/colleagues you've identified?
- How much do/don't you tend to make generalizations/assumptions about those people?
- Are those generalizations realistic?
- Is it possible that your reactions are distorted in ways that reflect your past experience?
- Can you identify any aspects of your personal history/experience in earlier relationships that might inform your reactions with your clients/colleagues in the here-and-now?

The goal of this exercise is really to deepen your understanding of the Rigidity-Flexibility Continuum model and tool, so that you have new pathways into figuring out why your clients and colleagues may behave as they do (and perhaps why YOU behave as you do) and to offer a model for helping you know what kinds of techniques may be most helpful with different people. Remember, though, that everyone moves up and down the Continuum, becoming more rigid during times of stress and more flexible when life is smooth.

Chapter 4: Introduction to the Professional Container

You saw it earlier, but here again is a diagram illustrating the way the authors conceptualize the professional Container in our work with separating and divorcing clients. To review: the Container is

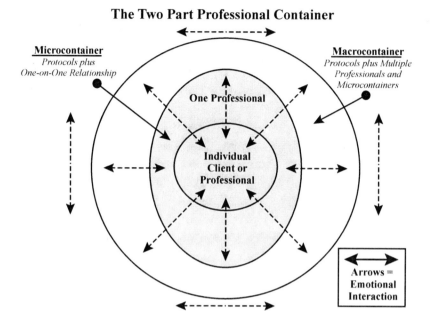

The Two Part Professional Container

made up of two parts: The Macrocontainer (represented here by the outer white circle) and the Microcontainer (represented here by the inner gray oval and the smaller gray oval within it.

The Macrocontainer has two components: The "rules of the road" in a given case (protocols, guidelines, legal and ethical obligations of the professionals, etc.), and the one-on-one relationships among professionals working on the case (Microcontainers within the Macrocontainer). The Macrocontainer has two primary functions: To provide structure for the case and to support the healthy functioning of the Microcontainers.

The Microcontainer is any one-on-one relationship, either between two professionals or between a professional and a client. The function of the Microcontainer is to create and maintain the Three Conditions for Positive Change. The Microcontainer we think the most about is that between you and your client. But the professional-to-professional Microcontainers are equally important since it is very hard to do our work without them.

EXERCISE: MAPPING THE CONTAINER IN YOUR CASE

Think of a case you've worked in the past or are working on now. Start by mapping your Macrocontainer. On a piece of paper, write a list of the entire cast of characters (all the professionals working with the clients). Now, pair them into all the possible types of Microcontainers (one-on-one relationships)—those between professionals and those between professionals and clients. Next, jot down some general notes about the structure of your Macrocontainer. This will include the protocols specific to your legal process, structural elements that your team has set up (e.g., pre-meeting check-ins and post-meeting debriefs), and each professional's role and ethical obligations.

Now, consider a particular moment in your case in which you were working intensely with your client. In this moment you and your client are the central Microcontainer. Imagine yourself at the center of our diagram, doing your work to maintain the Three Conditions for Positive Change. Look outward at the Macrocontainer that encircles you. Do you feel connected to it? Supported by it? Is it sturdy enough? How does it help or hinder you in supporting your client?

Chapter 5: The First Step in Establishing the Container: Our One-on-One Relationship with Our Client

Chapter 5 is an exploration of the ways can create a state of mind (for ourselves and our client) that provides and supports the Three Conditions for Positive Change. Chapter 5 is admittedly chock-full of concepts. Since each of us is unique in our strengths and vulnerabilities, each of us will have our own experience of how easy or difficult it will feel to grasp specific concepts and put them to work with clients. But for most of us, implementing many of the concepts—the ones that require us to let go of old habits in favor of new approaches—will feel strange and unnatural at first.

Here's a quick rundown of the central concepts from Chapter 5:

Offering curiosity without judgment
Learning to notice
Maintaining presence of mind
Conducting a nondirective interview
Deciding how to begin

Dealing with silent or disorganized clients in a first interview
Following affect, not content
Listening for what the client doesn't say
Providing structure within the holding environment
Minimizing self-disclosure
Maintaining a stance of "involved impartiality"
Avoiding inauthentic communications
Avoiding premature pep talks
Utilizing tact and timing
Avoiding rhetorical questions

EXERCISE: MAINTAINING A STANCE OF INVOLVED IMPARTIALITY

We picked this concept as the topic for our Chapter 5 exercise because it's one of the toughest. If you're working with a difficult, high-conflict client, accepting them as they are—empathically and without judgment—is already a tall order. Once you layer in the job of avoiding getting pulled into their irrational positions without losing their trust—Oy!

In Chapter 5 we offered an example of a challenging comment from a positional client, followed by an unhelpful response and a helpful response.

Here it is, for your review:

Client: *I feel like you're not supporting me. I've told you that my husband is a liar. He says he wants time with the kids, but he's just taking them to punish me. When he has the kids, it's round-the-clock nannies. Tell me, how is this fair? On what planet does he deserve equal custody?*

The unhelpful response:

Professional: *I hear you. You're right. If he is going to have the kids then he has to be **with** the kids. Children should be with a parent, not a babysitter! He can't just take them to make a point. I'll e-mail his lawyer saying that you'll only agree to shared custody if your husband can prove that **he** is taking care of the kids. He won't be able to do it on his work schedule—he's probably trying to hide that fact.*

The helpful response:

Professional: *I get it. It's already painful for you to give up time with the kids, but it's doubly hard to feel that they're being cared for by a babysitter rather than by you. I also know it feels terribly unfair that even though you've been the go-to parent from the beginning, their dad is now asking to spend significant time with them. That means time away from you. But I take your point about the nanny situation. Maybe we can get some more information about how much time the kids are spending with nannies versus with their dad and go from there.*

Now, here's the exercise. Do this one with a colleague.

Think of a case in which you worked or are working with a rigid, demanding, positional client. Pick someone who often feels ignored, misunderstood, or victimized. This should be a client who sticks with you, but tenuously. Now, think of a one-on-one meeting in which your client expressed an irrational, unrealistic, or exaggeratedly self-centered belief, demand, or position, then challenged you to support it.

Explain the facts of your case to your colleague—including the content of the meeting in question. Role-play the scene, "with your colleague playing your client," experimenting with different responses. Remember: The task is to ensure that your client feels held and supported without saying or doing anything to convey the idea that you're signing on to his or her destructive ideas. After each exchange (the challenging moment, your balanced response) check in with your "client." Do they still feel you're on their side? If not, why not? How do *you* feel as the professional? Do you feel you've managed to maintain a state of "involved impartiality" or do you have the vaguely guilty feeling that you've said something you wouldn't have wanted the other spouse to hear?

Change roles, and try it again. If you feel like it, experiment with another fact pattern. If you have the right case and enough game colleagues, try a fact pattern that involves a large group (such as a Collaborative case with a full team). The more people in the room, the more interesting the action!

Chapter 6: The Second Step in Establishing the Container: Process Guidelines and Relationships among Colleagues

In Chapter 6 we illustrated the way a strong Macrocontainer can help repair ruptures in relationships between team members (usually caused by difficult dynamics in one or both clients), and in so doing expand everyone's understanding of the case—all leading to a better outcome.

EXERCISE: USING THE MACROCONTAINER TO REPAIR
RUPTURES ON THE TEAM

Identify a case in which a disagreement or personality clash between two professionals caused a rupture in their relationship that was so toxic it began to affect other people on the team (if there were any) and to negatively affect your work with clients.

In other words, the conflict started out like this (feel free to substitute the word "attorney" with the title(s) of professional(s) of any other discipline(s) . . .)

Conflict Spreads to the Professionals
Rupture in One Microcontainer

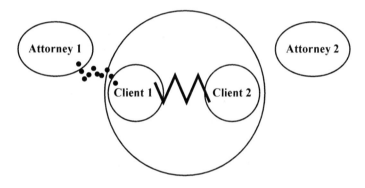

. . . then developed into this:

Ruptures Spread
Weakening of Microcontainer

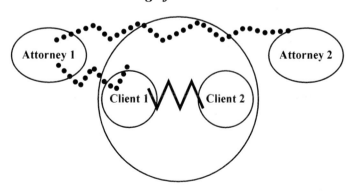

How far did the rupture spread? Did it affect other Micro-containers? Was there a moment when you·wondered if the case would tank? How did you and the other professional(s) handle the rupture(s)? What kinds of conversations did you have? Was there a turning point? If you were able to repair the various ruptures and reestablish the Macrocontainer, what did you learn about yourself, your colleagues, your clients, and how to work more effectively going forward?

Chapter 7: The Importance of Self-Awareness

Exercise 1: Where Is My Focus?

The next time you find yourself reading texts or e-mails at the same time as you're doing something else—walking down the street, cooking, cleaning, shopping, driving(!)—catch yourself in mid-stream. As you lower the electronic device of choice to your side, take a moment to stand still. If you're comfortable with it (and it won't result in your getting run over by a bicycle, or worse), close your eyes. Ask yourself the following questions:

1. Without opening my eyes, what can I describe about the people and objects around me?
2. What details can I include?
3. What aspects of the task in which I've been involved (other than looking at my phone) am I able to recall? The smell of the food I was cooking? The sense of frustration or mastery I had while scrubbing the bathtub? The faces and voices of others in the supermarket?
4. Did my mind move back and forth between focusing on my e-mails and the activity in which I was engaged? If so, how did that affect my experience of both tasks? How did it affect my competence or efficiency? How did it affect my mood?
5. Consider your experience—try it a few times! Note insights you find especially important or helpful. Then apply your learning to your work with clients and colleagues.

Exercise 2: Finding the Edge—a Doorway into Mindfulness[1]

Start by locating an ordinary household object. Pick one that has some weight, but that you can lift with a moderate amount of effort—a stool, perhaps, or a cast-iron pan or heavy book.

Pick up the object, hold it aloft for a few seconds, then put it down.

Now do it again, but read these instructions carefully before proceeding.

1. Grasp the object. But this time, before you lift it, tune in to whatever muscles you'll need to engage. Pay attention to what your body will need to do in the moment you begin to lift the object. Tense the needed muscles, but don't begin the lift. This is "the edge" of lifting the object.

2. Once you're fully aware of what your body feels like in the seconds before actually lifting—go ahead and lift the object up slowly. Hold it aloft for ten seconds. Tune in to what your shoulders, your back, your neck, your legs—any parts of your body engaged in holding the object aloft—feels like. Pay attention to your breath. After a few moments, and without letting go of the exertion in your muscles (don't relax them!) begin to slowly, slowly, gently, gently put the object down. With your muscles still engaged, pay close attention to the sensation of the object settling onto the receiving surface. You have now reached the "outer edge" of the lift.

3. Now slowly release your grasp on the object and relax your muscles. Reset your posture to its natural state and take a deep breath in followed by an exhalation out. You are now done lifting. You're in "the drop."

---

1. The concept of "finding the edge" came to us from Ben King, a wonderful human being who (in addition to being our trainer and friend) is the founder of Mindful Personal Training, founder of the Mindful Memorial Day Foundation, president and CEO of Weloo, LLC, and creator of Armor Down.

Compare the two experiences. First, you mindlessly lifted the object and put it down. The second time, your mind and body were engaged in every stage of the exercise. You began by finding the edge of lifting, then you lifted, found the outer edge of lifting, consciously released the object, and settled into "the drop." Your body then returned to its ordinary state.

Think about entering a meeting with a client, starting a conversation with a colleague, or beginning a conference call with your team. Imagine what it might feel like find "the edge" of each experience before entering it. How would each interaction be transformed if you remained engaged, aware, and attuned—from the moment you met the leading edge of the experience, and for the entire duration until you met the outer edge and moved into "the drop?"

Try it!

PS: Lisa loves this one; she sees "edges" everywhere! But that's how mindfulness works—everything starts to feel connected.

Exercise 3: Countertransference—Taking Your Own Temperature

Think back to Roberta from Chapter 6; she's the wife who is always late. To remind you, here are the first two sentences of that vignette:

The four-way settlement meeting is set for 9 a.m., but Roberta is running late—again. Mark waits in the law firm's reception area while his attorney (Michael) and Roberta's attorney (Renee) are in the conference room looking over documents.

Consider the following questions:

- What thoughts or feelings do you have about the fact that Roberta showed up late again and didn't even bother to apologize?
- What thoughts or feelings do you have about her tendency to minimize the importance of her lateness, or to project the blame onto others?

On this scale of 1–5, where does your reaction to Roberta's lateness fall in terms of the following emotions?

1. Curious
2. Resigned
3. Impatient
4. Quite irritated
5. Angry

If you rated yourself anything other than a one, try to name the feelings that Roberta's lateness engendered in you. Did you feel disrespected? Abandoned? Frightened of her husband's reaction? Frustrated that she was making it hard for you to do your job? Did you experience her lateness as a personal affront?

Now that you've identified your feelings, can you link them to any aspect of any important relationship in your history? Did you have an unpredictably available parent? Perhaps a critical grandparent who made you feel incompetent? A nasty grad school professor who repeatedly accused you of being disorganized and scattered (like Roberta)?

Can you imagine having a conversation with Roberta about her lateness? Would your negative feelings be evident? Would they intrude into your work with the couple?

Repeat this exercise substituting other common problematic behaviors in clients and colleagues. If you need help, there are a lot of examples of seemingly irrational, self-defeating behaviors in clients in Chapter 3, and a list of issues that commonly trigger divorce professionals in Chapter 7. Which of these behaviors and issues elicit personal responses in you? Identify the feelings associated with those responses, then, in your mind, try to trace them back to their source.

EXERCISE 4: CHECKING YOUR OWN BIASES—FEELINGS ABOUT MONEY

Let's start with a vignette;

Pat and Jesse have been married for 22 years. Both parents were engaged in rearing their two children. Pat worked part-time from the time the kids entered school and was home most afternoons. She still works part-time, though the children are now in college.

Jesse grew up in poverty and overcame many challenges to obtain an advanced degree and a high paying job. Pat grew up in a middle class family. She's never had professional ambition, but she's always had expensive tastes. Pat has always prioritized luxury family vacations over saving money. Her spending patterns have been a source of contention in the marriage. Jesse has spent countless hours in marital therapy imploring Pat to work with him on a budget they can live with. But Pat has been intractable. In order to avoid going into debt, Jesse has kept an eagle eye on the family's money, investing it wisely and shopping carefully. Jesse has set up college savings plans for the children, and has contributed to them whenever possible.

The event that catalyzed the end of the marriage was Jesse's discovery that Pat had been having an affair with a coworker. Given the length of the marriage and the fact that she had worked part-time, Pat is asking for alimony in an amount that would come close to equalizing the clients' standards of living over many years.

Consider the following questions:

- Do you think Pat deserves long-term alimony? Why or why not?
- Does it sound to you like Pat is an entitled or spoiled person? Why or why not?
- How do you feel about Pat's spending habits?
- How do you feel about Jesse's thriftiness?
- Does the fact that Pat had an affair affect your reactions to her alimony requests?
- If Jesse had had the affair and Pat had ended the marriage, do you imagine your reactions would be any different? The same?
- Does the fact that Pat is female and Jesse male have an impact on your feelings and reactions? If so, how so?
- What if Pat were male, and Jesse female? Would that affect answers to any of the above questions? What if they were the same gender?
- At any point in this exercise, have you considered what role Pat might play in the couple's difficulties? If not, why not? If so, what thoughts have you had?

Based on your answers to these questions, have you identified any biases you carry in relation to gender? Money habits? Professional ambition? Infidelity? The connection between infidelity and alimony? The connection between overcoming hardship and entitlement?

Exercise 5: Checking Your Own Assumptions

Read each question below and write down your "off-the-cuff" response. Try not to think too much.

1. Do you think infants and toddlers should spend most of their time with their mothers rather than their fathers?
2. Do you think children should have one "home base" rather than moving fairly equally between two homes?
3. Do you have an opinion about how long separated parents should wait before introducing a new romantic partner to their children? How about before having the new partner spend the night while the children are there?
4. Do you think it's a good idea for parents to celebrate holidays and birthdays together with their children after a divorce?
5. Do you think a nonworking spouse who has been financially dependent on a working spouse and will require alimony to live comfortably post-divorce should (assuming they are able-bodied) take action to find employment? What if the couple has young children? What if the children are in college? What if the couple has no children?
6. Do you think it's a good idea for a future stepparent to attend parent-teacher conferences, go to school functions, or host neighborhood parties soon after the divorce? Do your feelings change if the future stepparent becomes a stepparent? Are your feelings any different if we're talking about a stepmother versus a stepfather?
7. Do you think gay couples should be able to raise children? Do you have any concerns abut gay men rearing daughters, or gay women rearing sons? When negotiating a custody agreement for gay parents, how does the fact that one parent never formally adopted the child play into your thinking? What if the child is the biological offspring of one parent and not the other? Do you feel differently about heterosexual couples in which the child is the legal or biological child of only one parent?

8. What are your thoughts about custody arrangements for families in which the breadwinner works long hours and travels frequently for business? How would you react if the working parent wanted joint custody and flexibility to spend time with the children whenever he or she is available?

9. Do you have any thoughts about what it's like to work with clients of any specific religious, ethnic, or cultural heritage? African Americans? Spanish Americans? White Anglo-Saxon Protestants? Jewish people? Asian people? Middle Eastern People? Muslims? Mormons?

If, as you read through that list you notice that certain ideas, beliefs, or fixed opinions spring to mind, pay attention! Ask yourself if your ideas, beliefs, or opinions are based on empirical data that you have studied, or on your own experiences. Lack of awareness in these areas is toxic in our work. On the other hand, awareness of one's own perspective brings opportunities for change, and growth.

EXERCISE 6: STRATEGIES FOR RESETTING WHEN YOU'RE TRIGGERED

Think about how you reestablish your sense of being grounded after you've been triggered? What are your go-to techniques for turning moments of disequilibrium into opportunities for growth? If you don't yet have them, we suggest you work on building a repertoire of at least three good strategies. Try asking colleagues what techniques work for them.

EXERCISE 7: CONSIDERING THE ORIGINS OF YOUR RELATIONSHIP TO CONFLICT

Conflict management styles, just like biases, assumptions, and triggers, develop early in our lives. Explore the origins of your own conflict management style by thinking back to how conflict was treated in your family of origin. It's often useful to begin this exploration by having a conversation with a family member who knows you well and has a fairly high emotional IQ If you don't have a family member that fits the bill (or even if you do), try sharing your personal narrative with a friend or colleague and listening to theirs. You'll both likely learn a lot. Think about whether your feelings about and reactions to conflict are different with various people (or types of people) in our life. Do you experience conflict differently when it crops up in your personal life than you do at work? Or are you pretty consistent across the board?

As part of the exercise, consider these specific questions:

- What were/are your parents' conflict styles—first think about one parent, then the other (if you had two). If you had/have stepparents, think about them as well.
- Did your parents ever fight? What was it like for you to witness or overhear your parents fighting?
- When your parents did argue, did their exchange typically devolve or did they reach a satisfactory resolution?
- Did you ever witness or were you ever the victim of emotional or physical violence (domestic or otherwise)?
- What strategies did you begin to develop as a child and adolescent for navigating conflict within your family? With friends? With romantic partners? Do you typically run from conflict? Are you a peacemaker, provocateur, fighter?
- Do you have a current go-to style in your personal life, but another style for professional situations?
- Does your style of conflict management look different when you are part of the conflict than when you are working with clients to help them resolve their own conflicts?
- How do your conflict styles reflect, echo, or represent a reaction against the conflict styles you experienced in your family of origin?

As you explore these questions, privately or in conversation with others, consider whether there's anything about your approach to conflict that you'd like to change. What adjustments could you make that would allow you to be more effective as a friend, partner, parent, family member, colleague, or helping professional?

Chapter 8: What Should I Do? What Should I Say? Factors to Consider in the Moment (Please refer back to page 145 for a list of Factors.)

EXERCISE 1: EXPERIENCING THE IMPACT OF FACTORS

Seven-year-old Jake has been trying for weeks to gather the courage to jump off the diving board, but he hasn't managed it yet.

As you study the photo, imagine yourself into the scene. Consider the following questions:

- What is Jake's developmental challenge?
- What are the polarities that Jake is struggling with?
- What might Jake be thinking and feeling?
- What do you think Jake needs in this moment?
- If you were standing on the pool deck, what would you say or do?

Now we're going to add in a few more facts about Jake.

Jake has a troubled older brother named Dylan who, sadly, is a bully. For months Dylan has been teasing Jake over the younger child's fear of jumping off the diving board. Dylan has relentlessly accused Jake of being a "sissy" and a "momma's boy." Often Dylan has pulled other kids into the action, so Jake has frequently been humiliated by groups of jeering peers. In *this* moment, Dylan and a handful of his friends are sitting on the edge of the pool watching Jake and yelling nasty comments.

With this new information in mind, reconsider the questions we posed earlier:

- What is Jake's developmental challenge?
- What are the polarities that Jake is struggling with?
- What might Jake be thinking and feeling?
- What do you think Jake needs in this moment?
- If you were standing on the pool deck, what would you say or do?

As you formulate your answers, consider how the new information affected your perception of Jake, his situation, his needs, and what you'd be tempted to do or not do if you were present in the moment. Ask yourself questions like:

- What feelings were stirred up in me when I first looked at the photograph (before I had the information about Jake's brother)? Was I aware of any particular agenda or wish for Jake (e.g., that he jump off the board during this attempt)?
- What personal memories, if any, came to my mind?
- What Factors did I consider when I was imagining what I might say or do in the moment?
- What feelings were stirred up in me after I learned about Jake's older brother? If I had been carrying an agenda or wish for Jake, (e.g. that he jump off the diving board) did it shift? If so, why?
- After I learned about Jake's brother, was there a shift in my perception of Jake's needs?
- After I learned about Jake's brother, did I change my mind about what I'd want to do or say in the moment?
- If so, what new Factors did I consider?

EXERCISE 2: PUTTING THE FACTORS TO USE

Start by reading the below fact pattern.

Cast of Characters

Clients: William and James
Son: Charley, 11 years old
William's Attorney: Wayne
Neutral Coach: Allie
James's Attorney: Marion
Neutral Financial: Carl

William and James have been married for 18 years and are going through a Collaborative divorce. William initiated the divorce. He cites James's bad temper, negativity, and constant criticism as his reasons for leaving the marriage. James feels that William's decision came out of the blue, and sees it as an unforgiveable betrayal. William has expressed sadness about his decision, and says he wants James to be "ok" when the process is over.

The clients have previously met twice with Allie (their neutral coach) to work on their parenting plan. Those meetings have been contentious, as James feels strongly that Charley should live with him during the school week and spend only alternate weekends with William. William wants equal time with Charley, but is eager to hire a child specialist to meet with Charley and offer both parents feedback about what arrangement might work best. James has refused to use a child specialist, saying that he knows Charley best and doesn't need the advice of a stranger.

William and James have also met twice with Carl (their neutral financial) to gather and organize information about their finances. During one meeting, James became upset when Carl failed to endorse James's notion that William should be required to pay long-term alimony. Carl explained that the team would help the clients generate options about spousal support. James later called Marion (his lawyer) to say Carl was allied with William and therefore wasn't trustworthy.

The attorneys, Wayne and Marion, have worked well together on prior cases, and they both trust and respect Allie. Carl is a newly trained Collaborative professional, and has never before worked with the other professionals on the team.

The team has been having weekly conference calls to debrief each meeting and to prepare for the next. During one call they discuss the challenges Allie faces in helping William and James agree on a time-sharing schedule. Marion reports that James believes Carl has a bias in favor of William; the team reassures Carl that he has handled James's aggression well. Wayne reports that William views Carl as competent and neutral. Allie says that she views her relationship with both William and James as strong; she believes they both view her as trustworthy. Marion and Wayne report that they both feel good about their respective clients thus far, though Wayne notes that he doesn't feel much connection with William, who has a hard time staying in touch.

The Potentially Transformative Moment

Twelve weeks into their process the professionals schedule their third full team meeting with the clients. In preparation for the meeting, Marion and Allie have spoken with James about staying calm, focused, and relaxed even if he doesn't like some of William's options. Wayne has also prepared his client, by reminding William of his tendency to clam up in meetings and by encouraging him to speak up during the meeting, rather than waiting until the meeting was over to articulate his views and ideas.

We enter the scene ten minutes into the meeting; the clients are engaged in generating options for dividing their retirement and cash accounts.

*William is discussing an option in which he would keep his premarital retirement account while he and James would each keep half of their marital retirement accounts. As William speaks, James loses his temper. His face becomes bright red, and in a loud, aggressive voice he barks, "Oh, is **that** how this process is going to go, William? With you keeping every nickel and dime that you earned, so you can give me and Charley as little as possible?"*

Meanwhile Carl, who has been assigned the task of recording options on the flip chart, continues to record William's suggestion. He labels it "Option 1."

James, growls at Carl, "So, you're writing down that William will keep everything he saved before we were married? How is that fair? We had already been living together for three years! I can't believe this!"

Allie tries to help by reminding James that they'd anticipated that both he and William would have negative reactions to each other's options. She attempts to reassure him that an option is simply one person's idea, and that writing it down doesn't imbue it with any particular significance or constitute an endorsement.

William ignores Allie, turns to Wayne, and says (in a tone of uncharacteristic anger), "This is ridiculous. We're never going to get anywhere. You told me to speak up, and I just did. Look where that got me!"

Wayne looks at Marion. Marion looks blankly back. Carl, inscrutably, continues to write. Allie looks like a deer in the headlights. The clients sit, arms crossed, glaring into space.

Now, consider the following questions. As you do, refer back to the fact pattern and make use of specific facts, phrases, words, and actions to support your ideas. Feel free to write your ideas down, or just let them float freely in your mind.

Question 1

What was the "topical context" of the moment (e.g., primary task(s), team members present, time allotted, emotional nature of the topic at hand)?

Question 2

What is the "temporal context" of the moment (e.g., where the moment falls within the trajectory of the case and of the present meeting)?

Question 3

What are the "intrapersonal" factors at play in this moment (e.g., rigidity and flexibility of the people in the room, level of cognitive functioning of the people in the room in this moment and in general, attachment styles of the people in the room, known triggers of the people in the room)?

Question 4

What is the "interpersonal context" of the moment (e.g., the nature of the relationships in the room, whether the case is generally high or low conflict)?

Question 5

What is the "recent or impending occurrence context" of the moment (e.g., any recent upsetting events, people involved, place and time the event occurred, anticipated significant upcoming events)?

Question 6

What is the state of the two-part container in this moment (e.g., level of comfort and trust between professionals and clients, changes in quality of the containers since the last meeting)?

Question 7

What might be one of the developmental tasks that each client, and each professional, are faced with in this meeting, and at this moment?

Chapter 9: Facilitating Positive Change: The Essence of Technique

Following is a series of brief fact patterns that lead to verbal "prompts." As you read each fact pattern, consider how you might respond. As you do, try to be mindful of the Factors we discussed in Chapter 8. Pay particular attention to finding the right balance between tending to (or opening up) emotion and remaining focused on the task at hand. Try to craft responses that do both in the appropriate measures.

Do this exercise on your own (either in your head or while writing down some of your responses to review later) or pair up with a colleague and have fun improvising new prompts of your own! Challenge each other!

1(a). You are having your first meeting with a female client, age 32. You know nothing about her, but earlier, when you went to fetch her from your reception area, you overheard her complaining to your receptionist that it took "forever" to find parking in the neighborhood. She also grumbled that she'd had trouble locating your suite number on the directory in the lobby. We join you during your initial interview.

Client: *My husband just canceled my credit card. I'm going to be completely ruined by this whole thing. I'm going to be out on the street.*

Choose a paraphrase or reframe.

Why did you choose that response? Are there other kinds of responses you could also have chosen that would potentially be just as helpful?

1(b). You have been working with this same female client for four months, and you feel you and she have a good working relationship. You know her to be very anxious, a "glass half-empty" person. You also know that she and her husband possess marital assets worth approximately three million dollars.

Client: *My husband just canceled my credit card. I'm going to be completely ruined by this whole thing. I'm going to be out on the street.*

Choose a paraphrase or reframe.

Why did you choose that response? Are there other kinds of responses you could also have chosen that would potentially be just as helpful?

2(a). Your client is a 62-year-old man. You have been working with him for nine months, and he is impatient to finish his divorce process. You and he have a good working relationship, but you find him difficult to manage. He frequently becomes irritated with you and with the pace of the process—though most delays have been due to his busy work schedule and inability to get his homework done in a timely manner. His wife complains about his bullying behavior, and you have experienced that behavior yourself.

During a one-on-one meeting with this client, he says the following:

Client: *Why didn't you send me these notes before last night? I find it completely unacceptable to receive your e-mails the day before we meet. How am I supposed to get this friggin' divorce done if we can't make progress faster than this?*

Choose a curious question, an empathic statement, or make a link.

Why did you choose that response? Are there other kinds of responses you could also have chosen that would potentially be just as helpful?

2(b). Your client is the same 62-year old man. You are about to walk into a one-on-one meeting with this client. As you head to your office, you recall an incident that occurred during another one-on-one meeting you had with this client the week before. During that meeting, the client suddenly stood up as you both were talking, and walked to the window. While standing with his back to you, he had talked with a great deal of emotion about his memories of his own parent's divorce when he was in college. He told you that his mother left his father suddenly, and that his father then plunged into a deep depression from which he never recovered. That meeting had ended with the client quite subdued, but you finished up with him effectively.

Client: *Why didn't you send me those notes before last night? I find it completely unacceptable to receive your e-mails the day before we meet. How am I supposed to get this friggin' divorce done if we can't make progress faster than this?*

Choose a curious question, an empathic statement, or make a link.

Why did you choose that response? Are there other kinds of responses you could also have chosen that would potentially be just as helpful?

3(a). You are in a four-way meeting with at least one other colleague (co-mediator, coach, a financial neutral, or all three— it doesn't matter) and a divorcing couple, partner "A" and partner "B." This is the fourth meeting you have had with the clients. The meeting has just begun. Both clients are participating in an engaged and civil manner.

Client A: *We have to make a decision about when to put the house on the market. And we haven't figured out how to pay for the bathroom repair—I'm not going to receive my bonus for another month, and anyway I'm not sure it's really fair for us to use my bonus money to fund the repair.*

Client B: *We already agreed to use that bonus money, and the house needs to go on the market by the end of this month. Have you talked to the contractor about giving us an estimate for the repair?*

Choose a curious question, paraphrase, or reframe.

Why did you choose that response? Are there other kinds of responses you could also have chosen that would potentially be just as helpful?

3(b). You are in a four-way meeting with at least one other colleague (co-mediator, coach, a financial neutral, or all three— it does not matter) and the same divorcing couple. This is the fourth meeting you have had with the clients. The meeting has just begun. Your client, Client B, has been struggling in each meeting to stay calm (versus tearful or angry). She finds her spouse's disorganization upsetting, and tends to get lost in her spouse's thought processes.

Client A: *We have to make a decision about when to put the house on the market. And we haven't figured out how to pay for the bathroom repair—I'm not going to receive my bonus for another month, and anyway I'm not sure it's really fair for us to use my bonus money to fund the repair.*

Client B: *We already agreed to use that bonus money, and the house needs to go on the market by the end of this month. Have you talked to the contractor about giving us an estimate for the repair? (Client's voice sounds tense, and her volume is growing louder.)*

Choose a curious question, a paraphrase, or reframe.

Why did you choose that response? Are there other kinds of responses you could also have chosen that would potentially be just as helpful?

EXERCISE 2: ASSESSING YOUR OWN COMFORT WITH TECHNIQUES, A DATA-GATHERING EXERCISE

The next time you meet with a client, either in a group or one-on-one, pay attention to the techniques you rely on most often. Within a few minutes after the meeting ends, take a minute or two to jot down the kinds of responses you offered during the meeting and how helpful they seemed to be for the client(s).

Try to track your responses again in other meetings with this client or with different clients. Keep a journal of "my go-to techniques."

When you have a fair amount of data on the range of techniques you most often use, look over your notes and consider the following questions:

1. Do I have certain ways of responding to my clients that I feel comfortable with? Is that because I am good at responding in those ways? Is that because those responses seem particularly effective with many of my clients?
2. Are there certain techniques and ways of responding that I rarely rely on? Why is that? Are those techniques simply less familiar to me, or are those techniques not suited to my personality or approach?
3. Do I want to augment my own toolbox of techniques by practicing new ways of responding in upcoming meetings with clients? If so, how will I remind myself to practice?

Conclusion

EXERCISE 1: MATCHING

Do this one with a colleague or in a group of pairs. Have one person in each pair act as the client who speaks each of the following statements (trying as best they can to *get into* the role—go "Method" here, people!).

The other member of each pair will play the professional. In each scenario, the professional should reply in a manner that conveys the basic message, "I understand what you're saying. I understand how you feel. I'll do my best to help you reach an outcome you can live with." In each case, the professional should try to match the client's emotional make-up and style of speech in such a way that the client experiences the professional as being attuned to them.

You can switch roles whenever you like so each member of your pair has a chance to ham it up. Play! Have fun!

Client 1: Dorinda (55-year-old sassy lady from the deep South)

Darlin', I am NOT gonna budge one tiny little inch on my alimony numbers. He can just kiss my sweet patootie. You know what I'm sayin? Don't talk to ME about takin' a "position!" Child—I KNOW what "position" I'm in, and I'm NOT bendin' over any further!

Professional: ??????

Client 2: Henry (65-year-old corporate banker from Boston in a tailor-made suit)

I feel strongly about this. I am not going to change the alimony numbers we already discussed. She might not like it, but I'm not offering any more. I'd appreciate you backing me up on this. It's important to me.

Professional: ??????

Client 3: Dez (30-year-old hipster from Silicon Valley who earns ten times more money than you do and comes to meetings in jeans and a t-shirt)

I'm not doin' it, dude. I'm not down. We came up with some tight numbers and we're stickin' with 'em. She might walk, but it's a free country. Finito. Peace out.

Professional: ??????

Client 4: Catherine Ann (40-year-old woman in tennis whites. She's head of the PTA and a docent at a local art museum)

(Tearful) I can't get by with any less. I won't be able to make it. He's a tightwad who just got a big fat bonus! He can afford more than that. He's going to get a bonus every year!

His offer is simply insulting. I can't deal with this anymore—when is this going to end? (Blows her nose)

Professional: ??????

Client 5: Lindsey (28-year-old former model, reed thin. She's just returned from jet-setting around the world with her new beau. You wonder if she's on a stimulant.)

So he's offering how many years at how much? Like, I can't follow this; it freaks me out. I KNOW we haven't been married for that long but, like, he's got a lot of money. A LOT of money. You've seen the numbers, right? Didn't we, like, go over the accounts in the last meeting? I can't remember, but I think we did. He promised me he'd take care of me—doesn't that mean he needs to come through? Isn't that, like, an agreement we made? He's totally changing his mind here—that seems completely unfair. Isn't there something we can do to make him offer more? Didn't you tell me there's, like, a formula or something—like some kind of a guideline or something? What was it you said? I know my sister got a HUGE amount from her jerk of a husband and she wasn't, like, married for that much longer than me. (She continues in this vein until she is firmly interrupted.)

Professional: ??????

We hope these exercises are helpful, stimulating, informative . . . and fun.

Index